Online and Adaptive Signature Learning for Intrusion Detection

Kamran Shafi

Online and Adaptive Signature Learning for Intrusion Detection

An Application of Genetic Based Machine Learning

VDM Verlag Dr. Müller

Impressum/Imprint (nur für Deutschland/ only for Germany)
Bibliografische Information der Deutschen Nationalbibliothek: Die Deutsche Nationalbibliothek verzeichnet diese Publikation in der Deutschen Nationalbibliografie; detaillierte bibliografische Daten sind im Internet über http://dnb.d-nb.de abrufbar.
Alle in diesem Buch genannten Marken und Produktnamen unterliegen warenzeichen-, marken- oder patentrechtlichem Schutz bzw. sind Warenzeichen oder eingetragene Warenzeichen der jeweiligen Inhaber. Die Wiedergabe von Marken, Produktnamen, Gebrauchsnamen, Handelsnamen, Warenbezeichnungen u.s.w. in diesem Werk berechtigt auch ohne besondere Kennzeichnung nicht zu der Annahme, dass solche Namen im Sinne der Warenzeichen- und Markenschutzgesetzgebung als frei zu betrachten wären und daher von jedermann benutzt werden dürften.

Coverbild: www.purestockx.com

Verlag: VDM Verlag Dr. Müller Aktiengesellschaft & Co. KG
Dudweiler Landstr. 99, 66123 Saarbrücken, Deutschland
Telefon +49 681 9100-698, Telefax +49 681 9100-988, Email: info@vdm-verlag.de
Zugl.: Canberra, University of New South Wales @ Australian Defence Force Academy (UNSW@ADFA), 2008

Herstellung in Deutschland:
Schaltungsdienst Lange o.H.G., Berlin
Books on Demand GmbH, Norderstedt
Reha GmbH, Saarbrücken
Amazon Distribution GmbH, Leipzig
ISBN: 978-3-639-13630-2

Imprint (only for USA, GB)
Bibliographic information published by the Deutsche Nationalbibliothek: The Deutsche Nationalbibliothek lists this publication in the Deutsche Nationalbibliografie; detailed bibliographic data are available in the Internet at http://dnb.d-nb.de.
Any brand names and product names mentioned in this book are subject to trademark, brand or patent protection and are trademarks or registered trademarks of their respective holders. The use of brand names, product names, common names, trade names, product descriptions etc. even without a particular marking in this works is in no way to be construed to mean that such names may be regarded as unrestricted in respect of trademark and brand protection legislation and could thus be used by anyone.

Cover image: www.purestockx.com

Publisher:
VDM Verlag Dr. Müller Aktiengesellschaft & Co. KG
Dudweiler Landstr. 99, 66123 Saarbrücken, Germany
Phone +49 681 9100-698, Fax +49 681 9100-988, Email: info@vdm-publishing.com
Canberra, University of New South Wales @ Australian Defence Force Academy (UNSW@ADFA), 2008

Printed in the U.S.A.
Printed in the U.K. by (see last page)
ISBN: 978-3-639-13630-2

Abstract

This thesis presents the case of dynamically and adaptively learning signatures for network intrusion detection using genetic based machine learning techniques. The two major criticisms of the signature based intrusion detection systems are their i) reliance on domain experts to handcraft intrusion signatures and ii) inability to detect previously unknown attacks or the attacks for which no signatures are available at the time.

In this thesis, we present a biologically-inspired computational approach to address these two issues. This is done by adaptively learning maximally general rules, which are referred to as signatures, from network traffic through a supervised learning classifier system, UCS. The rules are learnt dynamically (i.e., using machine intelligence and without the requirement of a domain expert), and adaptively (i.e., as the data arrives without the need to relearn the complete model after presenting each data instance to the current model). Our approach is hybrid in that signatures for both intrusive and normal behaviours are learnt. The rule based profiling of normal behaviour allows for anomaly detection in that the events not matching any of the rules are considered potentially harmful and could be escalated for an action.

We study the effect of key UCS parameters and operators on its performance and identify areas of improvement through this analysis. Several new heuristics are proposed that improve the effectiveness of UCS for the prediction of unseen and extremely rare intrusive activities. A signature extraction system is developed that adaptively retrieves signatures as they are discovered by UCS. The signature extraction algorithm is augmented by introducing novel subsumption operators that minimise overlap between signatures. Mechanisms are provided to adapt the main algorithm parameters to deal with online noisy and imbalanced class data.

The performance of UCS, its variants and the signature extraction system is measured through standard evaluation metrics on a publicly available intrusion detection dataset provided during the 1999 KDD Cup intrusion detection competition. We show that the extended UCS significantly improves test accuracy and hit rate while significantly reducing the rate of false alarms and cost per example scores than the standard UCS. The results are competitive to the best systems participated in the competition in addition to our systems being online and incremental rule learners. The signature extraction system built on top of the extended UCS retrieves a magni-

i

tude smaller rule set than the base UCS learner without any significant performance loss.

We extend the evaluation of our systems to real time network traffic which is captured from a university departmental server. A methodology is developed to build fully labelled intrusion detection dataset by mixing real background traffic with attacks simulated in a controlled environment. Tools are developed to pre-process the raw network data into feature vector format suitable for UCS and other related machine learning systems. We show the effectiveness of our feature set in detecting payload based attacks.

Keywords

intrusion detection, evolutionary computation, classification, data mining, genetic based machine learning, supervised learning, learning classifier system, knowledge extraction.

Contents

List of Publications

Journal Articles

1. Shafi, K. and H. A. Abbass (2008). An Adaptive Genetic-Based Signature Learning System for Intrusion Detection. *Expert Systems With Applications*, Elsevier, *To Appear*.

2. Shafi, K. and H. A. Abbass (2007). Biologically-inspired Complex Adaptive Systems approaches to Network Intrusion Detection. *Information Security Technical Report 12*(4), Elsevier, 209–217.

3. Shafi, K., T. Kovacs, H. A. Abbass, and W. Zhu (2007). Intrusion Detection with Evolutionary Learning Classifier Systems. *Natural Computing 8*(1), Springer, 3–27.

Conference Proceedings

1. Shafi, K., H. A. Abbass, and W. Zhu (2007). Real Time Signature Extraction From A Supervised Classifier System. In *Proceeding of the IEEE Congress on Evolutionary Computation, CEC 2007, 25-28 Sept., 2007*, pp. 2509–2516.

2. Shafi, K., H. A. Abbass, and W. Zhu (2006a). An Adaptive Rule-based Intrusion Detection Architecture. In *Proceedings of the RNSA Security Technology Conference, Canberra, Australia, 19-21 Sept., 2006*, pp. 345–355.

3. Shafi, K., H. A. Abbass, and W. Zhu (2006b). The Role of Early Stopping and Population Size in XCS for Intrusion Detection. In *Proceedings of the 6th International Conference on Simulated Evolution and Learning*, Lecture Notes in Computer Science (LNCS), 4247, pp. 50–57. Springer, Heidelberg.

4. Dam, H. H., K. Shafi, and H. A. Abbass (2005). Can Evolutionary Computation Handle Large Datasets? A Study into Network Intrusion Detection. In *Proceedings of the 18th Australian Joint Conference on Artificial Intelligence*, Lecture Notes in Computer Science (LNCS), 3809, pp. 1092–1095. Springer, Heidelberg.

List of Figures

xiii

List of Tables

List of Acronyms

CPE	Cost Per Example Score
DOS	Denial Of Service
EC	Evolutionary Computation
FA	False Alarms
FN	False Negatives
FP	False Positives
GA	Genetic Algorithms
GBML	Genetics Based Machine Learning
IDS	Intrusion Detection System
KDD	Knowledge Discovery in Databases
LCS	Learning Classifier System
NIDS	Network Intrusion Detection System
R2L	Remote to Local
U2R	User to Root
UCS	Supervised Classifier System
UCSD	UCS with Dixon's rule reduction algorithm
UCSSE	UCS Signature Extraction System
UCSx	Extended UCS
XCS	Extended Classifier System

Chapter 1

Motivation

1.1 Computer Security

With the evolution of computer networks, computer security has also evolved from securing giant mainframes in the past to securing large scale unbounded computer networks. The nature of threat has changed from physical infiltration and password breaking to computer viruses, self propagating and self replicating worms, backdoor software, trojan horses, script kiddies, computer criminals and terrorists to name but a few (UPI 2008).

The need for computer security has become even critical with the proliferation of information technology in every day life. Businesses and critical services are becoming increasingly reliant on computer networks and Internet. The increase in dependability on computer systems and the corresponding risks and threats has revolutionised computer security technologies. New concepts and paradigms are being adopted, new tools are being invented and security conscious practices and policies are being implemented. Vendors and users are equally taking the nature of threat seriously and strengthening their defenses. The latest FBI/CSI survey[1]

---

[1]An annual joint survey of computer security incidents by USA's Federal Bureau of Investigations and Computer Security Institute.

shows that 34 percent of the respondent organisations spent more than 5 percent of their total information technology (IT) budget on security in 2006 (Gordon, Loeb, Lucyshyn, and Richardson 2006).

Despite the increase in security arsenal and awareness, however, the threat has neither being eliminated nor mitigated. In fact, computer crimes have become more organised and sophisticated as the intents and motives of these crimes are changing from mere fun and bragging to high financial gains, information gathering for information warfare and terrorism. The 2006 E-crime watch survey reported an overall loss of 740,000 US Dollars in 2006 vs. 507,000 US Dollars in 2005 (Survey 2006), despite the decrease in number of security incidents from 86 in 2005 to 34 in 2006. IT security has emerged as the second most critical security challenge for organisations in 2007, according to EDUCAUSE (Camp and Deblois 2007).

There are various reasons behind this aggravation of attacks and threats. A primary reason is that network protocols and Internet was never developed with security in mind. Additionally, building absolutely secure systems of this magnitude is unlikely anyway due to the complexity of these systems and likelihood of human errors in implementing these systems. As an example, the Computer Emergency and Response Team (CERT) reported 2,874 software vulnerabilities for the first two quarters of 2005 (CERT Coordination Center 2005). A vulnerability can be quite damaging; Blaster worm (CERT Coordination Center 2003) that infected at least 100,000 Microsoft Windows machines in 2003 was launched within 15 days of discovery of a buffer overflow vulnerability in the RPC interface of Microsoft Windows. To further complicate matters, the level of skills required to carry out computer crimes have decreased with the increase in easily available automated attack tools. These trends show that the computer security problem is there to stay for at least many decades to come.

1.1.1 The Role of Intrusion Detection

The field of computer security is vast and can be classified under various domains including but not limited to cryptography, authentication, access control, perimeter security, intrusion detection, forensics and auditing, risk and vulnerability assessment. The basic purpose is to serve the fundamental criteria of assuring the confidentiality, integrity and availability of all components of a computer system.

A computer system can be protected from the threats it faces using many techniques; for example, by implementing risk and vulnerability assessment schemes and tools to avoid threats in the first place and then by using a prevention system, such as firewalls and anti virus software, to stop well known threats and attacks. However, defense in depth principle requires that a good security mechanism be complemented with an Intrusion Detection System (IDS) in order to monitor security breaches when other prevention systems are evaded. IDS is defined by Denning (Denning 1987) as a system that *aims to detect a wide range of security violations ranging from attempted break-ins by outsiders to system penetrations and abuses by insiders.* Denning provided four important factors necessitating the use of intrusion detection systems, underlining the fact that replacing existing systems with security flaws is infeasible and developing absolutely secure systems is almost impossible. This assertion is still valid after almost two decades and probably will remain applicable in the future given the evolving nature of threats.

Intrusion detection systems can be classified in various ways (e.g., based on the protected system or the detection principle). An IDS can be host based, network based or hybrid protecting both networks and hosts. The two basic approaches to intrusion detection are misuse based detection and anomaly based detection. The former deals with intrusions by looking for known patterns of attacks in protected system activities, while the latter models the normal behaviour of a system and flags deviations from normal as anomalous.

One of the major challenges in the intrusion detection domain is the identification of novel attacks. Anomaly based systems use various techniques to address this problem; for example, statistical models profile users and system behaviours using event histories and audit logs; probabilistic models use prior and posterior distributions to predict abnormal events; classification models learn decision boundaries based on the training data to distinguish future intrusive behaviour from that of the normal; time and frequency models use the rate and number of events to point out the anomalous behaviour and so on. While these techniques are aimed at detecting most of the unknown attacks, there is hardly any defence to ward off zero-day attacks and there are a few schemes that are implemented in real world security systems. This is either because of the sensitivity of these techniques which often bury true alerts under the myriad of false alarms or that they require intensive processing or simply because new attacks are too covert and innocent to be detected.

On the other hand, misuse detection approaches generally rely on rules, or so called signatures, for known intrusions. They are considered efficient and are used in most real time systems as they need less processing resources. The rules however need to be updated persistently in order to cope with the ever changing attacks and threats to the information system. Currently, rule creation and update is mainly a manual process (Roesch 1999; Paxson 1998). Thus signature based models suffer from the delay between updating the signatures and new attacks. Very often by the time signatures are made available, the damage had already been done.

A hybrid approach is to combine the strengths of both approaches in a single framework. Despite the fact that many researchers believe in the effectiveness of hybrid approaches (Axelsson 2000; Bace and Mell 2001; Kemmerer and Vigna 2002), most practical intrusion detection systems remain signature based and a handful with anomaly based components (Vigna and Kemmerer 1999). Our choice therefore, is to use a hybrid approach which is self sufficient in learning attack signatures, dynamically, profiling normal traffic and updating the model accordingly.

In summary, adaptability, or in other words reacting to a changing threat environment, is a key requirement for modern intrusion detection systems. It is obvious from the exponential growth of the enabling technologies and the increasing demand in the autonomy and mobility of these systems that traditional techniques of dealing with the protection of these systems will not suffice and we need alternative approaches that can adapt to these drifting concepts over time.

1.2 Problem Formulation

In this thesis, we attempt to address the problem of *dynamically and adaptively learning interpretable rules or signatures that can classify the intrusive and normal behaviour from live network traffic with minimal involvement of human experts.*

1.2.1 Approach

We take a biologically-inspired machine learning approach to this problem. Systems found in Nature, often referred to as complex adaptive systems, are highly robust and resilient that can adapt to environmental changes and constantly evolve their states for their betterment. The study of adaptation in natural systems is the basic theme of complex adaptive systems theory. It generally refers to the ability of an organism to survive in a new environment by accommodating changes in the environment (Holland 1975) (for example, acclimatisation of species from hot weather to cold weather). Natural systems achieve adaptation in various ways such as by promoting biological diversity. Computational complex adaptive system based approaches mimic these natural models to achieve similar objectives in man-made systems.

Thus our approach to learning signatures for intrusion detection is based on a genetic-based machine learning technique called Learning Classifier Systems (LCS) (Holland, Booker, Colombetti, Dorigo, Goldberg, Forrest, Riolo, Smith, Lanzi, Stolzmann, et al. 2000). LCS are parallel production systems that have been designed to exploit the implicit parallelism of genetic algorithms (Goldberg 1989). Genetic algorithms are implicitly parallel meta-heuristic search procedures that are inspired by the natural evolutionary process. The strength of LCS lies in its ability to adapt to changes in the environment.

There are three key features which make LCS quite promising within the intrusion detection domain.

- LCS are rule-based learners that employ genetic algorithms as their generalisation mechanism to learn accurate, maximally general and interpretable rules. The rule based representation allows domain experts to understand the evolved knowledge. Further the rules can be easily ported to existing signature based intrusion detection systems.

- LCS learn incrementally (i.e., they update their knowledge after seeing each input instance) but without needing to re-evaluate the whole model or to keep data instances in memory, a traditional approach to incremental learning. Thus they suit the streaming data requirements where the data is considered virtually lost after seeing it once.

- Various representations and learning schemes can be incorporated into LCS with ease, allowing to build prototype intrusion detection systems around its framework.

All of these characteristics are highly desirable from intrusion detection viewpoint.

In this thesis, we analyse and extend UCS, a supervised LCS (Bernadó-Mansilla and Garrell 2003), for intrusion detection. Several key challenges posed to UCS by the intrusion detection domain are highlighted and mechanisms are provided to address them. A framework is proposed for dynamically and adaptively extracting signatures of normal and anomalous behaviour from network traffic (extendable to other audit sources) discovered adaptively by UCS.

We take the rule based approach because signature based intrusion detection systems are considered most efficient in real world implementations as they require less computational resources and produce fewer false alarms than anomaly based intrusion detection systems. Moreover, rules provide an intuitive way for experts to interact with the learnt knowledge and understand the nature of intrusions. Dynamically learning signatures is an important problem in intrusion detection that has not received much attention. As Axelsson (Axelsson 2000) noted in his famous survey of intrusion detection systems:

> The lack of detectors in the signature self-learning class is conspicuous, particularly since detectors in this class would probably prove useful, combining as they do the advantages of self-learning systems - they do not have to perform the arduous and difficult task of specifying intrusion signatures - with the detection efficiency of signature based systems.

The two main criticisms of signature based intrusion detection systems are their inability to detect novel attacks and hard to maintain signature bases. The signatures are mainly created manually by domain experts and are usually updated only after new intrusions had compromised the security of protected systems.

We place our focus on addressing these two issues using a signature based hybrid detection approach. Firstly, rules are used to detect intrusive activities, as generally done by signature based systems, as well as for profiling normal behaviours. Secondly, the goal is to learn these rules *automatically* from live network/host activities (i.e., using machine intelligence without the need of domain experts; albeit for labelling sufficient training instances), and adaptively (i.e., as the data arrives without the need to relearn the complete model after presenting each data instance to the current model). This could also facilitate the dynamic updates of rule bases without delays. In current signature based systems, an activity that does not trigger an alert is considered normal. We aim to complement this by learning signatures for legitimate activities along with malicious ones. Any instance not matching both profiles is considered potentially harmful and thus could be escalated to the security supervisor for appropriate action.

We evaluate the algorithms developed in this thesis on a benchmark intrusion detection dataset used in the 1999 KDD Cup competition. This data is extracted from a simulated traffic dump on a real network. A standard confusion matrix approach is used to report the accuracy achieved by the developed systems. Further, a cost per example score is measured for each classification model using a given cost matrix. Both of these measures are used in the KDD Cup competition to rank the participating systems. In addition to these two measures, we also report *false alarm rate*, *hit rate* and the number of rules or signatures learnt by the tested systems.

Despite its usefulness, the KDD Cup dataset has some limitations. Some researchers have argued its inappropriateness for training machine learning algorithms (Sabhnani and Serpen 2004), while others have pointed out its staleness. But a major problem when using the KDD Cup dataset is that it does not provide access to raw network data and one has to stick with the provided set of features. This is not a problem for those techniques focusing on improving their prediction accuracy on the given test set. But for those systems that intend to address the intrusion detection problem in general and not limited to this dataset, it poses an inherent limitation and require developing tools that can independently preprocess network data in the required format for the detection engine or learning algorithms. Consequently, to overcome this problem we develop a new methodology to build labelled datasets from real network traffic. This involves capturing real network data from a university departmental server and mixing it with attacks that are simulated in a controlled environment. A state-of-the art signature based IDS is used to label this data and tools are developed to process the raw data into feature vector format. This processing is done offline because the intrusive traffic cannot be generated on a live network; however the tool can be extended easily for real time implementation. Finally, the algorithms presented in this thesis are tested on the real dataset using the same evaluation metrics as those used for the KDD Cup dataset.

1.2.2 Research Questions

The basic research question arising from the problem statement that this thesis is trying to answer is:

Can we adaptively and efficiently learn effective signatures from live network activities, using evolutionary learning classifier systems, which can be used to classify intrusions and normal behaviour of the monitored system?

There are several sub questions that arise from the approach taken to address the problem:

- *How effective are LCS, in particular UCS, in classifying intrusions and normal events from network traffic and/or other audit sources?*

- *Can UCS be extended to improve its accuracy and false alarm rate when tested with intrusion data to a satisfactory level?*

- *Can UCS evolve effective and compact rule sets in real-time that can be used in signature based intrusion detection systems?*

- *How can we evaluate the performance of supervised learning algorithms, such as UCS, for intrusion detection?*

1.3 Thesis Contributions

This thesis contributes to both the genetic based machine learning and intrusion detection fields in the following ways.

- **Analysis and extension of UCS for intrusion detection** - The use of learning classifier systems, specifically UCS, has not been previously explored for intrusion detection and ours is the first attempt to study their usefulness for this domain.

The effects of several key UCS parameters on its performance are analysed using the KDD Cup dataset. In particular, the effects of population size, genetic search, related operators and the covering operator on UCS performance are analysed.

A fixed covering interval heuristic is introduced to better guide the genetic search in finding the maximally general rule sets in UCS.

Distance-metric based prediction - We bring to light the problem of coverage gaps in the test feature spaces in UCS and introduce a distance-metric based approach for dealing with this case.

Strategies to deal with imbalance class distribution - The performance of UCS is analysed in the presence of noise and class imbalance in the data. Several modifications including a new accuracy function, techniques for adapting the rate of applying the GA, class-sensitive deletion and cost-sensitive prediction techniques are introduced to address the class imbalance problem in UCS. These techniques are compared comprehensively with existing ones and their generalisation advantage is shown on synthetic datasets.

Finally, the performance of the extended UCS is evaluated using the KDD Cup dataset and results are compared against the baseline setup.

- **A framework for real-time signature extraction** - A new algorithm is introduced to extract maximally general rules learnt by UCS during its adaptive discovery process. The algorithm is validated using learning bounds from existing LCS theory. New generalisation operators are introduced that can modify rule boundaries to resolve overlaps and redundancies among the signatures.

  Adaptive tuning of the signature extraction algorithm's parameters for noisy and imbalance class problems - The performance of signature extraction algorithm is analysed in the presence of noise and class imbalance through synthetic datasets. Control mechanisms are introduced to adapt important algorithm parameters to deal with these problems.

Finally, the signature extraction system is evaluated on the KDD Cup dataset and its performance is compared with UCS, extended UCS and another offline rule reduction algorithm that we implemented in UCS.

- **A methodology to build intrusion data for supervised learning algorithms** - A new methodology is developed to evaluate UCS, the signature extraction system and their variants, with real data captured from a university departmental server. Intrusion traffic is generated by simulating hundreds of attacks tailored to trigger alerts in a state-of-the art signature based intrusion detection system. The captured traffic is mixed with the attack traffic to build the raw dataset. A detailed analysis of the raw data is provided. Tools are developed to process this raw network traffic into feature vectors. The developed algorithms are evaluated with the constructed dataset.

1.4 Thesis Structure

The rest of this thesis is structured as follows: In Chapter 2, we set out the context of the problem and provide a summary of the related literature. The first half of the chapter covers background materials on intrusion detection, traditional machine learning with emphasis on rule induction algorithms and genetic based machine learning. The latter half covers existing work related to our proposed approaches. In particular, we survey existing hybrid approaches, rule learning approaches and nature-inspired computational approaches applied to intrusion detection.

In Chapter 3, the KDD Cup dataset is introduced and the details about its feature set, attack types and class distributions are presented. We also highlight the advantages and criticisms of this dataset. Next, the experimental methodology and evaluation metrics used in this thesis are explained in detail and a baseline performance of UCS is established on the KDD Cup dataset.

In Chapter 4, we analyse different effects of key UCS components on its performance and propose modifications to improve upon the baseline performance. A distance metric based prediction technique is introduced to handle uncovered test cases in UCS. The performance of UCS in the presence of imbalance class datasets is studied in detail and different strategies to handle class imbalance in UCS are compared comprehensively. Finally, the extended UCS is evaluated using the KDD Cup dataset.

In Chapter 5, an algorithm to extract effective generalisations evolved by UCS in real-time is presented. The performance of the signature extraction system is analysed in noisy and imbalanced class environments and mechanisms for the online adaptation of its parameters are presented. At the end of the chapter, adaptive and non-adaptive versions of the signature extraction systems are evaluated on the KDD Cup dataset and their performance is compared with UCS and another rule reduction algorithm implemented in UCS.

In Chapter 6, we develop a methodology for evaluating UCS and other systems proposed in this thesis with real network traffic and simulated attacks. The motivation of developing such a methodology is discussed and a detailed analysis of the captured traffic and the dataset built from this traffic is presented. Finally, the baseline UCS, extended UCS and the signature extraction system developed in the previous chapters are evaluated with the dataset built in this chapter.

In Chapter 7, we summarise our contributions in this thesis, point out the limitations of our work and discuss the future directions that stem from this work.

Chapter 2

Background and Related Work

2.1 Chapter Objectives

This chapter sets the context of the thesis and provides a brief introduction to intrusion detection and different approaches to deal with this problem. Our goal is to provide both anomaly and misuse (i.e., hybrid) intrusion detection by learning rules of normal and abnormal behaviour. We take a Genetic Based Machine Learning (GBML) approach to adaptively learn effective rules of normal and abnormal activities from network traffic. Therefore, we provide a brief background on machine learning with emphasis on rule induction and GBML algorithms. A review of the work in the intrusion detection domain related to our approach is also presented. Specifically, brief surveys of techniques that use a hybrid detection principle, machine learning to generate rules for intrusion detection and nature-inspired machine learning approaches for dealing with intrusion detection are presented.

2.2   Intrusion Detection

Intrusion detection was identified promptly as an important area of computer security when computer professionals started to realise the significance of protecting computer systems. The basic purpose of intrusion detection is to classify illegitimate and malicious activities into a computer system, which aim to gain unauthorised access, gather crucial information about the system (i.e., to compromise systems confidentiality) or simply disrupt the normal operation (i.e., to compromise integrity and availability of the system and services it is providing), from the normal operation (Bace and Mell 2001).

The work on intrusion detection dates back to the early 1980's when James Anderson published his work on the importance of audit trails to detect misuse and identify user behaviour (Anderson 1980). The idea of an Intrusion Detection System (IDS) was first introduced formally by (Denning 1987) based on her work on a government project. These two seminal works are the basis of the current state of IDS research. A history and evolution of intrusion detection systems can be found in (Kemmerer and Vigna 2002; Bruneau 2001).

2.2.1   Approaches to Intrusion Detection

Intrusion detection approaches can be classified in several different ways. A detailed taxonomy and classification can be found in (Axelsson 2000). Here we concentrate on four aspects of intrusion detection techniques.

- **Detection Principles** - The two fundamental detection principles in intrusion detection are misuse and anomaly detection. The former detects intrusions by matching patterns or signatures of known attacks and vulnerabilities while the latter by flagging deviations from normal behaviour. As discussed in the previous chapter, the aim of the anomaly based techniques is to detect previously unseen attacks. The underlying assumption driving these techniques is that malicious activities has substantially different characteristics than the normal activities and thus can be detected by monitoring deviations from the profiles built from normal traffic. In practice, however, this simple assumption does not always work as the normal behavior patterns change over time giving rise to false alarm rates. In addition, attackers often conceal their activities by adapting to normal profiles used by anomaly techniques. The biggest challenge for signature based techniques is to keep up with the evolving nature of attacks. Given that these signatures are often hand crafted by the domain experts, this becomes a bottleneck for these techniques. A third way is to combine the strengths of both misuse and anomaly detection techniques into a hybrid approach. One way this can be done is by providing the hybrid detection through signatures of malicious as well as normal traffic. This particular area has received little attention and is the concentration of this thesis.

- **Detection Locale** - The detection can be performed on host or network level. Host based systems audit host logs, system calls and file systems etc., whereas the network based systems consider network traffic as the main source of audit data. A hybrid approach is to use both host and network based audit sources for the detection of illegitimate activities. Machine learning techniques can play a vital role in detecting from hybrid sources. Since these techniques mostly work with pre-process data, they can easily generalise to different source of information. However, it would be important to tune the bias of such techniques to deal with different pieces of information, even though it is provided in a similar format. An ensemble of learning machines would be a better choice in such situations, where disparate information is fed to corresponding expert algorithms and the final outcome is determined by some sort of a gating mechanism.

- **Detection Time** - Intrusion detection can be performed in real-time or offline. The real-time systems aim to detect intrusions in the flow of network traffic or during live host based activities. Offline systems operate on the collected traces and logs in the past and aid in forensic testing and other related domains. Both techniques have their own merits. Generally speaking, an intrusion detection system is supposed to perform in real-time so that protection can be provided before the damage occurs. Real-time detection, however, is challenging, especially for anomaly based systems that often use sophisticated machine learning and artificial intelligence techniques that are computationally expensive and does not scale well with high speed data. It is thus essential to drive these techniques towards better scalability in addition to achieving high precision.

- **Learning Ability** - Intrusion detection systems can be pre-programmed such as in the form of hand-crafted signature bases, expert-drafted detection policies or pre-built statistical profiles. Other systems use machine learning and other artificial intelligence techniques to learn signatures, policies and profiles automatically from a training dataset and then generalise to predict future intrusions. Anomaly detection techniques inherently use different learning mechanisms. It would be ideal to completely automate the process of signature generation for misuse detection systems and would give them the flexibility to adapt to changing environment without human intervention. The work presented in this thesis is a step towards this approach.

2.2.2 Challenges in Intrusion Detection

It is obvious from the evolving nature of threats and attacks against the computing infrastructure that the job of intrusion detection systems is far from over. The two key desirable characteristics that exist among others is the effectiveness and adaptability of intrusion detection systems.

- **Effectiveness** - corresponds to the ability of an intrusion detection system to detect attacks accurately without raising too many false alarms. High number of false alarms can overly burden human operators, bury the actual attacks under them or crash the system. It is important to note, however, that there is always a tradeoff between the detection rate and the false alarm rate (see e.g. (Mahoney 2003)). An IDS can be fine tuned to produce less number of false alarms but only at the cost of increased number of false negatives (i.e., by missing the actual attacks); conversely, it can be made general to cover more attacks but only at the cost of increased number of false alarms. In addition, the efficiency of an intrusion detection system also contributes to determining its effectiveness. Efficiency is often measured by the cost of learning and updating a detection model and the cost of actual detection in terms of both time and resources.

- **Adaptability** - corresponds to the ability of an intrusion detection system to perpetually learn changes in the environment over time and adjust to them accordingly. Adaptability is a major challenge and arguably the most desired characteristic for an IDS. Generally, achieving adaptability automatically is a harder problem for misuse detection systems which rely on a manual creation of signatures. Anomaly detection systems by definition look for novel attacks but they also need to adapt their learnt models of normal behaviour relative to changes in the environment.

2.3 Machine Learning

Machine learning is a field of artificial intelligence (AI) that is concerned with constructing programs that can improve their behaviour with experience (Mitchell 1997). In general, machine learning algorithms aim to find a functional mapping, also referred to as a *concept* or a target *hypothesis*, between a given input or *feature space* and an output or *label space*. The input space is often represented in the form of a set of *instances*, where each instance consists of a set of features or attributes. The task of a machine learning algorithm is to find the target class each instance belongs to. For example, in an intrusion detection task, the instances may represent the network connection records or host log entries and the set of features could be the types of protocols and services in a packet header or the source and type of an event in a log file respectively. The goal of a machine learning algorithm (at least from a classification viewpoint) would be then to assign an attack or normal class to each instance. Usually, supervised machine learning algorithms require training with already labelled data before they could assign labels to test or future instances.

There are several ways in which machine learning techniques can be applied to intrusion detection problems. For instance, they can be used

- to automatically generate signatures or rules for misuse or signature based intrusion detection systems,

- in building and extracting interesting features that improve the effectiveness of existing detection systems, and

- to learn the normal behaviour of a protected system or its users in an anomaly detection context.

A variety of machine learning algorithms have been proposed which can be categorised in several different ways such as based on the inference technique they employ (Michalski, Carbonell, and Mitchell 1986). Below we provide a brief discussion of common machine learning methods.

- **Inductive Learning** - Inductive learning methods attempt to find the most general hypothesis that best fits the given training data. They do not use any prior knowledge about the given hypothesis space and learn by exploiting the statistical properties of the data. Inductive learning methods include decision tree learners, conditional rule learners, inductive logic programming and neural networks.

- **Analytical Learning** - Analytical learning methods use deductive inference. In addition to the training examples, they use background domain knowledge to deduce generalised hypotheses. In contrast to some inductive learning methods such as inductive logic programming, that use prior background knowledge to enrich instance description, analytical learning methods use this knowledge to reduce the hypothesis search space. An example of analytical learning methods is explanation based learners such as those presented in (Mitchell, Keller, and Kedar-Cabelli 1986).

A hybrid approach is to combine the strength of both inductive and analytical learning techniques to minimise the reliance on both prior background knowledge and training. Knowledge Based Artificial Neural Network (KBANN) is an example of such a hybrid approach.

- **Instance Based Learning** - Instance based learning methods are localised by definition. Instead of learning a generalised hypothesis of the feature space, they learn by memorisation of the training data. Any new instance is assigned a target function value of the closest category. The distances are usually measured in the Euclidean space. Instance based learning methods include case based reasoning and k-nearest neighbours.

- **Bayesian Learning** - Bayesian methods provide a probabilistic approach to learning. They combine prior knowledge of probability distributions of the candidate hypotheses with the observed data to determine the posterior probability of target hypotheses. Thus they can be applied inherently to problems whose output require probabilistic predictions. They also provide a framework for analysing the bias of other algorithms that do not deal directly with probabilities. The naïve Bayes classifier is an effective algorithm that uses Bayesian reasoning.

2.3.1   Rule Induction Algorithms

Rules are considered as one of the most expressive and human readable form for representing a learnt hypothesis (Mitchell 1997). In general, the rule-based models are represented as a set of if-then rules in a disjunctive normal form (DNF), where each rule has an antecedent, consisting of a conjunction of conditions imposed on attribute values, and a consequent specifying the predicted class of the matching instances.

Many rule induction algorithms exist in the literature at present. Sequential covering algorithms are one of the most widely used approach to learn disjunctive sets of rules (Mitchell 1997). This family of algorithms are sometimes also referred to as the separate-and-conquer algorithms. In the simplest form, these algorithms iteratively learn one rule at a time with high accuracy and low coverage (i.e., a rule which covers maximum number of target class instances with minimum number of other class instances). Then the instances covered by this rule are removed from the data set and the process is repeated until all the data is covered. The outcome of the algorithm is a set of rules that can be ordered in terms of rule accuracy so that the most accurate rules are considered first when predicting the class of a new instance.

A possible way that this type of algorithms can be classified is the direction of rule search, which can be either specific-to-general or general-to-specific. The specific-to-general techniques, such as (Domingos 1995), start with the most specific rule (i.e., a rule that does not match any instance) and then generalise progressively by covering instances of the target class. These algorithms scale poorly with increasing number of features. The general-to-specific techniques, such as AQ (Michalski 1969), CN2 (Clark and Niblett 1989) and IREP (Furnkranz and Widmer 1994), begin their search with the most general rule and then specify its conditions to improve its performance over the training set.

Another way of distinguishing the sequential covering class of algorithms is based on the pruning techniques they use to reduce the generalisation error of the learned rule sets.

A variation of the sequential covering algorithm is to learn rules for only the most interesting class, for example the attack classes in an intrusion detection context, and use a *default* rule for the prevalent class in the data.

Association rule learning (Agrawal and Srikant 1994) is another popular approach that is used to discover interesting patterns in databases. In a strict sense, association rule induction is considered different from classification rule induction methods. Association rule learning algorithms first find large sets of items that *support* a minimum number of transactions in a database and then generate rules from these large *itemsets* which have a minimum *confidence* level.

An indirect way of rule induction is to first learn a classification model through a non-rule-based approach such as decision trees or support vector machines and then generate rules from these output models (Quinlan 1987; Burges 1996).

2.4 Genetic-Based Machine Learning

In this section, we will focus on the specific machine learning paradigm used in this thesis (i.e., GBML). GBML approaches employ evolutionary computation (EC) techniques as their learning mechanism to search the hypotheses space (Michalewicz 1996).

EC techniques are meta-heuristic search techniques which loosely imitate the process of natural evolution by simulating principles of natural selection and reproduction. Similar to natural systems, which evolve over many generations to adapt to their environments using natural selection, reproduction and diversification, EC techniques evolve a set of candidate solutions to adapt to the requirements of a problem. EC techniques have been applied to various machine learning tasks including function approximation, learning sets of rules for classification and control problems, and optimising the parameters of other machine learning algorithms such as neural networks, decision trees and support vector machines.

Traditionally, evolutionary algorithms are classified under four categories, that are, Evolutionary Strategies (ES) (Rechenberg 1973), Evolutionary Programming (EP)

(Fogel 1964), Genetic Algorithms (GAs) (Holland 1975) and Genetic Programming
(GP) (Koza 1992). GAs are the most widely used and popular evolutionary algorithms (Jones 1998) and are an integral part of learning classifier systems - the type
of GBML techniques we are concerned with in this thesis.

2.4.1   Genetic Algorithms

Unlike specific-to-general or general-to-specific approaches, GA search large hypothesis spaces by first randomly generating a collection of hypotheses (i.e., individuals),
referred to as a *population*. It then iteratively selects the best individuals from this
population and reproduce the next generation of individuals by crossing over and
mutating the individuals in the selected subset. The selection of best individuals is
performed stochastically according to some desired performance measure, denoted
as the *fitness* of the individual.

Figure 2.1 illustrates a pseudo code for a canonical GA (Goldberg 1989). Each *individual* in a population of hypotheses is traditionally represented as a bit string,
referred to as a *Chromosome*, where each bit in the chromosome is called a *Gene*.
The *selection* procedure chooses individuals from the population for reproduction
proportional to their fitness. Several selection procedures have been proposed in
the literature; among the most commonly known are roulette wheel and tournament selection (Goldberg and Deb 1991). The *crossover* and *mutation* operators
create offspring by mixing and altering the genes of parents respectively. Similar to
selection, crossover and mutation can be performed in several different ways.

GA are implicitly parallel and have proven robust in many fields of applications.
The success of GA is often explained by the *building block hypothesis* (Goldberg
1989) which in turn is built on Holland's *schema theorem* (Holland 1975). A schema
is defined as a template that matches a subset of all possible input states. For
instance, the schema 1##1 describes a subset of 4 strings that must have a 1 at
position 1 and 4 in a set of all possible 4 bit binary strings. The # sign represents

the don't care symbol or wild card. The schema order is defined as the number of non-don't care bits in a given schema. The schema theorem states that the number of short, low-order and above average fitness schemata increases in successive generations. Goldberg termed these short, low order and above average schemata as building blocks and proposed that these schemata receive exponentially increasing trials in the subsequent generations of a classic GA whereas the below fitness schemata receive exponentially decreasing trials.

Figure 2.1: Pseudo code for a simple Genetic Algorithm

$t \leftarrow 0$

Initialise $P(t)$

Evaluate $P(t)$

while Stopping condition is not true **do**

    $t \leftarrow t + 1$

    $P'(t) \leftarrow$ Select a parent population from $P(t)$

    Apply crossover to $P'(t)$

    Apply mutation to $P'(t)$

    Evaluate $P'(t)$

    $P(t+1) \leftarrow$ Replacement $(P(t), P'(t))$

end while

return Best individual of $P(t)$

2.4.2 Learning Classifier Systems

Learning Classifier Systems (LCS) are described as GBML systems by (Goldberg 1989). LCS are rule based production systems that use GA for rule discovery and traditional machine learning techniques like reinforcement or supervised learning to evaluate the fitness of rules. The rules in LCS are referred to as *classifiers*, thus the name Classifier Systems.

There are two common approaches to LCS. Pittsburgh style LCS represent complete rule sets as an individual classifier. GABIL (De Jong and Spears 1991) and more recently GAssist (Bacardit and Butz 2004) belong to this category of LCS. Michigan style LCS on the other hand consider each individual rule as a classifier. It is the latter approach which we are concerned with in this thesis and will refer to it as LCS from hereon.

LCS combine a sequential covering algorithm with a GA based search technique to learn rules in a disjunctive normal form. The GA module empowers LCS to adaptively learn new rules as well as provide generalisation mechanism that enables the system to classify future cases. LCS are not merely rule learners but they also provide an interface with live environments where data can be received continuously and processed using the learnt knowledge of the system. Further, LCS are incremental and online rule learners, which means they update their classification model after seeing each data instance and without storing the instance in the memory. These powerful features make LCS an interesting approach to be used for intrusion detection.

LCS were originally introduced by Holland in 1975 (Holland 1975) and later simplified and revised in (Holland and Reitman 1978). Stewart Wilson's XCS (Wilson 1995) is considered the current state-of-the art LCS. A main difference between XCS and its older counterparts is the evaluation of rule fitness which is based directly on the accuracy of rules instead of the rules' strength as used previously. This major shift allowed XCS to overcome several weaknesses of the strength based LCS (Kovacs 2000). XCS incorporates temporal-difference learning in its framework and thus suits reinforcement learning problems, although we note that it has also been applied to supervised learning tasks, among others (Bernadó-Mansilla, Llorà, and Guiu 2002). Recently UCS, a very close variant of XCS, has been introduced for specifically supervised learning tasks. In this thesis, our focus is on this LCS, thus we give a description of UCS in the following section, highlighting its differences from XCS.

2.4.3 A Supervised LCS

UCS (sUpervised Classifier System) (Bernadó-Mansilla and Garrell 2003; Bernadó-Mansilla 2002) is an LCS derived from XCS. Both use the same classifier representation and a niche Genetic Algorithm (GA) (Goldberg 1989) as their search mechanism. The fitness of individuals (classifiers) in the population is based on their accuracy. UCS is specifically designed for classification tasks and benefits directly from known labels during training. In contrast, XCS uses a reinforcement learning approach and can be used in single or multi-step tasks. It receives an immediate or delayed reward from the environment upon predicting an action or a label for an input state. Consequently, the classifier parameters in XCS and UCS are updated according to their respective learning schemes. In the following subsection, a discussion of several key UCS components and their operations is provided.

2.4.3.1 Classifier Representation

UCS, like XCS, evolves a *population* (a set of rules denoted as $[P]$) of rules in DNF representation called *classifiers*. Each classifier consists of two parts; a *condition* and an *action* or the label of the predicted class. The condition is essentially a conjunction of predicates, where each predicate can be coded using one of several available representations. The original XCS was mainly applied to binary tasks and used a ternary representation of the form $\{0,1,\#\}$, where # represents the don't care symbol meaning it can match either of the input values. Wilson later on introduced an interval based representation for dealing with continuous value variables (Stewart W. Wilson 2000; Wilson 2001b); some variations of which are proposed in (Stone and Bull 2003; Dam, Abbass, and Lokan 2005). Using the interval representation, each predicate takes the form (l_i, u_i), where l_i and u_i corresponds to the lower and upper bounds of each interval. An interval predicate matches a continuous input value if it lies between the lower and upper bounds of that interval. The handling of unordered attributes has not been mentioned explicitly in the literature. Usually, such attributes can be coded using a binary string where each bit in the string corresponds to a specific category of the unordered attribute or by mapping the categories to integral values.

Given the flexible framework of both LCS, various other non-symbolic representations have been used for coding the classifiers including S-expressions (Lanzi 1999), kernel functions (Butz 2005) and neural networks (Dam, Abbass, Lokan, and Yao 2008). In this thesis, however, we will stick to the symbolic representations described above.

2.4.3.2 Classifier Parameters

In addition to the condition and action, each classifier has a set of parameters that are used for keeping various statistics and measuring rule's confidence. The main classifier parameters listed below are essentially a subset of XCS parameters.

- **accuracy** - The accuracy (acc) is a measure of the correctness of a rule.

- **fitness** - The fitness (F) of a rule in UCS is a direct function of rule's accuracy.

- **experience** - The experience (exp) is a count of the number of times a classifier matches an input instance.

- **numerosity** - The numerosity (num) of a classifier corresponds to the number of its copies in the population.

- **niche size** - The niche size (ns) is an average of correctset (described in the next section) sizes to which a classifier has belonged. It is similar to the *action set size* (as) parameter in XCS.

The *prediction* and *prediction error* parameters used in XCS are not required in UCS.

2.4.3.3 System Parameters

An additional set of parameters are used in UCS to control the operation of different components in the system. Similar to classifier parameters, UCS inherits its system level parameters from XCS. These parameters can be divided into following three sets:

- **Covering parameters** - Covering (detailed in the next section) is applied in UCS to create new rules at the time of system initialisation or when no matching rules are found for an input feature vector. The specificity of the new covering rules is controlled by a parameter $P_{\#}$ that represents a user-defined probability of including don't cares (#) in a rule's condition. A higher $P_{\#}$ value means more general rules. In the case of numeric attributes, specificity (width) of initial covering intervals is controlled by r_0.

- **Learning parameters** - The learning parameters in UCS are used when updating classifier parameters described in the previous section. Parameter acc_0 refers to an optimum rule accuracy. Any rule above this threshold is considered 100% accurate. Parameter ν relates rule's fitness to its accuracy (more discussion to follow). Finally, there are two more parameters α and β that are used only when fitness sharing is applied in UCS in which case they act as accuracy discount factor and system learning rate respectively.

- **GA parameters** - There are several GA parameters that include the usual crossover and mutation probabilities, population size and selection related parameters. Other parameters include θ_{ga} - a threshold to control the rate of applying GA to individual niches (or correctsets), θ_{sub} - a rule's experience threshold above which a rule is allowed to subsume another rule provided certain other conditions are met, θ_{del} - another experience threshold below which rules with low fitness are discounted for deletion and δ - a deletion discount factor.

2.4.3.4 Operation

Both XCS and UCS interact with the environment in a similar fashion. An instance is presented to UCS in a standard feature vector format, where each feature can be of discrete, continuous or nominal type. There are two distinct phases in which an instance can be processed; namely training and test phases. Traditionally, these two phases have been referred to as *explore* and *exploit*, respectively, in LCS jargon. Figure 2.2 depicts the interaction of different components and a typical working cycle of UCS in both phases.

During training, UCS learns from the labelled examples incrementally in a supervised mode. In each iteration, an instance is presented to the system and a *matchset* $[M]$ is built of all the matching classifiers in $[P]$. A classifier matches an instance only if all of its conditions satisfy the corresponding feature values of the input instance. The parameters of all classifiers participating in $[M]$ are then updated as explained in §2.4.3.5. Those classifiers in $[M]$ that predict the same class as the label of the current input example form the *correctset* $[C]$ (equivalent of *actionset* $[A]$ in XCS). If $[C]$ is empty, then the *covering* operator is used to create a new matching rule with the same class as the label of the matched example. Note that this is different from XCS, where parameter update is carried out in $[A]$ and the covering operator is used to create a rule for every class not present in $[M]$. The covering classifier is generated by creating a matching condition for every attribute of the current input instance according to its respective representation discussed above. Finally, GA is applied to $[C]$ as explained in §2.4.3.6.

During the test phase, the learning and induction processes do not take place and the system predicts a test case using the population of classifiers it has evolved during training. For each test input, $[M]$ is formed as usual and a *system prediction* for each class (P_c) is calculated as a fitness-weighted vote:

$$P_c = \sum_{cl_i \in [M]} \gamma \cdot F \cdot num$$

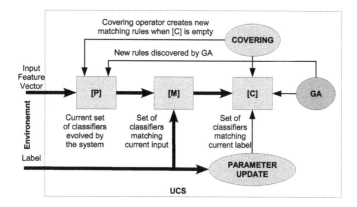

(a) Training Phase

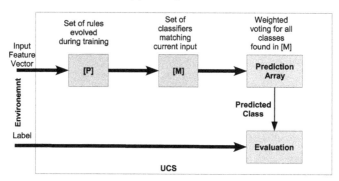

(b) Test Phase

Figure 2.2: A typical UCS working cycle.

where F is the classifier fitness and γ is a discount factor given by:

$$\gamma = \begin{cases} 0.01 & \text{if } exp < 10 \\ 1 & \text{otherwise} \end{cases}$$

The class label with the highest prediction vote is selected as the output.

2.4.3.5   Parameter Update

Unlike XCS, where only classifiers participating in $[A]$ get updated, parameters in UCS are updated in $[M]$. First, a classifier's exp is incremented by one. Next, the accuracy is calculated as the proportion of correctly classified examples matched by a classifier:

$$acc = \frac{\text{number of correctly classified examples}}{experience}$$

This is different from XCS, where the accuracy of a classifier is calculated inversely proportional of its *prediction error*. Finally fitness is calculated as a function of accuracy given by:

$$F = (acc)^{\nu}$$

where ν is a constant that controls the slope of the curve.

Originally, fitness sharing was not tested in UCS but was pointed out as a potential extension. A recent work by (Orriols-Puig and Bernadó-Mansilla 2006a) investigated the use of fitness sharing. In fitness sharing, the fitness update is done similar to XCS. First a new accuracy κ is calculated for each classifier participating in $[C]$ as follows:

$$\kappa_{cl \in [C]} = \begin{cases} 1 & \text{if } acc > acc_0 \\ \alpha(acc/acc_0)^{\nu} & \text{otherwise} \end{cases}$$

where acc_0 is a user-defined accuracy threshold (usually set to 0.999 for noise free problems) above which a classifier is considered accurate and α is the rate of distinction between accurate and inaccurate classifiers. Also note that κ is set equal to 0 for those classifiers not belonging to $[C]$ in a $[M]$.

Next, a relative accuracy $\acute{\kappa}$ is calculated as:

$$\acute{\kappa} = \frac{\kappa_{cl} \cdot num_{cl}}{\sum_{cl_i \in [M]} \kappa_{cl_i} \cdot num_{cl_i}}$$

In addition to the above updates, the niche size parameter ns is updated every time a classifier is included in $[C]$.

2.4.3.6 GA Component

UCS adopts the search and generalisation mechanism from XCS as it also uses a niche GA. The GA is applied in $[C]$ when the time elapsed since the last application of GA in $[C]$ exceeds a user-defined threshold θ_{GA}.

During GA process, two parents from $[C]$ are selected stochastically, in proportion to their fitness. The two most commonly used selection schemes are roulette-wheel selection and tournament selection. Two offspring are generated by probabilistically reproducing, crossing over and mutating the parents. In crossover, the genetic materials of two offspring (i.e., the rule conditions) are exchanged. Similar to selection schemes any of the crossover techniques can be applied (e.g., single-point, two-point or uniform crossover). The interval predicates for real representations can be crossed over either at the boundaries or within. Likewise, mutation is applied to individual offspring based on a user-defined mutation probability. In mutation, the values of classifier predicates are changed by a small step probabilistically according to their respective representation.

The resultant offspring are first checked to see if they can be *subsumed* by their parents (i.e., if the parents are more general than children in all attributes), sufficiently experienced and accurate then the *numerosity* of the parents is incremented by one and the children are discarded; otherwise children are inserted in the population. If the insertion of the new classifier causes the population size to exceed its user defined maximum threshold, then a classifier is deleted stochastically to create room for a new one. For a higher fitness pressure and to keep a balance between the size of all niches, deletion of classifiers is biased towards those with lower fitness and larger niche sizes. The deletion vote for each classifier is computed as follows:

$$dv = \begin{cases} ns \cdot num \cdot \frac{\overline{F}}{F} & \text{if } exp > \theta_{del} \text{ and } F < \delta\overline{F} \\ ns \cdot num & \text{otherwise} \end{cases}$$

where $\overline{F}$ is the average fitness of the population.

2.4.3.7   Macro Classifiers

Both XCS and UCS are implemented using macroclassifiers (Wilson 1995), which extend classifiers with the numerosity parameter that indicates the number of virtual classifiers that a macroclassifier represents. This is an implementation technique which can speed up the processing time considerably by removing the need to process identical classifiers.

2.4.4   Other Uses of GBML

Although LCS are considered the main stream GBML systems, the scope of GBML systems has grown with the increase in the application of evolutionary algorithms as search techniques in various contexts. For instance evolutionary algorithms have been used in evolving artificial neural networks (Abbass 2002; Yao and Liu 1997), inducing decision trees (Cantu-Paz and Kamath 2003), clustering (Maulik and Bandyopadhyay 2000) and so on. There are many variations of rule induction algorithms based on GA and other evolutionary algorithms including (Bonarini 1996; Freitas 1999; Chiu and Hsu 2005).

2.5 Related Work

In this section we review some of the prominent work related to our approach.

2.5.1 Hybrid Approaches

Hybrid intrusion detection systems incorporate both misuse and anomaly detection approaches. These systems generally attempt to complement signature based misuse detection with anomaly detection techniques to detect novel attacks for which no signatures are available. Since anomaly detection techniques are prone to high false alarm rates the systems are designed generally in stages or hierarchies, so that anomaly detection module is used only when needed.

NIDES (Next-Generation Intrusion Detection Expert System) (Anderson, Frivold, and Valdes 1995) is a host based IDS that employs a statistical anomaly detection component and a rule base component for detecting known attacks. User profiles are created using the short and long term behaviour of the user's activities and are updated regularly. Rule creation and update are manual processes but can be carried out while the system is in operation. The processed audit records from the target hosts are sent to the statistical and signature analysis modules simultaneously. A resolver filters out redundant alarms before prompting the users through email or popup windows.

EMERALD (Event Monitoring Enabling Responses to Anomalous Live Disturbances) (Porras and Neumann 1997) is a large scale intrusion detection framework, which combines statistical anomaly detection models with a signature based misuse detection engine. The signature base is a forward chaining production expert system called *P-Best*. The rules are first written in a proprietary specification language, which are then translated into a C language expert program. The anomaly detection engine called *eBayes* uses Bayesian inference. eBayes work on sessions rather than individual connections; a group of TCP connections within a short time is considered a session. It models the probability of occurrence of attribute value pairs and then classifies sessions using naïve bayes inference based on the observed values.

(Lee, Stolfo, Chan, Eskin, Fan, Miller, Hershkop, and Zhang 2001) extended their data mining framework for building intrusion detection models in real time. They combined algorithms for anomaly detection to complement misuse based detection in the same framework. One of the methods they used is *artificial anomaly generation*. In this method, artificial anomalies are introduced at the edges of the sparse regions to avoid creating overgeneral rules. The rules are then created for normal events, known attacks and unknown intrusions (i.e., artificial anomalies). They also tried a clustering technique for unsupervised learning in their framework. The feature extraction module developed earlier (Lee and Stolfo 2001) is decomposed to extract different levels of features as required to speed up this process for real time application.

ADAM (Audit Data Analysis and Mining) (Barbara, Wu, and Jajodia 2001) is a two stage system; the first stage is a rule mining stage that creates a network traffic profile in the form of association rules based on attack free training data. Another component of this stage, fed with training data including attacks along with the normal profile rules, generates attack rules dynamically (i.e., over a pre-specified window size). A third component of this stage extracts other features from the training data. The outputs of the last two components (i.e., attack rules and extracted features) are used as a training set for the second stage - a classifier based on pseudo-Bayes estimators. The purpose of the classifier is to further analyse the attacks' predictions before passing it onto the security expert. Training is done offline. During testing, the same process is repeated except that normal profiles are not computed. The dynamic miner generates suspicious rules based on the itemsets that do not match the normal profiles created during training and pass them to the classifier along with the extracted features. The classifier then decides finally if the suspicious events are attacks; in which case an alert is generated. Note that our framework is also multi-stage, however our first stage is a signature based stage that contain both normal and attack signatures. We also treat events not matching with any of these rules as suspicious and send them to the next stage classifier which is an LCS.

SPADE (Statistical Packet Anomaly Detection Engine), originally developed as a module in SPICE (Stealthy Portscan and Intrusion Correlation Engine) (Staniford 2002), is an anomaly detection plug-in for Snort (Roesch 1999), an open source, real time and popular signature based intrusion detection system. SPADE is a frequency based approach; it keeps track of the number of occurrences of specific packet fields and constructs a joint probability model of different field combinations such as destination IP/port. However, SPADE is not used for learning new signatures and the process of signature update for Snort remains manual.

MINDS (Minnesota INtrusion Detection System) (Ertoz, Eilertson, Lazarevic, Tan, Kumar, Srivastava, and Dokas 2004) is a network level anomaly detection system that also incorporates a signature component. The input to the system is the packet header information captured through Cisco's NetFlow tool every 10 minutes and stored in a flat file. This data is first filtered to remove uninterested connections (e.g., transactions to/from trusted sources). Next, a feature extraction module extracts features very similar to the work of (Lee and Stolfo 2001). This featured vector is then passed through a signature base module to check for known attacks. The remaining data is sent to an anomaly detection module which assigns an anomaly score to each connection based on a Shared Nearest Neighbour (SNN) clustering approach (Ertoz, Steinbach, and Kumar 2002). The output of the anomaly detection module is sent to a security expert, who can create new signatures after performing analysis of the interesting alerts. Note that intrusion detection is near real time and not instantaneous. Further, the number of alarms generated from each 10 minutes data is in thousands. In addition, the new signature creation is still a manual process.

(Martin and Sewani 2004) applied a multi-level detection approach for offline host based intrusion detection. They built user profiles using user commands entered on Unix command line interface. A fuzzy rule-based expert system is used to first reduce the set of commands for each user. In the second step, k-means clustering is applied on the reduced command set followed by a Learning Vector Quantization (LVQ) technique to refine these clusters.

As noted earlier, despite its potential, hybrid modelling is still a less explored area. Not all of the systems discussed above are network level; others plug-in separate anomaly modules into existing rule based systems that rely on manual signature creation and update. Our focus on the other hand is to develop online (i.e., in real time or using a single-pass through the data) profiles of both attacks and normal activities. As opposed to many other hybrid systems, our emphasis is on creating rules dynamically. Problems of intrusion detection can be approached in many different ways. Given the nature of the threat, diversity in the detection methodology is essential. Our approach based on GBML adds another defence mechanism against intruders.

2.5.2 Rule based Approaches

Automatic rule learning for intrusion detection is an active area of research. Many machine learning techniques are applied to the problem of intrusion detection, however, there are few that emphasise on automatic rule learning and a fewer that learn rules online (i.e., in a single-pass). Here, we detail some of the prominent techniques for learning rules; specifically for intrusion detection.

RIPPER (Repeated Incremental Pruning to Produce Error Reduction) (Cohen 1995) is a sequential covering based rule learner, extended from IREP (Incremental Reduced Error Pruning) (Furnkranz and Widmer 1994), that has been used by several researchers for learning rules for intrusion detection. The RIPPER algorithm works by breaking the training dataset into two sets; a growing set and a pruning set. It learns a single rule at a time by greedily adding conjunctions to its condition part that maximise information gain until the rule covers no negative examples from the growing set. The rule is then pruned immediately by minimising its generalisation error over the prune set. The rule discovery is stopped using Minimum Description Length (MDL) principle (i.e., when the MDL of the current rule set exceeds a minimum user-defined threshold). The ruleset is further optimised by replacing existing rules with their variants such that the new rules minimise the generalisation error of the entire rule set over the prune set.

Apriori (Agrawal and Srikant 1994) learns association rules by mining the frequent episodes and has also been used for intrusion detection by many researchers.

(Ramesh and Mahesh 2001) proposed a framework to learn rules in two stages. First, the sequential covering algorithm is used to learn highly accurate P rules indicating the presence of a target class. Two rules for every distinct value of all categorical attributes in a feature vector are generated that take the form R1: (A = v) ? C and R2: (A != v) ? C, where C denotes the target class. Multiple ranges are used to cover continuous variables. The strength of each rule is calculated in terms of its coverage and accuracy on the subset they are generated from. The strongest rule is then selected and the examples it covers are removed from the training set. This procedure is repeated with the reduced set at each step until the best rule's strength remains above a minimum user-defined accuracy and coverage thresholds. In the second stage, rules classifying the negation of the target class (!C) are learnt on the subset covered collectively by all positive rules. A score is calculated for each rule based on its statistical significance on the training data. This score is also weighted by a cost matrix (note that a score here is not a probability). During testing, the conflict between P and N rules is resolved based on this score.

(Mahoney and Chan 2003b) introduced a randomised rule generation algorithm which they called LERAD (Learning Rules for Anomaly Detection). LERAD generates simple if then conditional rules similar to association rules. It first randomly selects a pair of instances (an attribute vector based on TCP streams) from a subset sampled randomly from the training data. It then searches and randomly orders k matching attributes between the pair. The first attribute among the sorted attributes becomes the consequent of the rule and the rest are taken as antecedents. The generated rule set is then pruned by first discarding redundant rules (i.e., the rules having the same consequents) with lower scores on the sample data and rules which perform poorly on the full training set (i.e., rules having a higher number of unique attribute values) towards the end of training. Note that rules are not learnt incrementally and require two passes through the training data. During testing a rule fires if the antecedent matches the test instance but the consequent does not. Recently, this system is extended also to learn rules from system call sequences (Tandon and Chan 2005).

(Maloof 2003) extended the AQ11 algorithm, the incremental version of the sequential covering based AQ algorithm to AQ11-PM (i.e., AQ11 with partial memory). AQ11 is a memory less system that learns rules incrementally but suffers from ordering problems. AQ11-PM keeps a memory of representative examples derived from past experience; the representative examples are those which contribute to the evolution of concepts or in other words that lie near concept boundaries. As new rules are learnt, some of the old examples are forgotten when they no longer enforce boundary conditions. Similarly old instances are removed from the memory over a window whose size is adjusted dynamically.

JAM (Stolfo, Fan, Lee, Prodromidis, and Chan 2000) and ADAM (Barbara, Wu, and Jajodia 2001) mine association rules from the training data and then use them to detect intrusions in the test data. The former works in a misuse detection mode while the latter in the anomaly detection mode.

Some other researchers have explored the application of meta-classification algorithms in the intrusion detection domain. Among others (Sabhnani and Serpen 2003) developed a multi-classifier model using three of the nine best performing pattern recognition and machine learning algorithms such as neural networks, clustering techniques and decision trees and applied it to the 1999 KDD Cup data. (Giacinto, Roli, and Didaci 2003) divided connection records in KDD Cup dataset into six categories based on different network services. Three dedicated classifiers, each relating to a different feature subset of the KDD Cup dataset, are then applied to these service modules. The best performing classifiers are fused to classify intrusions using different voting methods. They reported that the majority voting method performed the best among all methods.

2.5.3 Nature-Inspired Approaches

Nature inspired approaches, including the GBML techniques discussed above, are being applied to various domains of computer security including cryptology, secure protocol design and intrusion detection. Techniques like Genetic Algorithms, Genetic Programming, Artificial Immune Systems and Swarm Intelligence are used for the detection of attack patterns, adaptively learning rules from network traffic and implementing the overall frameworks of intrusion detection and response systems. Below we present a brief survey of some of the work in this area with a focus on the intrusion detection problem.

2.5.3.1 GA Based Approaches

The use of GA based approaches for intrusion detection problems is not entirely new. In fact, in 1990 (Heady, Luger, Maccabe, and Servilla 1990) proposed an offline network anomaly detection system architecture using Holland's strength based classifier system described in (Booker, Goldberg, and Holland 1990). They proposed to use classifier system rules for profiling the normal network traffic. However, they did not provide any results on the evaluation of such a system.

(Ludovic 1998) developed a tool called GASSATA (Genetic Algorithms for Simplified Security Audit Trail Analysis) for audit trail analysis in the misuse detection context. GASSATA works in offline mode and uses a GA to search for a binary hypotheses vector H, where each binary value indicates an occurrence or absence of an attack, from an attacks-events matrix built from the observed data in an audit trail. The objective of GA is to maximise $R \times H$ where R is a weight vector that signifies the risk associated with the particular attacks involved.

NEDAA (Network Exploitation Detection Analyst Assistant) (Sinclair, Pierce, and Matzner 1999) is a network level intrusion detection system that used GA among other machine learning techniques for offline rule learning which can then be used in signature bases of the real time IDS. They modelled source/destination IP/Ports and the protocol values in the IP packet header. Each chromosome consisted of 29 genes corresponding to the modelled features. Random rules are generated first to create a population which are then trained on labelled data using genetic operators and a fitness function which drives them to accurate attack detection. Rules matching the intrusion patterns in the training dataset get higher fitness values. The algorithm is augmented with a variation of crowding technique based on hamming distance metric to promote diversity in the rule sets.

(Helmer, Wong, Honavar, and Miller 2002) used GA based search to reduce the rule set size learnt by RIPPER using system call traces. Each attribute in the feature vector represented a system call sequence and was encoded in binary. A standard GA with rank based selection was used then to select a feature subset among the rules learnt by RIPPER. A weighted sum of rule accuracy, number of conditions and attributes in each rule was used as the fitness function of each individual. By using this technique, they were able to reduce the number of attributes used in feature vectors from 1832 to 840.

(Chittur 2002) applied a GA on the 10% of the KDD dataset to evolve best fit rules based on the accuracy of predicting anomalous connections from the normal. They used Ephemeral Random Constants to assign weights to individual attributes in the dataset.

(Gomez and Dasgupta 2002a) used adaptive-parameter genetic algorithm with special genetic operators (gene addition and deletion) to evolve fuzzy classifiers and applied it to the KDD Cup dataset. The rules for Denial of Service (DOS) attacks in the dataset were evolved independently of the other attacks because of the high number of instances belonging to DOS category. They showed equivalent performance to traditional machine learning algorithms in all categories and improved performance in one of the categories.

(Pillai, Eloff, and Venter 2004) manually created a rule set from the network connections and then used GA to evolve new rules to detect novel intrusions in the network traffic.

Several other researchers have explored the use of GA for intrusion detection problems in various contexts. However, here we restrict overselves to the brief overview of GA approaches presented above in the rule based context.

2.5.3.2 Artificial Immune Systems

Natural immune systems provide an intuitive metaphor for applying nature-inspired computation to the intrusion detection problem. Artificial Immune Systems (AIS) are learning algorithms that attempt to mimic some of the processes found in natural immune systems.

In a typical AIS based intrusion detection system (Hofmeyr and Forrest 1999; Kim and Bentley 2001), the normal behaviour is considered as self and the intrusive behaviour as non-self. Initially, the detectors or patterns of network traffic or the host activities are randomly generated to mimic the generation of T cells. During training, the negative selection process occurs where these detectors are exposed to the normal events and any matching detectors are removed from the detector sets. The remaining detectors are then used to detect the abnormal behaviour. The detectors which correctly match the anomalous behaviour are memorised for future use. These detectors also go under the clonal selection process which is simulated using a GA.

AIS resembles with LCS in many respects (Forrest and Hofmeyr 1999). Similar to LCS, a typical AIS also uses genetic operators for learning self and non-self behaviour. Usually these profiles are learnt in the form of binary strings that represent network packets or host processes. These binary strings can actually be considered a form of if-then rules as used in LCS.

Various researchers have used AIS based approaches for intrusion detection problems due to the similarities between the two domains. (Dasgupta 1998) and (Aickelin, Greensmith, and Twycross 2004) provide a good review of the field. Many early researchers have provided frameworks for host and network based intrusion detection systems such as (Forrest, Hofmeyr, Somayaji, Longstaff, et al. 1996; Dasgupta 1999; Kim and Bentley 2001). Recent research is concentrating on the advanced features of natural immune systems benefiting from the advances in the biological research of immune systems, among others (Aickelin, Bentley, Cayzer, Kim, and McLeod 2003; Kim, Greensmith, Twycross, and Aickelin 2005).

2.5.3.3 Swarm Intelligence

Swarm Intelligence (SI) is yet another example of the powerful phenomenon of learning and adaptation observed in many natural systems (mainly social insects and birds) that have got the attention of recent research. A swarm is defined as a *set of (mobile) agents which are liable to communicate directly or indirectly (by acting on their local environment) with each other, and which collectively carry out a distributed problem solving* (Hoffmeyer 1994). The individual agents themselves are simple entities that interact with other agents using simple rules, yet overall they emerge as completely self-organised systems. Moreover, these systems work in a completely distributed and decentralised manner which makes these systems quite robust against environmental changes. Common examples of such natural systems include colonisation of ants, flocking behaviour of many bird species and emergence of belief systems in human social networks.

In a computing environment, software mobile agents emulate the behaviour of social insects. They perform different tasks such as finding the shortest path between two nodes on a computer network. To achieve the tasks, agents communicate with each other using the electronic version of pheromone (e.g., by registering information about the number of remaining hops to a destination host on an intermediate router).

SI is relatively a new area of study in computer science. Nonetheless, quite a few intrusion detection schemes have already been proposed using swarm behaviour metaphors. In (Foukia and Hassas 2004; Foukia 2005) a mobile agent based intrusion detection and response system (IDRS) is proposed using the AIS and SI approaches. The detection part of the system is based on a self non-self AIS (see §2.5.3.2) where mobile intrusion detection agents (IDAs) take the role of T cells and travel around the network to detect intrusive behaviour using the sequence of events such as system calls. The response part of the system is based on ants behaviour. Similar to ants, the intrusion response agents (IRAs) roam in the network to find an attacked node and perform a countermeasure for that attack. Analogous to ants, IRAs rely on an electronic pheromone, build and deposited by IDAs upon detecting an intrusion, to locate the infested host. The electronic pheromone comprises of different information related to the detected events; for example, the information about the type and severity of an attack.

In other works, (Dozier, Brown, Hurley, and Cain 2004) used Particle Swarm Optimization (PSO) to simulate hackers in order to provide vulnerability assessment of an AIS based IDS. (Tsang and Kwong 2005) used ant colony based clustering models for unsupervised classification in distributed IDS architectures.

2.6   Summary and Way Forward

This chapter covers concepts related to the scope of this thesis; namely intrusion detection, machine learning, rule induction and nature-inspired machine learning techniques. The basic approaches and challenges faced by the intrusion detection domain are highlighted and the motivations for opting hybrid intrusion detection approach are spelled out. An overview of traditional machine learning techniques with the emphasis placed on the rule induction algorithms is provided. Special attention is given to genetic based machine learning and the working of genetic algorithms is elaborated. We highlighted the main differences between two state-of-the art learning classifier systems and provided a detailed description of UCS and its working principle.

A literature review of existing techniques relating to our work in this thesis is presented. In particular, we looked at some of the work on hybrid intrusion detection, automatic rule learning for intrusion detection and nature-inspired computational approaches for intrusion detection.

After setting out the context of the problem and presenting some of the relevant work in this chapter, we move on to investigate the performance of UCS in the next chapter.

Chapter 3

Experimental Setup

3.1 Chapter Objectives

In this chapter, we introduce the 1999 KDD Cup benchmark intrusion detection dataset, the experimental methodology and metrics used for the evaluation of the proposed algorithms, and establish a baseline performance of UCS, a GBML system introduced in the last chapter, by evaluating it through the KDD Cup dataset.

3.2 KDDCUP Datasets

In 1998, the MIT Lincoln Lab under the DARPA and US Air Force Research Labs (AFRL) sponsorship conducted the first Intrusion Detection Evaluation (IDEVAL) program. The two main objectives of the exercise were to evaluate intrusion detection approaches by analysing their weaknesses and strengths against a wide range of attacks and to promote future research providing a common, security and privacy concerns free, testing platform in the form of a data corpus (Haines, Lippmann, Fried, Tran, Boswell, and Zissman 2001). The corpus collected during this program was later made public and provides a benchmark for the evaluation of intrusion detection systems. The traffic was generated on a simulated network resembling a portion of typical AFRL network and collected through tcpdump network sniffer (Jacobson, Leres, and McCanne 1989). The training data was developed from seven weeks of simulated traffic and audit records and included twenty-four attack types. The test data was developed from another two weeks of traffic and contained additional fourteen attack types not present in the training data.

KDD Cup is an annual Data mining and Knowledge Discovery competition organised by ACM SIGKDD. The focus of the 1999 KDD Cup (Hettich and Bay 1999) was intrusion detection and the task was to build a predictive classification model that can distinguish between good (i.e., normal) and bad (i.e., attack) connections. The datasets used for the KDD Cup, originally provided by (Stolfo, Fan, Lee, Prodromidis, and Chan. 2000), are derived from the IDEVAL data mentioned above. The raw traffic dump collected from simulated traffic was converted into unique connection records. A connection here corresponds to a time-stamped session of data transfer between two computers, in the form of network packets, using a specified protocol. The training dataset consists of approximately five million connection records extracted from seven weeks of traffic dump. The test set yielded approximately 0.3 million connection records extracted from the additional two weeks of traffic dump. A ten percent version of the training dataset is also provided which contains almost half a million records with similar class distribution as the original KDD dataset. We will refer to these two datasets as 10% and full datasets respectively.

These two datasets are used frequently by researchers working in the domain of intrusion detection. In particular, the KDD Cup dataset is used predominantly by the researchers working with classification algorithms such as (Sabhnani and Serpen 2003; Ramesh and Mahesh 2001). In the following sections, we present a detailed description of its features and related statistics.

3.2.1 Features

Each connection record in the KDD Cup dataset is a labelled feature vector consisting of forty-one features in total. These include 9 basic or *intrinsic* features, nine
temporal or *time-based traffic* features, ten statistical or *host-based traffic* features
and thirteen *content-based traffic* features (Lee and Stolfo 2001).

Table 3.1: Intrinsic features in KDD Cup data.

Feature Name	Description	Type
duration	length of the connection in seconds	continuous
protocol_type	type of protocol, e.g. tcp, udp, etc.	nominal
service	network service on the destination, e.g., http, telnet, etc.	nominal
src_bytes	number of data bytes from source to destination	continuous
dst_bytes	number of data bytes from destination to source	continuous
flag	normal or error status of the connection	nominal
land	1 if connection is from/to the same host/port; 0 otherwise	binary
wrong_fragment	number of "wrong" fragments	continuous
urgent	number of urgent packets	continuous

The basic features are related to fields in the network packet headers and session
timeouts. These features could help in identifying attacks that target protocol and
service vulnerabilities. Table 3.1 lists the intrinsic features along with their description and value types.

Table 3.2: Time-based traffic features in KDD Cup data.

Feature Name	Description	Type
count	number of connections to the same host as the current connection in the past two seconds	continuous
serror_rate	% of same host connections that have "**SYN**" errors	continuous
rerror_rate	% of same host connections that have "**REJ**" errors	continuous
same_srv_rate	% of same host connections to the same service	continuous
diff_srv_rate	% of same host connections to different services	continuous
srv_count	number of connections to the same service as the current connection in the past two seconds	continuous
srv_serror_rate	% of same service connections that have "**SYN**" errors	continuous
srv_rerror_rate	% of same service connections that have "**REJ**" errors	continuous
srv_diff_host_rate	% of same service connections to different hosts	continuous

The time-based traffic features are constructed particularly to detect high volume fast rate DOS[1] attacks based on the number of connections made to the same destination host or service in the past two seconds. These are listed in Table 3.2.

Table 3.3: Host-based traffic features in KDD Cup data.

Feature Name	Description	Type
dst_host_count	number of connections to the same host in the past 100 connections	continuous
dst_host_serror_rate	% of connections that have "SYN" errors	continuous
dst_host_rerror_rate	% of connections that have "REJ" errors	continuous
dst_host_same_srv_rate	% of connections to the same service	continuous
dst_host_diff_srv_rate	% of same host connections to different services	continuous
dst_host_srv_count	number of connections to the same service in the past 100 connections	continuous
dst_host_srv_serror_rate	% of same service connections that have "SYN" errors	continuous
dst_host_srv_rerror_rate	% of same service connections that have "REJ" errors	continuous
dst_host_srv_diff_host_rate	% of same service connections to different hosts	continuous
dst_host_same_src_port_rate	% of connections from the same source port	continuous

---

[1]attack types are discussed in the next section

Similar to time-based features, host-based traffic features capture the number of connections to the same host, port or service by a destination host in the past 100 connections. Their main target is slow scanning Probe attacks. These are listed in Table 3.3.

Table 3.4: Content-based traffic features in KDD Cup data.

Feature Name	Description	Type
hot	hot indicators e.g., access to system directories, creation, and execution of programs, etc.	continuous
num_failed_logins	number of failed login attempts	continuous
logged_in	1 if successfully logged in; 0 otherwise	binary
num_compromised	number of compromised states on the destination host (e.g., file/path "not found" errors, and "Jump to" instructions, etc.)	continuous
root_shell	1 if root shell is obtained; 0 otherwise	binary
su_attempted	1 if "su root" command attempted; 0 otherwise	binary
num_root	number of "root" accesses	continuous
num_file_creations	number of file creation operations	continuous
num_shells	number of shell prompts	continuous
num_access_files	number of operations on access control files	continuous
num_outbound_cmds	number of outbound commands in an ftp session	continuous
is_host_login	1 if the login belongs to the "host" list; 0 otherwise	binary
is_guest_login	1 if the login is a "guest" login; 0 otherwise	binary

The content-based traffic features are constructed using domain knowledge. Their aim is to detect stealthy U2R and R2L attacks by monitoring statistics manifested in the audit logs or in the payload section of the packets. Content based features are listed in Table 3.4.

3.2.2 Attack Types

Each connection record in the data is labelled either as normal or as an attack. There is a total of thirty-nine intrusion types including both training and test datasets. All of these types can be classified into four major categories (Kendall 1999) described in the following sections.

3.2.2.1 Probe

The probe attacks are carried out usually for reconnaissance purposes; for instance, a network can be probed to gather information about the types and number of computers connected to a network, a host can be probed to find out the types of installed services or the types of user accounts configured on it. Attackers usually use probing prior to launching an actual attack to scan a large number of machines and services. Various techniques are used for probing such as brute force pinging of IP addresses, testing of open ports by sending connection requests and so on.

3.2.2.2 Denial Of Service (DOS)

DOS attacks are targeted at disrupting a normal service or completely making it unavailable for normal usage. For example, a web service can be denied access to legitimate users if the server is flooded with unfinished connection requests or if it is crashed altogether by exploiting some bug in its implementation. A variety of known DOS attacks exist that use different mechanisms of operation; such as, taking advantage of vulnerabilities or implementation bugs in network protocols or

Table 3.5: Attack types in KDD Cup data and their categorisation

Category	Attack Types
Probe	ipsweep, mscan, nmap, portsweep, satan, saint
DOS	apache2, back, land, mailbomb, neptune, pod, processtable, smurf, teardrop, udpstorm
U2R	buffer_overflow, loadmodule, perl, ps, rootkit, sqlattack, xterm
R2L	ftp_write, guess_passwd, httptunnel, imap, multihop, named, phf, sendmail, snmpgetattack, snmpguess, spy, warezclient, warezmaster, worm, xlock, xsnoop

services at end hosts, choking the computing or memory resources with high volumes of traffic or requests.

3.2.2.3 User to Root (U2R)

In these types of attacks the aim of the attacker is to gain illegal access to the super-user or administrative account privileges to abuse resources or to get access to classified documents. First, the attacker gains access to a normal user account by sniffing passwords or other social engineering techniques and then exploits a vulnerability, implementation bug or administrative discrepancies to obtain super-user access.

3.2.2.4 Remote to Local (R2L)

R2L (also called Remote to User) attacks provide illegal access to an attacker, who has access to send packets to a remote network, to the local users accounts. A basic type of R2L attacks is the brute force password guessing attack, where an attacker tries to crack an easy password by hit and trial or through running automated scripts.

More sophisticated attacks involve software vulnerability exploitation or multi-step attacks where an attacker first installs a sniffing tool to capture passwords and other user information before penetrating into the system.

A complete listing of all the attacks used in the KDD Cup data placed under the above mentioned four categories is given in Table 3.5.

3.2.2.5   Label Inconsistency

The KDD Cup official website states that the *datasets contain a total of 24 training attack types, with an additional 14 types in the test data only* (Hettich and Bay 1999). However, our calculations show that there is a total of 39 attacks in both datasets. The training dataset contains 22 of them and the test dataset contains an additional 17 attacks not present in the training dataset.

Another inconsistency is found in the categorisation of *httptunnel* attack, which only exists in the test dataset. In the KDD Cup competition, this is categorised as a U2R attack (Elkan 2000), while actually this is an R2L type of attack (Kendall 1999). This has a significant impact on the class distribution of the rarest classes in the test dataset (refer to Table 3.6), since the scoring procedure maps attack types to their respective categories, as is done in this thesis (see §3.3.1). Thus in our experiments we have mapped *httptunnel* as an R2L attack.

Other researchers have also found some inconsistencies in the data; such as, (Ramesh and Mahesh 2001; Levin 2000). (Ramesh and Mahesh 2001) found problems in the labelling of the test dataset which was later corrected. They have also reported 39 attack types (as shown by our calculations) in their work.

As a side note, it is worth mentioning that R2L attacks are sometimes referred to as Remote to User attacks which should not be confused with User to Root (U2R) type of attacks.

3.2.2.6 Class Distribution

Table 3.6 shows the number of instances in the full and 10 percent training datasets as well as the test dataset along with their respective percentages. All attack types are mapped to their respective categories while the non-intrusive instances are labelled as normal. Note that mapping *httptunnel* attack to R2L reduces the number of U2R instances from 228 to 70 and increases the R2L instances from 16189 to 16347.

Table 3.6: Class distribution in KDD Cup datasets

Class	Full Training Dataset		10 % Training Dataset		Test Dataset	
	No.	%age	No.	%age	No.	%age
Normal	972,780	19.86	97,277	19.69	60,593	19.48
Probe	41,102	0.84	4,107	0.83	4,166	1.34
DOS	3,883,370	79.28	391,458	79.24	229,853	73.9
U2R	52	0.001	52	0.01	70	0.02
R2L	1,126	0.023	1,126	0.23	16,347	5.26
Total	4,898,430		494,020		311,029	

3.2.3 Advantages and Criticism

Intrusion detection is a practical problem which requires the development of techniques that can be deployed in securing real systems. Obviously, this implies that intrusion detection techniques be evaluated on real world data. Unfortunately, scarcity of such test data is one of the major issues in intrusion detection research. Not that there is a shortage of network traffic or host logs and events, but the privacy and secrecy issues make such data collection a difficult exercise. Even if such data could be obtained with restrictions; making it available for general access is often not possible. Furthermore, collecting data from a production environment also raises concern about its normalcy and labelling. For example, most anomaly detection systems require training with an attack free data, however, this may not be guaranteed when the data is collected from a real network. Such data also needs to be labelled for training most of the misuse detection systems. Manually labelling a huge amount of data is next to impossible and is also error prone. Automatically labelling the data also carries the risk of wrong labelling. Intrusion detection evaluation thus is also a hot research issue in the domain.

The DARPA and KDD Cup datasets overcome these difficulties as they are publicly available, fully labelled and do not raise any privacy concerns. Further, using these dataset the results of individual algorithms can be compared with that of already published results. Another advantage of the KDD Cup dataset is that it is provided in a ready-made feature vector format suitable for most classification algorithms. This eliminates the need for dealing with binary traffic dumps used in the DARPA datasets. This, however, also puts an inherent limitation on the performance of intrusion detection systems that are evaluated using these datasets only; since they have to stick with the provided feature set and they do not guarantee similar performance if tested with real data.

Traditionally, machine learning techniques have shown poor performance on the two very rare classes of attacks (i.e., U2R and R2L) in the KDD Cup dataset. Some researchers have attributed this to the dissimilar probability distribution of classes in the training and test datasets (Ramesh and Mahesh 2001; Levin 2000). (Sabhnani and Serpen 2004) has argued that the KDD Cup datasets should not be used to train machine learning algorithms for the two rare classes (i.e., U2R and R2L) in the misuse detection context because the target hypotheses in training and test datasets are dissimilar. However, it is worth noting that the presence of previously unknown attacks is one of the major challenges of intrusion detection research and the machine learning algorithms targeting this domain should be able to deal with such variations.

In addition to the above, the KDD Cup dataset is also criticised for being outdated because of the changes in computing and networking technologies and increased sophistication of attacks since it was created. Despite that, the taxonomy used to classify attack types in DARPA evaluation remains relevant today regardless of the modernisation of attacking methods. Nevertheless, as discussed above, this data provides an easy access and a common platform for IDS evaluation and is being extensively used in the intrusion detection research.

3.2.4 Complexity

The KDD Cup dataset poses interesting challenges from machine learning viewpoint. The first obvious observation is the severe class imbalance in the training datasets. One attack category (i.e., Probe) is very rare and is only 0.84% of the whole dataset; whereas two other attack classes (i.e., U2R and R2L) are severely rare and constitute only 0.001% and 0.02% of the full training dataset, respectively. Generally, machine learning algorithms assume equal distribution of the classes which can lead to a bias towards majority class in case of imbalanced class distribution. This problem becomes even pronounced for online (single-pass) learners, like LCS, which do not learn in a batch mode. Additionally, the class distribution in the test dataset is different from the training dataset (e.g., the R2L class, which is only 0.02% of the training, amount to 5.2% of the test dataset). Subsequently, a poor generalisation of this class in training can significantly affect the performance of a learner on the test data. Another difficulty of the data is the highly overlapped classes; many records belonging to different classes differ only in very few attributes, thus making the problem hard for generalisation. These problems together with a large search space make the KDD dataset a challenging problem for machine learning algorithms.

3.3 Methodology

Our approach for evaluating UCS for intrusion detection is to test it on the KDD dataset using appropriate parameter settings and then analyse the results to identify problem areas which are then addressed in the subsequent chapters. This section explains the setup used for the experiments.

In our experiments, UCS is trained using the pre-processed KDD training dataset and then the learnt model (i.e., the rule set) at the end of each training pass is used for the classification of the test dataset. Note that we train UCS using only a single-pass through the data, unlike traditional batch learning systems. Although multiple passes can be made through the training data, in this thesis however, our focus is on learning rules in real time. Since UCS is a stochastic algorithm, each experiment is repeated 30 times with a different seed and results are averaged over all runs.

In our UCS implementation, each feature type (i.e., real, integer, binary and nominal) in the KDD dataset is handled independently according to its respective representation as discussed in §2.4.3.1. In these experiments, UCS is trained using the 10% pre-processed dataset and then tested on the provided test set. As mentioned, 10% dataset consists of half a million records and maintains almost the same class distribution as the full dataset.

3.3.1 Data Pre-Processing

Features in the KDD dataset have mixed data types (i.e., continuous, discrete and nominal) with a highly skewed distribution of values. The data was pre-processed as follows:

- All attack types were mapped to their respective categories and given an integer value, i.e., Probe=1, DOS=2, U2R=3 and R2L=4. Normal connections were mapped to 0.

- All binary attributes were left as is.

- All continuous value attributes with a range greater than 1 were scaled linearly between 0 and 1. Except *src_bytes* and *dst_bytes* attributes, which were scaled logarithmically because of their very large ranges.

- There are three nominal attributes; *protocol_type* attribute has only three categories and is thus treated using the sparse representation discussed in §2.4.3. The other two attributes (i.e., *service* and *flag*) have 70 and 11 categories respectively. To avoid inflating the classifier length these were mapped to integer values from 0 to N-1, where N corresponds to the number of categories in an attribute.

Two attributes, *num_outbound_cmds* and *is_host_login*, which have zero values all over the data are removed from the datasets, leaving the number of attributes to 39 from 41.

3.3.2 Evaluation Metrics

The contestants of the 1999 KDD Cup were evaluated on two measures. First, the classification accuracy for each class was reported by using the standard confusion matrix approach. A confusion matrix is an $n \times n$ square matrix where n represents the number of classes, which summarises the errors made by a classification model. It is calculated by comparing the actual class labels in the test set with that of the predicted ones by a classifier.

Second, a cost per example (CPE) score was assigned to each classification model using a cost matrix (given in Table 3.7) based on the rarety of the classes. The cost per example score is computed by multiplying the cost and confusion matrices and dividing the sum of the resultant matrix by the total number of test instances. A lower cost-based score means better classification model. In the results, we will also use these two measures to report the accuracy of different classification models.

Table 3.7: Cost matrix used for scoring intrusion detection techniques in the KDD Cup competitions.

	Normal	Probe	DOS	U2R	R2L
Normal	0	1	2	2	2
Probe	1	0	2	2	2
DOS	2	1	0	2	2
U2R	3	2	2	0	2
R2L	4	2	2	2	0

In addition, *false alarm rate* and *hit rate* are two other measures that are used commonly in the intrusion detection domain to measure the performance of an IDS. False alarms refer to the benign activities reported as intrusions by an IDS whereas hits refer to the true intrusions flagged by an IDS regardless of their particular type. Table 3.8 illustrates the calculation of these two measures along with the overall accuracy using confusion matrix.

Table 3.8: Confusion matrix for a two-class problem and evaluation metrics.

$$\text{accuracy} = \frac{a+d}{a+b+c+d}$$
$$\text{false alarm rate} = \frac{b}{a+b}$$
$$\text{hit rate} = \frac{d}{c+d}$$

		Predicted	
		Normal	Attack
Actual	Normal	a	b
	Attack	c	d

Table 3.9 shows the confusion matrix and other related measures achieved by the winner of the 1999 KDD Cup. Note that in these results httptunnel attacks are labelled as U2R as opposed to R2L (see §3.2.2.5).

In our experiments, we will also report the number of rules evolved by each classification model and their overall coverage of the test feature space. These factors give an indication of the model complexity and the generalisation ability.

Table 3.9: Performance of 1999 KDD Cup Winner.

Confusion Matrix

Predicted

		Normal	Probe	DOS	U2R	R2L	Accuracy
	Normal	60262	243	78	4	6	99.50%
	Probe	511	3471	184	0	0	83.30%
Actual	DOS	5299	1328	223226	0	0	97.10%
	U2R	168	20	0	30	10	13.20%
	R2L	14527	294	0	8	1360	8.40%

Other Performance Measures

Overall Accuracy = 92.71%

False alarm rate = 0.55%

Hit rate = 91.81%

Cost per example = 0.2331

3.3.3 UCS Parameter Settings

There are quite a few UCS parameters that need external setting as discussed in §2.4.3. To ensure the best performance, we used the best practice parameter settings to suit the KDD dataset. Several studies have looked into the effect of different parameters on the performance of XCS and have recommended appropriate settings. Since UCS parameters are essentially a subset of the XCS parameters with only few differences, same settings can be applied to UCS. (Butz, Kovacs, Lanzi, and

Wilson 2004b) identified two important challenges namely *covering challenge* and *schema challenge* to guarantee the application of right fitness pressure to evolve accurate and general rule sets in XCS. The covering challenge requires that classifiers are initialised with high enough generality to overcome the *cover-delete* cycle that can be triggered if the population is too specific in the beginning, in which case, useful classifiers start getting deleted quickly to give room to newly created covering classifiers. On the other hand, the schema challenge requires that the classifiers are specific enough for GA to work properly. Together, these two challenges can be met by appropriately setting the value of $P_{\#}$, for binary and nominal attributes and r_0 for continuous attributes (see §2.4.3.1 for details). (Butz and Goldberg 2003) also derived a *reproductive opportunity bound* which states that the population size (N) should grow exponentially in problem difficulty and polynomially in the string length (i.e., the number of features). Note that the exact formulation of problem difficulty and schema order is not always possible in many real world problems and thus estimated values are used in such cases.

In the following experiments we set $P_{\#} = 0.6$ and $r_0 = 0.4$ as used by (Bacardit and Butz 2004) in their data mining exercise . As for the population size they used N=6400, however, taking account of Stewart Wilson's recommendations we increase the population size to 8000 in our experiments (Wilson 2005). Wilson also recommended to increase the values of θ_{sub} and θ_{del} by a factor of 10 so that the majority class classifiers get sufficient online experience before they can be considered for subsumption or deletion (Wilson 2005). The covering operator is used as described by Wilson in (Wilson 2001b). Both the covering threshold r_0 and mutation threshold m_0 are set in a problem independent way as a percentage of feature values. Proportionate selection is used in the GA procedure which has shown to evolve more compact solutions in XCS (Kharbat, Bull, and Odeh 2005). The *actionset subsumption* is also turned off according to Wilson's suggestion (Wilson 2005). The rest of the parameters are set as given in (Butz 2004), except the UCS specific parameters which are set according to (Bernadó-Mansilla and Garrell 2003). A complete listing of the parameter settings is given below:

$\alpha = 0.1$, $\beta = 0.2$, $\delta = 0.1$, $\upsilon = 10$, $\chi = 0.8$, $\mu = 0.04$, $m_0 = 0.2$, $r_0 = 0.4$, $\theta_{GA} = 50$,

$\theta_{sub} = 200$, $\theta_{del} = 200$, $N = 8000$, $acc_0 = 0.99$, GASubsumption=YES,

ASSubsumption=NO

The same parameter settings will be used in all the experiments throughout this chapter unless otherwise stated explicitly.

3.3.4   UCS Implementation

UCS and all other algorithms developed in this thesis are implemented in C++ programming language and compiled on a Red Hat Linux gcc 3.2.2 compiler. All experiments in this thesis (unless otherwise mentioned) are run on a high performance parallel computing Linux Beowulf cluster with 152 dual 3GHz Pentium-IV computing nodes maintained by Australian ac3 super-computing facilities.

3.4   Baseline UCS Performance

We begin our investigations with the original UCS as described in (Bernadó-Mansilla and Garrell 2003). Table 3.10 summarises the performance of UCS on the KDD dataset. The tabular at the top shows the average confusion matrix along with percentage accuracies and their standard deviations from the mean for each class. The middle tabular shows the average number of rules evolved by UCS, along with their variances, for each class at the end of training runs. Note that the number of rules are rounded to their nearest integer for better readability. The bottom tabular provides the score for the other evaluation metrics discussed above.

The results show that overall, UCS performance is worse than the top entries in the KDD Cup competition. UCS achieves lower accuracy on almost all of the classes in comparison to the winner of the KDD Cup (see Table 3.9). It also generates significantly higher number of false positives which suggests that UCS is evolving

Table 3.10: Baseline UCS performance on the KDD Cup dataset.

Confusion Matrix

Predicted

	Normal	Probe	DOS	U2R	R2L	Accuracy
Normal	59062.30	434.80	396.23	356.47	343.20	97.47(0.36%)
Probe	418.73	2548.47	390.83	432.33	375.63	61.17(9.22%)
DOS	12282.03	7273.80	195674.20	7271.00	7351.97	85.13(7.89%)
U2R	34.47	7.33	8.10	10.57	9.53	15.10(4.87%)
R2L	14919.63	374.57	279.03	266.77	507.00	3.10(1.58%)

(Actual)

Number of Rules

Normal	Probe	DOS	U2R	R2L	Overall
6068(64)	510(24)	916(53)	105(8)	180(13)	7779(15)

Other Performance Measures

Average accuracy =	82.89(5.85)%
False alarm rate =	2.53(0.36)%
Hit rate =	88.96(2.05)%
Cost per example =	0.41(0.10)

a high number of overgeneral rules for the Normal class. Although the overall hit rate is around 89%, the cost per example score is much higher because of the misclassifications within the attack types. Also note that UCS performs poorly on the two rare classes (i.e., U2R and R2L).

Interestingly, the evolved number of rules remain near the maximum population size limit at the end of the training run. This suggests that UCS is having difficulty in converging to an optimal representation. Overall the rule population is dominated by the Normal class rules that accounts for almost 78% of the total population. This is counter-intuitive as one would expect the DOS class rules to have the highest proportion in the population, given its majority in the training set. However, this is the nature of intrusion detection problem where the attackers try to hide their intrusive activities under the normal activities to make their detection hard. If normal activities are scattered all over the search space, a greater number of rules would be required to cover them; especially using the hyper-rectangular rule representation as used by UCS. Fortunately, UCS is able to maintain rules for rare classes despite their extremely small representation in the training set.

3.5   Summary and Way Forward

This chapter provided a detailed introduction to the KDD Cup dataset used as a benchmark in intrusion detection research. The advantages and criticisms of using this dataset are discussed. The experimental methodology, including evaluation metrics, experimental setup and parameter settings, used in this and the following chapters are presented.

One of the objectives of this chapter was to establish the effectiveness of UCS for the intrusion detection domain. We conducted this feasibility study by evaluating UCS on the KDD Cup dataset. UCS achieved an overall accuracy of around 83% in a single training pass. It produced a false alarm rate of 2.53% and cost per example score of 0.41. The number of rules evolved by UCS also remains near the maximum population size limit, signifying the existence of a memorisation phenomenon.

In the next chapter, we will analyse some of the key components and parameters in UCS to identify issues that led to the inferior UCS performance on the KDD Cup dataset.

Chapter 4

Extending UCS for Intrusion Detection

4.1   Chapter Objectives

In the last chapter, UCS was tested on the KDD Cup dataset and the baseline evaluation metrics achieved by it were presented. In this chapter, we analyse key UCS operators in details, identify several issues that contribute to UCS's inferior performance and propose modifications that significantly improve the baseline UCS performance on key evaluation metrics using the KDD Cup dataset.

4.2   Effect of Different Operators on the System Performance

In this section, we attempt to understand the underlying reasons for the inferior UCS performance by analysing its important parameters and search mechanisms.

4.2.1   The Effect of Population Size

The maximum population size is an important factor in determining the learning complexity of the LCS. Difficult problems with high dimensions and oblique classification boundaries need a higher number of rules to cover the space. (Butz and Goldberg 2003) derived a *reproductive opportunity bound* for XCS and suggested that the population size bound needs to be satisfied to ensure that the GA will get enough reproduction opportunities for each niche representative before it gets deleted from the population. Simply put, the bound guards against the deletion of good classifiers from the population by increasing the maximum population size according to problem difficulty.

Ironically, increasing the population size can significantly increase the learning time and may still not result in a significant improvement in system performance. In this section, we analyse this trade-off by experimenting with different population sizes. To test our hypothesis, we run UCS with the same setup (i.e., using the same parameters) as used for the baseline experiments but with increasing population sizes.

Table 4.1 provides a summary of UCS performance with varying population sizes on the KDD Cup dataset. The top tabular compares the mean per class accuracy along with their standard deviations for each of the five different population sizes represented by N. The bottom tabular shows other key performance metrics achieved by UCS for each of the population sizes along with the mean CPU time taken by each system to complete an experiment. A one-way analysis of variance (ANOVA) test is also carried out between these results achieved by UCS to determine their statistical significance. In addition, a multiple comparison of ANOVA estimates is performed using Tukey-Kramer test at 95% significance level to determine which group of means is significantly different. Figure 4.1 shows the comparison result for each of the five evaluation metrics. The x-axis on each graph represents the corresponding measures for each evaluation metric. The horizontal bars show comparison intervals and the $\ominus$ symbol represents the corresponding means. Two means

Table 4.1: UCS Performance on KDD Cup dataset with varying population sizes. UCS Performance on KDD Cup dataset with varying population sizes. N stands for population size. Numbers in parentheses show standard deviation from the mean.

Class Accuracy

N	Normal	Probe	DOS	U2R	R2L
1000	89.21(5.29)	21.07(0.94)	23.81(3.99)	18.24(4.81)	7.34(6.18)
5000	96.53(0.93)	35.84(8.46)	78.69(6.73)	16.76(5.12)	2.80(1.24)
10000	97.83(0.37)	66.37(2.20)	93.29(5.70)	14.81(4.88)	3.21(1.47)
15000	98.10(0.33)	67.35(0.98)	95.78(3.46)	14.29(3.92)	3.96(2.02)
20000	98.10(0.31)	67.14(1.31)	96.65(0.26)	14.05(5.19)	3.86(1.76)

Number of Rules

N	Normal	Probe	DOS	U2R	R2L	Overall
1000	885(8)	18(3)	58(6)	11(3)	7(3)	980(5)
5000	3889(49)	303(18)	517(31)	69(6)	102(9)	4880(11)
10000	7573(81)	605(18)	1177(69)	128(10)	222(16)	9704(19)
15000	11430(94)	813(27)	1779(76)	174(11)	315(20)	14510(22)
20000	15226(168)	923(29)	2520(151)	223(12)	375(17)	19267(29)

Other Performance Measures

N	Avg Accuracy	FA Rate	Hit Rate	CPE	Time
1000	35.64(3.05)	10.79(5.29)	77.04(1.58)	1.21(0.05)	16.57(0.19)
5000	77.59(5.00)	3.47(0.93)	87.66(2.05)	0.50(0.09)	84.10(0.88)
10000	89.07(4.24)	2.17(0.37)	90.81(1.53)	0.30(0.08)	178.71(1.75)
15000	91.00(2.54)	1.90(0.33)	91.27(0.87)	0.27(0.04)	238.49(15.34)
20000	91.64(0.23)	1.90(0.31)	91.49(0.56)	0.26(0.01)	286.96(3.27)

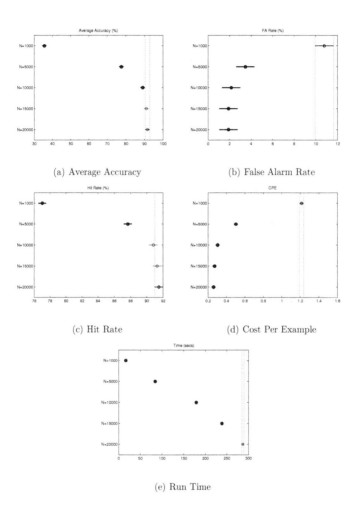

(a) Average Accuracy

(b) False Alarm Rate

(c) Hit Rate

(d) Cost Per Example

(e) Run Time

Figure 4.1: Multiple group comparison of key performance metrics achieved by UCS with increasing population sizes using ANOVA. The system with the highest population is highlighted and vertical rule lines are drawn to compare its significance with other methods. The intervals that are completely disjoint (plotted in bold) are significantly different.

are significantly different at the given significance level if their intervals are completely disjoint. The intervals plotted in bold are statistically different from the selected interval highlighted through vertical rules.

The results indicate that the average test accuracy increases significantly as the population size is increased from 1000 to 15000. However, there is no further significant improvement in the accuracy with increase in the population size. Also, the main improvement is obtained through the better performance of UCS in the three most prevalent classes. The false alarm rate, hit rate and CPE scores show a similar trend. The time statistics, however, show almost a linear increase in CPU time when growing the population size.

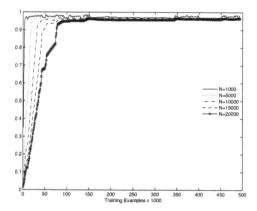

Figure 4.2: Evolution of macroclassifiers in UCS during training with varying population sizes on the KDD Cup dataset. Y-axis shows the percentage of macroclassifiers.

The middle tabular in Table 4.1 shows the number of rules evolved by UCS for each class for each population size. It can be seen that, despite the increase in the population sizes, UCS does not show any sign of population convergence and the post training number of rules reach the maximum limit. This effect is clearly depicted in Figure 4.2. The curves represent the number of rules evolved by UCS and are normalised to their respective maximum population sizes. For each population size, the number of macroclassifiers quickly fill in the maximum allowable limit and stay at this level throughout the training run.

The empirical results suggest that only increasing the population size might not lead the system to converge on a simpler representation. In addition, we observed that the system performance does not improve with an increase in the population size after reaching a maximum level. Similar observations were made by (Orriols-Puig and Bernadó-Mansilla 2006b) for XCS. In fact, a further increase in population size could even lead to the overfitting of training data. On the other hand, we saw that the system run time increases linearly with an increase in the population size. Therefore, a trade-off can be made between the maximum population size and the computational cost without a significant amount of loss in accuracy.

4.2.2 The Effect of Evolutionary Search

There are two ways in which new rules are induced in UCS: through covering and/or GA operations. In this section, we analyse the GA operators to see how they affect UCS's performance. In the following section, we will look at the operation of covering.

In an ideal situation, the covering occurs only minimally and at the start of a training run. Genetic search then discover new useful rules and drives the system to evolve a compact and maximally general rule set for the problem. If, however, nearly the entire rule population is needed to represent a solution the system can enter a cover-delete cycle in which an unmatched input triggers covering, which results in the deletion of an existing rule to make room for the covering rule, which in turns results in a new unmatched input. One way of addressing this problem is to increase the maximum population size so that GA can get enough reproduction opportunities. But increasing population size might not necessarily overcome this problem, as observed in the last section, and can significantly increase the processing times.

To provide a baseline, we ran UCS without the genetic algorithm. In these systems, rules are generated solely by covering. Note that without GA search, UCS essentially becomes a memorisation system that does not provide any explicit generalisation ability. The only generalisation in this case comes through the random generation of the covering predicates that remain static after their creation. The fitness of these covering rules is updated as they match and predict some training instances without changing their decision boundaries.

Genetic search in UCS consists of two generative operators: crossover and mutation. In order to continue our investigation, we also evaluated UCS with crossover alone or mutation alone. We used the same setup (i.e., the same parameter settings and experimental methodology) for these experiments as in the baseline experiments (§3.4) except that the different evolutionary operators were disabled alternatively.

The results of running UCS with different evolutionary operators on the KDD Cup dataset are presented in Table 4.2. The *No GA* system refers to UCS with the GA component completely deactivated. *No Mut* refers to the system without the mutation operator while the rest of GA operations are activated. Likewise, *No XO* refers to the system running without crossover. For comparison and better readability, the baseline results are also listed. Similar tests of significance are performed for the key performance metrics as was done in the last section. Figure 4.3 graphically shows the means along with the confidence intervals of overall accuracy, false alarm rate, hit rate and CPE.

From the results, it can be seen that UCS without GA (i.e., *No GA*) performs best in terms of the overall accuracy, hit rate and CPE score among all the systems. It significantly improves the baseline test accuracy on Probe, DOS and R2L attack classes. It also evolves the smallest number of rules overall among the three systems. The system without crossover (i.e., *No XO*) performs worst in terms of test accuracy and evolves the largest number of rules among the three systems. However, its performance degradation in comparison to the baseline system is not statistically significant.

Table 4.2: Effect of evolutionary search in UCS when evaluated with KDD Cup dataset.

Class Accuracy

System	Normal	Probe	DOS	U2R	R2L
Baseline	97.47(0.36)	61.17(9.22)	85.13(7.89)	15.10(4.87)	3.10(1.58)
No GA	97.43(0.34)	67.30(1.33)	96.87(0.22)	16.76(4.04)	5.94(1.77)
No Mut	97.53(0.48)	65.70(3.78)	88.49(8.86)	15.33(5.59)	4.17(2.51)
No XO	96.69(1.77)	53.75(10.67)	81.57(4.36)	15.67(4.68)	3.86(2.34)

Number of Rules

System	Normal	Probe	DOS	U2R	R2L	Overall
Baseline	6068(64)	510(24)	916(53)	105(8)	180(13)	7779(15)
No GA	2837(45)	326(11)	463(14)	37(1)	102(5)	3764(54)
No Mut	3631(89)	331(15)	443(23)	35(2)	93(7)	4533(88)
No XO	6036(68)	479(24)	851(49)	103(7)	173(13)	7640(23)

Other Performance Measures

System	Avg Accuracy	FA Rate	Hit Rate	CPE
Baseline	82.89(5.85)	2.53(0.36)	88.96(2.05)	0.41(0.10)
No GA	91.79(0.21)	2.57(0.34)	92.52(0.82)	0.25(0.01)
No Mut	85.49(6.57)	2.47(0.48)	90.34(2.46)	0.36(0.12)
No XO	80.04(3.31)	3.31(1.77)	88.84(1.37)	0.46(0.06)

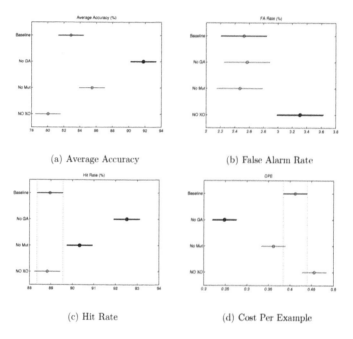

(a) Average Accuracy

(b) False Alarm Rate

(c) Hit Rate

(d) Cost Per Example

Figure 4.3: Multiple group comparison of key performance metrics achieved by UCS with different evolutionary operators using ANOVA. The baseline system is highlighted and vertical rule lines are drawn to compare its significance with other methods. The intervals that are completely disjoint (plotted in bold) are significantly different.

We also observe that the system with crossover alone (i.e., *No Mut*) produces the most unstable results characterised by the larger standard deviation figures while the No GA system understandably is the most stable, as the rule population is not being modified by the GA.

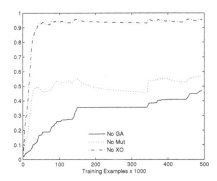

Figure 4.4: Number of macroclassifiers evolved by UCS using different evolutionary operators on the KDD Cup dataset.

Figure 4.4 shows the evolution of rules in the three systems as they train on the KDD Cup dataset. The No GA system curve shows a growing trend throughout the training run which suggests that covering is ongoing in this system and it could not find a stable representation for the training data. The curves for the other two systems show similar trends, although the system with mutation alone evolves much lower number of rules and have higher variations as also confirmed by the numerical results presented in the tables above. The number of rules for the system with mutation stays near the maximum population size suggesting the mutation continues to introduce changes in rule boundaries while the crossover alone will result eventually in a fixed population.

4.2.2.1 Discussion

Empirical evidences in this section suggest that UCS performs better in the absence of GA for the KDD Cup dataset. The question therefore is; is the system with no GA a better alternative? As mentioned above, UCS without the GA rule discovery and generalisation mechanisms merely acts as a memorisation system and at the very best a lookup table. It is therefore not interesting at all from a machine learning perspective. (Kovacs and Kerber 2006) showed that their version of XCS without GA can achieve 100% performance on small noise-free binary problems although they suggested it would not scale well to harder problems (particularly in terms of generalisation). This approach was not intended as a practical alternative to genetic search, but does provide a useful baseline and is much easier to analyse.

The results also clearly show that the genetic search and primarily mutation operator is the main cause of bloat in the rule population. A close look at the rule population tells us that many rules belonging to different classes overlap in many dimensions (i.e., they match in many attributes and vary in a few). Such rules may contribute little to the accuracy of the system and hence they are undesirable. However, it is difficult to avoid generating such rules when a high-dimensional real-valued space is searched by a stochastic method such as a GA, which generates and tests variations to existing rules. To complicate matters, such rules cannot be removed by the subsumption operator since their conditions do not logically subsume each other (at least not in a pair-wise manner).

Genetic search is difficult in this situation because the training set is sparse compared to the real-valued representation. Consequently making a small generalisation of an existing classifier, which may represent a step in the right direction, may not result in any additional inputs being matched. In other words, the fitness gradient of generalisation is a step function, and (partially) flat fitness landscapes are difficult to search.

Furthermore, in high-dimensional real-valued spaces, the GA's generation of redundant and similar rules can easily reach the maximum population size. When this occurs, cover-delete cycles start. This phenomenon results in a lower accuracy and a less consistent performance. Larger population sizes also increase run-times. Finally, cover-delete cycles prevent the system from finding compact representations of the problem.

In short, the tendency to find many partly-overlapping rules in high-dimensional real-valued spaces can stall genetic search and is thus a general and serious problem for learning classifier systems. The study in this section suggests that genetic operators need to be guided appropriately to achieve a better performance.

In the next section, we will investigate the effect of the covering operator on performance and introduce a simple heuristic to guide genetic search by fixing the initial covering intervals. In the next chapter, we will introduce a novel mechanism for extracting the optimal rules discovered by UCS during its learning. The extraction system allows to control the genetic search by exploring only those spaces where an optimal representation has not been found.

4.2.3 The Effect of Covering Operator

Recall that a classifier is created during training using the covering operator in UCS whenever $[C]$ is found empty, or in other words when no matching classifiers are found for a problem instance in the current population of classifiers.

During covering, the continuous valued features are covered by creating an interval around the current state of the input. The maximum width of this interval is controlled by a user-defined parameter r_0, which can be taken as a fraction of the feature range for a problem-independent representation. The upper and lower bounds of the intervals are then chosen uniform randomly from the range defined by this threshold.

As the random numbers are drawn from a uniform distribution, the intervals can be large or small. Classifiers with intervals which are too large will be overgeneral. Classifiers with intervals which are too small are likely to be redundant as described above. The optimal size of interval naturally depends on the problem and on what rules already exist. Since most of the features in the KDD dataset are continuous, in this section we investigate the effect of the size of the covering intervals. Our heuristic is to fix the initial covering interval instead of choosing it randomly. The *schema* and *covering* challenges identified by (Butz, Kovacs, Lanzi, and Wilson 2004b) imply that the setting of a correct initial covering interval is crucial for the proper working of the genetic search. We believe using the fixed covering technique should provide a better control for determining the search direction.

We experimented with various fixed covering interval sizes, rather than drawing them from a uniform distribution. Note that mutation is still able to modify intervals to more appropriate values; it is only the initial value which is fixed.

Table 4.3 provides a comparison of performance metrics for different fixed covering intervals as is done in the previous tables. The top tabular presents per class accuracies and the bottom tabular provides other key evaluation measures achieved by UCS. Again the same baseline setup was used for these experiments except that the initial covering intervals were generated using one of the given fixed interval thresholds. A multiple analysis of variance for each class and overall between all systems is also carried out and shown in Figure 4.5.

We can observe that for the two rarest classes (i.e., U2R and R2L) lower values of fixed covering intervals are better. For interval size of 0.2, UCS achieves the best U2R accuracy of 19.10% and 8.30% for R2L with an interval size of 0.1. The accuracy on these two rare classes start decreasing with the increase in the interval length. This indicates that a higher generalisation pressure for these two classes has a relatively higher deteriorating effect in terms of test accuracy. For the other three classes there is an optimum between intervals of size 0.3 to 0.6. For these classes very low intervals are suboptimal for UCS. Overall the fixed covering heuristic improves baseline UCS performance significantly using a fixed interval size range of 0.3-0.6.

Table 4.3: Effect of fixed covering interval sizes on UCS Performance.

Class Accuracy

CI Size	Normal	Probe	DOS	U2R	R2L
Baseline	97.47(0.36)	61.17(9.22)	85.13(7.89)	15.10(4.87)	3.10(1.58)
0.1	89.81(4.92)	29.31(4.74)	72.25(12.57)	18.62(5.61)	8.30(4.90)
0.2	98.06(0.24)	59.66(14.04)	83.84(3.17)	19.10(4.29)	2.89(1.24)
0.3	98.91(0.33)	68.48(0.59)	96.39(0.17)	13.38(4.32)	2.58(1.84)
0.4	99.07(0.52)	68.06(0.48)	96.02(2.60)	7.19(3.55)	0.79(0.99)
0.5	98.49(0.04)	68.29(1.16)	96.10(2.59)	4.76(1.47)	0.15(0.05)
0.6	98.51(0.02)	68.76(0.72)	96.52(0.23)	3.86(1.88)	0.14(0.22)
0.7	98.58(0.04)	65.09(2.18)	94.01(4.51)	2.12(1.30)	0.06(0.11)
0.8	98.63(0.05)	63.44(2.98)	96.52(0.17)	2.43(1.64)	0.02(0.02)
0.9	98.66(0.12)	45.69(14.25)	96.70(0.08)	0.45(0.92)	0.00(0.00)
1.0	94.50(5.54)	0.61(1.94)	96.98(0.15)	0.00(0.00)	0.00(0.00)

Other Performance Measures

CI Size	Avg Accuracy	FA Rate	Hit Rate	CPE
Baseline	82.89(5.85)	2.53(0.36)	88.96(2.05)	0.41(0.10)
0.1	71.72(9.24)	10.19(4.92)	88.97(3.63)	0.58(0.17)
0.2	82.02(2.32)	1.94(0.24)	88.91(1.32)	0.43(0.04)
0.3	91.55(0.19)	1.09(0.33)	90.97(0.15)	0.27(0.01)
0.4	91.22(1.95)	0.93(0.52)	90.18(2.39)	0.27(0.04)
0.5	91.13(1.92)	1.51(0.04)	90.06(2.39)	0.28(0.04)
0.6	91.45(0.17)	1.49(0.02)	90.30(0.22)	0.27(0.00)
0.7	89.56(3.34)	1.42(0.04)	87.81(4.17)	0.31(0.07)
0.8	91.40(0.14)	1.37(0.05)	90.01(0.18)	0.27(0.00)
0.9	91.30(0.19)	1.34(0.12)	89.99(0.10)	0.27(0.00)
1.0	90.08(1.04)	5.50(5.54)	91.11(1.13)	0.29(0.01)

The optimum interval size is around 0.4 where UCS achieves better overall accuracy than baseline system and also reduces the false alarm rate to 0.93% on average from a high 2.53%. It also achieves a cost per example score of 0.27 in comparison to the baseline score of 0.41.

In UCS, search is carried out mainly from specific to general rules because overgeneral rules have lower fitness and thus reproduce little. Thus, it makes sense that seeding UCS with small initial intervals is better, as they can then carry out their specific to general search. The best value for the covering interval is clearly problem dependent, although there is a strong suggestion that lower values are generally better for overall accuracy and we would take this as a heuristic for setting intervals on other, similar problems. In future we intend to investigate further the dynamics of the covering operator and a problem independent way of setting this value (refer to §7.3).

4.3 Strategies to Deal with Uncovered Test Cases

In this section, we highlight another important issue related to the test set performance of UCS. As discussed in §2.4.3.4, test cases are predicted in UCS by calculating a fitness-weighted average of all the matching classifiers. However, it is not clear from the literature what happens when there is no matching classifier found in the population for a test instance. For problems like intrusion detection, such situations can arise frequently (e.g., because of new types of attacks not found in the training data). This problem can further escalate when the system has difficulty in converging to an optimal representation (i.e., in the presence of cover-delete cycle discussed above).

A simple solution in this situation is to randomly select a class among the possible classes - the undocumented strategy used currently in UCS. Given N classes, the expected accuracy of uniform random prediction would be $1/N$. However, we can do better than random classification and introduce a distance-metric-based classifica-

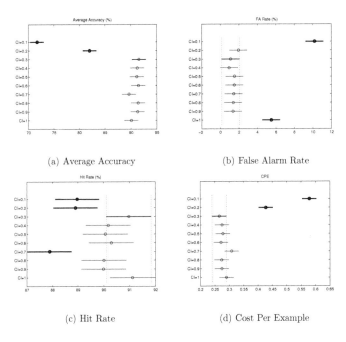

(a) Average Accuracy   (b) False Alarm Rate

(c) Hit Rate   (d) Cost Per Example

Figure 4.5: Multiple group comparison of key performance metrics achieved by UCS with varying fixed covering thresholds using ANOVA. The system with the optimum interval size ($CI = 0.3$) is highlighted and vertical rule lines are drawn to compare its significance with other methods. The intervals that are completely disjoint (plotted in bold) are significantly different.

tion for such cases. Upon encountering a test instance for which there is no matching classifier in the current population, we instead choose the nearest matching classifier based on the shortest distance D from the input, where D is calculated as follows:

$$D = \sum_{i=1}^{n} d_i$$

where d_i is the distance between the ith attribute of an input and the corresponding condition interval of a classifier, and n is the total number of attributes.

For continuous value attributes, d_i is calculated as follows:

$$d_i = \begin{cases} 0 & \text{if } l_i \leq x_i \leq u_i \\ l_i - x_i & \text{if } l_i > x_i \\ x_i - u_i & \text{if } x_i > u_i \end{cases}$$

where x_i is the ith attribute of the input instance, and u_i and l_i are the upper and lower bounds of the ith interval of a classifier respectively.

For discrete value attributes, d_i is calculated as follows:

$$d_i = \begin{cases} 0 & \text{if } c_i = x_i \mid c_i = \# \\ 1 & \text{otherwise} \end{cases}$$

where c_i is i^{th} predicate of the rule and $\#$ is the symbol used for a don't care. For nominal attributes, d_i is calculated as:

$$d_i = \sum_{j=1}^{m} \begin{cases} 1 & \text{if } x_i = 1 \ \& \ c_{i_j} = 0 \\ 0 & \text{otherwise} \end{cases}$$

where m is the number of categories in a nominal attribute and c_{i_j} is the jth category of the ith attribute.

In addition to the distance metric another option could be to use a default rule for the uncovered test cases (i.e., to choose a pre-selected default class upon encountering an uncovered test instance). The use of a default rule is common practice in many machine learning systems that use rule sets as ordered decision lists e.g. RIPPER

(Cohen 1995), CN2 (Clark and Niblett 1989) and AQ15 (Michalski, Mozetic, Hong, and Lavrac 1986). All of these methods use majority class in the training as their default class. Note, that the premise of using a default rule in these systems is to reduce the rule set size by avoiding to learn rules for most prevalent class. Our objective in contrast is to learn a complete map of the problem (i.e., rules for both normal and attack classes).

In this section, we run UCS independently with these three prediction approaches and evaluate their performance on the KDD Cup dataset. For the default class experiments, we also choose the majority class in training, which corresponds to DOS in the KDD dataset.

Table 4.4 provides a comparison of three approaches; namely random guess, default class and distance metric, to predict uncovered cases in the KDD Cup dataset. The first column of the top tabular shows the percentage of uncovered cases as a fraction of total test instances whereas the right three columns present the percentage of correct predictions by each of the three techniques respectively. The experiments with distance metric and default class modifications were run using the same setup as used for the baseline experiments 3.4 except that the uncovered test cases are now predicted using either distance metric or the default class. Each of these two systems are compared against the baseline or random guess technique using a pairwise student ttest at 99% significance level. A ▲ is used if either of the two systems (i.e., default class or distance metric) are significantly better than the baseline system. A ◆ shows that one of the two systems is significantly better than both the baseline as well as the other system. Similarly, a △ denotes that either of the two systems is significantly worse than the baseline system. A ◇ denotes that the selected system is significantly worse than both the baseline as well as the other system.

First note that 13.24% of the test cases are not covered by the UCS post training populations. This is significantly high and amounts to around 41,000 test instances on average. As expected, picking a class uniform randomly for these instances gets an accuracy of around 20%. Using the majority training class as a default class

Table 4.4: UCS Performance on KDD Cup dataset using Distance Metric.

Comparison of Three Strategies to Predict Uncovered Cases

Class	UnCovered	Random Guess	Default Class	Distance Metric
Normal	2.74(0.39)	19.77(0.98)	0.00(0.00)◊	86.48(8.01)◆
Probe	44.99(8.41)	19.97(0.90)	0.00(0.00)◊	45.32(9.01)◆
DOS	15.82(9.72)	19.91(0.28)	100.00(0.00)◆	80.54(22.23)▲
U2R	56.95(4.92)	20.17(6.45)	0.00(0.00)◊	19.95(6.52)
R2L	7.71(4.89)	19.76(1.35)	0.00(0.00)◊	14.20(11.14)
Overall	13.24(7.18)	19.92(0.26)	81.98(14.02)▲	77.37(20.06)▲

Overall Class Accuracy

Class	Random Guess	Default Class	Distance Metric
Normal	97.47(0.36)	96.93(0.42) △	99.30(0.32)◆
Probe	61.17(9.22)	52.18(10.47)	73.21(7.38)◆
DOS	85.13(7.89)	97.79(0.74)▲	95.77(3.33)▲
U2R	15.10(4.87)	3.76(3.80) △	15.05(5.33)
R2L	3.10(1.58)	1.58(1.03) △	2.63(1.19)

Other Performance Measures

Class	Random Guess	Default Class	Distance Metric
Avg Accuracy	82.89(5.85)	91.94(0.60)	91.24(2.47)
FA Rate	2.53(0.36)	3.07(0.42)	0.70(0.32)
Hit Rate	88.96(2.05)	92.13(0.87)	90.07(2.84)
CPE	0.41(0.10)	0.26(0.02)	0.27(0.05)

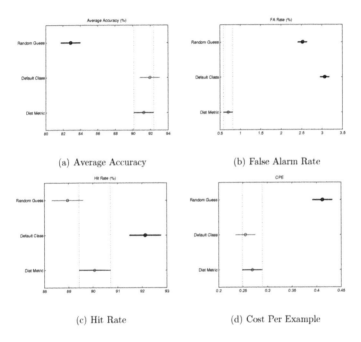

(a) Average Accuracy

(b) False Alarm Rate

(c) Hit Rate

(d) Cost Per Example

Figure 4.6: Multiple group comparison of key performance metrics achieved by UCS with different prediction strategies for uncovered test cases using ANOVA. The system with distance metric prediction is highlighted and vertical rule lines are drawn to compare its significance with other methods. The intervals that are completely disjoint (plotted in bold) are significantly different.

gives an overall accuracy of around 82% which is the best among the three methods. This essentially happens because the selected default class (i.e., DOS) is also the majority in the test set. In fact, the 15% uncovered cases of the DOS class accounts for around 89% of the total uncovered cases. Although the default class achieves best overall accuracy, it cannot predict cases belonging to any of the other classes. Moreover, choosing a default class pre-hand may not always be easy and can be misleading in other situations (e.g., when the default class is not a majority in the test set).

The distance metric based prediction on the other hand gets around 77% of the uncovered cases correct on average. It significantly improved accuracy than random prediction on 3 out of the 5 classes (i.e, Normal, Probe and DOS). On the two rare classes (i.e., U2R and R2L) there is no significant difference between the accuracies achieved by the two systems.

The middle tabular in Table 4.4 provides a comparison of overall accuracy on each class (i.e., including covered and uncovered cases) achieved by the three different methods that seems consistent with the results in the first tabular. The bottom tabular summarises the performance of three strategies on other key measures. Figure 4.6 shows a multiple comparisons of statistical significance among the three systems as has been done in earlier experiments. UCS with the distance metric significantly improves the overall baseline performance. It has also reduced the false alarm rate significantly from 2.53% to 0.7% and the cost per example score from 0.41 to 0.27.

We hypothesise that the distance metric introduces a bias for the following reason. Classes with more training set instances, and particularly those which occupy a greater volume of the instance space, are more likely to have low-distance rules for any given point in the test set. There should thus be a bias towards them. Of course the degree to which this bias improves generalisation depends on the extent to which decision boundaries generated from the training set match those in the test set. However, we should in general expect to see increased accuracy on the more common classes and decreased accuracy on the less common ones. This hypothesised bias fits the observed decrease in accuracy on the less common U2R and R2L classes and the common DOS and Normal classes, whereas the performance on the Probe class is around average which sits between the two levels of prevalence.

Given the supporting empirical evidence we believe that the distance metric method is a more appropriate way of making classifications on the test set than choosing a class randomly. Consequently, we recommend that it be adopted as a standard component of the XCS and UCS algorithms.

4.4 Strategies to Deal with Imbalanced Classes

In previous sections, we highlighted several factors that contribute to UCS performance, specifically on the KDD Cup dataset. We observed that the UCS performance significantly improves upon its baseline performance on Normal, Probe and DOS classes by increasing the population size, using a smaller fixed covering interval size and introducing a distance metric based prediction strategy for the uncovered test instances. None of the above techniques were, however, able to improve the performance on two very rare classes U2R and R2L. In fact, in some instances the accuracy on these two classes was worse than the baseline performance. Thus in this section we sought to investigate UCS's performance more profoundly on imbalanced class problems.

Imbalanced class distribution is an important challenge for data miners that exist in many real world domains. Since most classification algorithms assume an equal prior distribution of classes, their prediction models are generally biased towards the majority class. This has prompted research on analysing and addressing this problem in different ways ranging from varying the sampling rate of training data (Japkowicz 2002), making the classifiers cost sensitive (Drummond and Holte 2003) to boosting techniques (Joshi, Kumar, and Agarwal 2001). LCS, in particular XCS and UCS, have also been shown to be biased towards majority class in high class imbalance environments. In this section, we discuss and compare different strategies to deal with class imbalance issues in UCS.

(Orriols-Puig and Bernadó-Mansilla 2006b) and (Orriols-Puig and Bernadó-Mansilla 2006a) have also studied XCS and UCS on imbalanced binary multiplexer problems in, respectively. In an earlier study, (Orriols-Puig and Bernadó-Mansilla 2005) analysed the performance of UCS on an imbalanced checkerboard problem. It was shown that as the imbalance level increases, overgeneral classifiers covering the whole feature space take over XCS/UCS populations. This is because overgeneral rules become fitter as they match fewer minority class instances at higher imbalance levels. The following sections discuss different schemes to handle class imbalance in UCS.

4.4.1 Fitness Sharing

Fitness sharing has been shown to play an important role in the performance improvement of LCS, particularly dealing with the bias towards strong overgeneral rules (Bull and Hurst 2002; Wilson 1987). The original version of UCS did not implement the fitness sharing scheme. Recently, (Orriols-Puig and Bernadó-Mansilla 2006a) extended UCS by implementing fitness sharing similar to XCS. Under the fitness sharing scheme, the fitness of a rule is computed relative to the fitness of other rules participating in the same niche (i.e., the correctset - see §2.4.3.5 for details). The advantages of the fitness sharing scheme were demonstrated on some binary problems. In specific, UCS with fitness sharing was shown to outperform UCS without fitness sharing on high levels of class imbalance in a binary multiplexer problem.

4.4.2 Biased Accuracy Function

Recall from Section 2.4.3.5 that the fitness of rules in UCS (without fitness sharing) is computed as a direct function of accuracy. This causes a bias towards majority class rules because the accuracy in turn is calculated as a ratio between the correctly classified instances and total matches. Consequently, GA tends to evolve overgeneral rules as class imbalance increases. In (Orriols-Puig and Bernadó-Mansilla 2005), it was shown that a fitness function based on class-sensitive accuracy can discourage the evolution of strong overgeneral rules in UCS. The class-sensitive accuracy is calculated using Equation 4.1, where C_e corresponds to the number of classes a classifier is experienced in, C is the total number of classes, exp_i and acc_i are the experience and accuracy of a classifier in class i respectively. They showed that in imbalanced checkerboard problems, with the new accuracy measure, UCS can handle an imbalance level of up to 5 (i.e., when the ratio of imbalance between the two classes is 1:32).

$$acc = \frac{1}{C_e} \sum_{i=1|exp_i>0}^{C} acc_i \tag{4.1}$$

A side effect of the class-sensitive accuracy measure is that it does not discriminate between a completely overgeneral rule and a rule which is slightly overgeneral and hence discounts both rules equally. This could become a serious pitfall for such accuracy measure, especially in noisy or multi class problems. To overcome this problem, Orriols et al. introduced a weight term w_i on the right-hand side of Equation 4.1. The weighted accuracy is applied to only those classifiers which have an experience greater than a threshold (θ_{acc}) in one class and experiences lower than θ_{acc} in other classes, where θ_{acc} is again a user-defined parameter and is sensitive to problem complexity.

To overcome these problems, we introduce a new accuracy measure which is based on the rate of misclassifications and frequency of input examples in each class. The new accuracy function that we refer to as *class-distributive* accuracy is calculated as:

$$acc = \frac{\frac{exp_p}{\sum_{i=1}^{C} exp_i} \cdot \frac{\sum_{i=1}^{C} I_i}{I_p}}{\sum_{i=1}^{C} \left[\frac{exp_i}{\sum_{j=1}^{C} exp_j} \cdot \frac{\sum_{j=1}^{C} I_j}{I_i} \right]} \tag{4.2}$$

where C is the number of classes, exp_p corresponds to the experience of a classifier in the class it is predicting and I_p is the frequency of instances of the predicted class received so far by the system. The idea behind the class-distributive accuracy is to give more weight to the minority class rules. Since, the number of examples are calculated online, the parameter estimation reaches near equilibrium as more data arrives to the system.

4.4.3 GA rate Adaptation

GA provides generalisation mechanism in UCS and we studied the effect of different genetic operators above (see §4.2.2). UCS uses a niche GA, which implies that it allocates exploration resources according to the occurrence probabilities of different niches. As the class imbalance increase in the training data, the GA is applied more often to the correct sets belonging to the majority class rules. The overgeneral rules predicting majority class get more reproduction opportunities and also become fitter using the standard accuracy function discussed above and eventually takeover the whole population. One way to address this problem is to balance the rate of applying the among different niches according to their distribution in the training data.

(Orriols-Puig and Bernadó-Mansilla 2006b) proposed adaptive tuning of the learning rate (β) and the rate of applying GA to an action set (θ_{ga}) to deal with imbalance class problems in XCS. In contrast, UCS with a fitness sharing scheme is said to be less sensitive to parameter tuning (Orriols-Puig and Bernadó-Mansilla 2006a). The adaptation approach presented in (Orriols-Puig and Bernadó-Mansilla 2006b) works by first detecting an oscillating classifier based on the fluctuating *prediction* values and then measuring a niche level imbalance through the classifier experience in two classes. The algorithm uses a few new user-defined parameters to adapt θ_{ga}. It was unclear to us how it can be extended to UCS and multi-class problems. Consequently, in this work we use our own mechanisms to adapt θ_{ga}. Our approach is to update the GA rate at every discovery step. Here, we present two mechanisms; the first mechanism keeps a record of the global class imbalance level by counting the frequency of input examples for each class. The equation for adapting θ_{ga} is given below:

$$\theta_{ga_t} = C \cdot \theta_{ga} \cdot \frac{I_a}{\sum_{i=1}^{C} I_i} \tag{4.3}$$

where C is the number of classes, I_a is the current number of instances belonging to the class of the current example. We denote this scheme as the *global θ_{ga}* adaptation. The other mechanism is similar to the approach presented in (Orriols-Puig and Bernadó-Mansilla 2006b) in that it measures the imbalance level locally (i.e., based on the classifier experience). But unlike their approach, our method does not require any user-defined thresholds and is applied to all correct sets. The *local θ_{ga}* rate is adapted using the following equation:

$$\theta_{ga_t} = C \cdot \theta_{ga} \cdot \frac{\sum_{cl_i \in [C]} exp_a}{\sum_{cl_i \in [C]} exp} \tag{4.4}$$

where exp_a corresponds to the experience of a classifier in the class of the current example and exp is the sum of experiences in all classes. As noted in (Orriols-Puig and Bernadó-Mansilla 2006b), the local measure of imbalance is preferable because it is more likely to identify scarce unbalanced niches in otherwise balanced class problems.

4.4.4 Experiments with Imbalanced Checkerboard

In this section, we compare different schemes for handling class imbalance in UCS on a two dimensional, real-valued and binary class synthetic dataset; the *checkerboard*. The checkerboard dataset is relatively easy to analyse as data points and the evolved rules can be visually examined. Furthermore, checkerboard problem also suits the hyper planer rule representation used in UCS. Nonetheless, it is still a difficult problem because of interleaving class boundaries (Bernadó-Mansilla and Ho 2005). The dataset is created by uniformly sampling instances from a space bounded by [0,1] in both x and y dimensions and then choosing the class according to their respective coordinates. The complexity C of the dataset can be controlled by the number of class boundaries in each dimension. Further, varying levels of imbalance can be introduced in one of the classes by changing the probability of sampling. Figure 4.7 shows a checkerboard dataset with 5000 instances and $C = 4$.

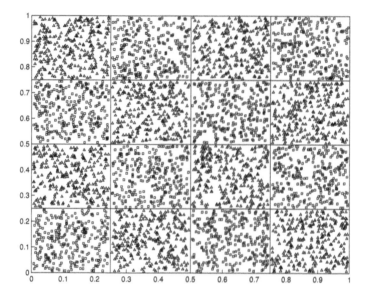

Figure 4.7: An example checkerboard dataset.

The datasets in these experiments are built similar to (Orriols-Puig and Bernadó-Mansilla 2005). However, our version of checkerboard is online (i.e., we generate data instances on the fly instead of feeding fixed samples in batch). Online training suits the requirement of a real time environment and avoids biases due to fixed errors and fixed example positions in noisy and imbalanced datasets. The test set consists of another 10000 instances randomly sampled from the same feature space. The test set is scanned during online training to ensure no test example is used for training the algorithms. To make the checkerboard imbalanced, the instances are sampled as usual, however to maintain the imbalance between the two classes, the minority class instances are sampled with a probability equal to the imbalance level given by $1/2^i$, where i is a monotonically increasing integer representing the imbalance level.

In Tables 4.5, 4.6 and 4.7, we compare the test set accuracies achieved by UCS using different strategies discussed above on increasing levels of imbalanced checkerboard problems. UCSs corresponds to UCS with fitness sharing, UCSns to UCS without fitness sharing, UCSx+wcs to UCS with and without fitness sharing plus the weighted class sensitive accuracy and UCSx+cda to UCS with and without fitness sharing plus the class distributive accuracy discussed above. Each of these systems is run with a fixed GA threshold and the two proposed adaptive mechanisms on 9 imbalance levels along with the balanced checkerboard. The results are averages over 30 independent runs.

The same parameter setting as described in §3.4 is used for UCS except the following changes $\theta_{GA} = 25$, $\theta_{del} = 20$, $\theta_{sub} = 20$, $N = 800$, which are set as in (Orriols-Puig and Bernadó-Mansilla 2005) for the checkerboard problem. Also, UCS was trained using a single-pass of 200,000 instances in these experiments before being evaluated on the test set.

Figure 4.8 shows a multiple comparison using ANOVA between the minority class accuracies achieved by UCS using different techniques to handle class imbalance. For $i <= 2$, almost all systems achieve near optimal performance and thus we do not show comparisons for $i = 0$ and $i = 1$. The x-axis on each graph represents the percentage of minority class accuracy achieved by each system listed on the y-axis. The horizontal bars show comparison intervals and the $\ominus$ symbol represents mean accuracy. The method with the highest mean accuracy is highlighted in each graph and vertical rule lines are drawn to compare its significance against all other methods. The methods with disjoint intervals are plotted in bold.

The results show that the performance of UCSns on minority class drops to zero percent for $i > 3$. The adaptation of θ_{ga} significantly improves the performance and for $i = 4$ UCSns achieves almost 50% minority class accuracy with global GA rate adaptation. But this also does not help with further increase in imbalance. On the other hand, UCSs performs well and reaches around 63% minority class accuracy at $i = 6$. Also we note that the θ_{ga} adaptation has little significant impact on the performance of UCSs and the accuracy drops to zero with or without θ_{ga} adaptation

Table 4.5: Comparison of UCSs and UCSns with and without θ_{ga} adaptation. See text for the explanation of symbols and notations used for significance tests and system names.

		No θ_{ga} Adaptation			Local θ_{ga} Adaptation			Global θ_{ga} Adaptation		
	I	Class 0	Class 1	Overall	Class 0	Class 1	Overall	Class 0	Class 1	Overall
UCSns	0	99.97	100.00	100.00	99.93	100.00	100.00	99.95	100.00	100.00
	1	100.00	99.92	99.96	100.00	99.60	99.97	100.00	99.90	99.95
	2	100.00	99.19	99.67	100.00	98.78	99.40	100.00	99.35	99.83
	3	100.00	96.59	98.23	100.00	97.30	98.60	100.00	98.20	99.20
	4	100.00	2.20	51.07	100.00	19.28	59.63	100.00	46.37	73.17
	5	100.00	0.14	50.03	100.00	0.56	50.27	100.00	1.04	50.43
	6	100.00	0.00	50.00	100.00	0.01	50.00	100.00	0.10	50.03
	7	100.00	0.00	50.00	100.00	0.00	50.00	100.00	0.00	50.00
	8	100.00	0.00	50.00	100.00	0.00	50.00	100.00	0.00	50.00
	9	100.00	0.00	50.00	100.00	0.00	50.00	100.00	0.00	50.00
UCSs	0	100.00	100.00	100.00	100.00	100.00	100.00	100.00	100.00	100.00
	1	100.00	99.96	99.97	100.00	99.96	100.00	100.00	99.99	100.00
	2	100.00	99.34	99.80	100.00	99.15	99.63	100.00	99.56	99.90
	3	100.00	96.49	98.20	100.00	96.94	98.47	100.00	97.91	98.87
	4	100.00	85.29	92.60	100.00	89.81	94.83	100.00	87.92	93.97
	5	100.00	62.62	81.27	100.00	74.27	87.17	100.00	75.10	87.50
	6	100.00	41.77	71.00	100.00	45.70	72.87	100.00	44.08	72.07
	7	100.00	0.00	50.00	100.00	0.00	50.00	100.00	0.00	50.00
	8	100.00	0.00	50.00	100.00	0.00	50.00	100.00	0.00	50.00
	9	100.00	0.00	50.00	100.00	0.00	50.00	100.00	0.00	50.00

Table 4.6: Comparison of UCSs+wcs and UCSns+wcs with and without θ_{ga} adaptation. See text for the explanation of symbols and notations used for significance tests and system names.

	I	No θ_{ga} **Adaptation**			Local θ_{ga} **Adaptation**			Global θ_{ga} **Adaptation**		
		Class 0	Class 1	Overall	Class 0	Class 1	Overall	Class 0	Class 1	Overall
UCSns+wcs	0	99.90	100.00	100.00	99.89	99.90	100.00	99.97	99.93	100.00
	1	99.99	99.80	99.93	100.00	99.80	99.93	99.96	99.95	100.00
	2	100.00	99.49	99.83	99.96	99.23	99.73	99.97	99.77	99.90
	3	100.00	97.75	98.80	99.96	98.08	98.90	99.97	98.60	99.23
	4	100.00	91.06	95.47	100.00	93.33	96.60	100.00	94.93	97.40
	5	100.00	70.93	85.53	100.00	79.71	89.93	100.00	79.44	89.80
	6	100.00	33.30	66.67	100.00	45.40	72.67	100.00	47.44	73.83
	7	100.00	10.21	55.07	100.00	17.33	58.60	100.00	18.29	59.13
	8	100.00	0.74	50.37	100.00	3.56	51.67	100.00	4.71	52.40
	9	100.00	0.00	50.00	100.00	0.02	50.00	100.00	0.03	50.00
UCSs+wcs	0	96.71	99.53	98.10	96.03	98.45	97.30	98.47	99.92	99.23
	1	99.97	99.97	99.93	99.12	99.85	99.50	99.73	99.97	99.90
	2	100.00	98.48	99.37	99.96	99.51	99.73	100.00	99.79	99.97
	3	99.93	98.47	99.30	99.97	98.49	99.13	100.00	98.93	99.47
	4	100.00	96.18	98.07	100.00	96.45	98.23	99.97	96.21	98.17
	5	100.00	85.68	92.73	100.00	89.69	94.73	100.00	89.92	94.87
	6	100.00	64.97	82.50	100.00	68.78	84.40	100.00	73.52	86.73
	7	100.00	47.77	73.87	100.00	47.72	73.83	100.00	51.11	75.57
	8	100.00	32.49	66.20	100.00	31.65	65.87	100.00	30.36	65.17
	9	100.00	14.92	57.53	100.00	18.05	58.97	100.00	16.27	58.17

Table 4.7: Comparison of UCSx+cda with and without θ_{ga} adaptation. See text for the explanation of symbols and notations used for significance tests and system names.

	I	No θ_{ga} **Adaptation**			Local θ_{ga} **Adaptation**			Global θ_{ga} **Adaptation**		
		Class 0	Class 1	Overall	Class 0	Class 1	Overall	Class 0	Class 1	Overall
UCSns+cda	0	100.00	99.96	100.00	100.00	99.99	100.00	100.00	100.00	100.00
	1	100.00	99.99	100.00	100.00	99.93	100.00	99.97	100.00	100.00
	2	99.99	99.76	99.97	99.97	99.83	99.97	100.00	100.00	100.00
	3	100.00	99.12	99.70	100.00	99.57	99.87	100.00	99.76	99.97
	4	100.00	97.49	98.77	100.00	98.53	99.10	100.00	98.38	99.07
	5	100.00	90.63	95.17	99.93	94.35	96.97	99.96	95.17	97.43
	6	99.67	70.82	85.20	99.93	82.55	91.17	99.90	81.69	90.73
	7	99.60	39.76	69.57	99.49	56.24	77.73	99.69	61.51	80.50
	8	99.14	18.75	58.90	99.27	33.96	66.57	99.50	31.58	65.47
	9	99.67	8.17	53.87	99.40	13.18	56.33	99.57	13.35	56.50
UCSs+cda	0	99.93	100.00	100.00	100.00	100.00	100.00	100.00	100.00	100.00
	1	100.00	99.97	100.00	99.99	99.90	100.00	99.97	100.00	99.97
	2	99.96	99.93	99.97	100.00	99.73	100.00	99.99	99.90	100.00
	3	100.00	99.19	99.80	100.00	99.19	99.60	100.00	99.56	99.87
	4	99.97	97.74	98.87	100.00	98.03	99.07	100.00	98.03	98.90
	5	100.00	92.36	96.20	100.00	93.29	96.57	99.97	93.67	96.70
	6	100.00	71.33	85.70	99.97	79.53	89.80	100.00	80.34	90.07
	7	99.97	44.18	72.13	100.00	55.15	77.43	99.90	55.47	77.77
	8	99.97	23.50	61.77	100.00	29.45	64.80	100.00	30.92	65.47
	9	100.00	9.89	54.97	100.00	16.31	58.23	100.00	15.43	57.70

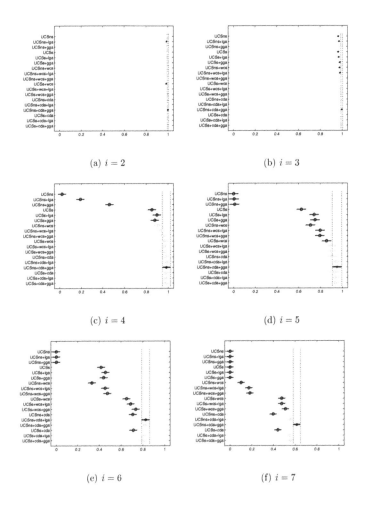

(a) $i = 2$ (b) $i = 3$

(c) $i = 4$ (d) $i = 5$

(e) $i = 6$ (f) $i = 7$

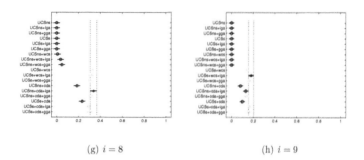

(g) $i = 8$ (h) $i = 9$

Figure 4.8: Multiple group comparison of minority class test accuracies achieved by UCS with various strategies to deal with class imbalance using ANOVA. X-axis represents the percentage of test set minority class accuracies achieved by each system listed on Y-axis. See text for the explanation of system names. The system with best mean is highlighted and vertical rule lines are drawn to compare its significance with other methods. The intervals that are completely disjoint are significantly different.

for $i > 6$. UCS with both biased accuracy functions perform consistently well. Fitness sharing significantly improves the performance of UCS with class sensitive accuracy but it does not have a significant impact on UCS with class distributive accuracy. The adaptation of θ_{ga} does not seem to improve the accuracy of these systems significantly, although we note that systems with global θ_{ga} adaptation methods almost always achieve higher mean accuracy than local θ_{ga} adaptation. The better performance of global θ_{ga} adaptation could be due to the uniform random sampling of feature space in these problems. However, local θ_{ga} adaptation seems to be a better choice to measure the imbalance at niche level. Finally, we note that UCS with class distributive accuracy has the highest mean accuracy in almost all imbalance levels except $i = 9$.

From this analysis, we conclude that UCS with fitness sharing, local θ_{ga} adaptation and class distributive accuracy is the best combination of strategies to deal with class imbalance in UCS without loosing the performance in balanced datasets.

4.4.5 Experiments with KDD Cup Dataset

In this section, we rerun UCS implemented with the class-distributive accuracy, local θ_{ga} adaptation and fitness sharing on KDD Cup dataset. Table 4.8 presents the evaluation metrics achieved by the modified UCS system on the KDD Cup dataset. The bold figures represent statistically significant improvement over the baseline results using a *t-test* at 99% significance level. Likewise, the figures in italics represent significantly worse results. The figures in plain are not statistically different.

Table 4.8: UCS Performance on KDD Cup dataset with class-distributive accuracy, local θ_{ga} adaptation and fitness sharing. Numbers in **bold** are significantly better and those in *italics* are significantly worse than the baseline UCS.

Class Accuracy				
Normal	Probe	DOS	U2R	R2L
97.28(0.51)	63.86(6.06)	**93.04(6.46)**	14.49(3.85)	**4.50(2.59)**

Number of Rules					
Normal	Probe	DOS	U2R	R2L	Overall
6174(62)	**476(21)**	**846(52)**	104(9)	178(12)	7778(16)

Other Performance Measures			
Avg Accuracy	FA Rate	Hit Rate	CPE
88.79(4.82)	2.68(0.41)	**91.31(1.88)**	**0.30(0.09)**

Although the modified UCS achieves significantly better accuracy on the DOS and R2L classes and overall than the baseline UCS, the gain in rare classes is not that significant unfortunately. The two most rare classes (i.e., U2R and R2L) have a very poor representation in the training data (an imbalance ration of almost 1/7,500 for

U2R and 1/347 for R2L with respect to the majority DOS class). Under such sparse representation this becomes a very hard generalisation problem for LCS with the given knowledge representation. Such lower representation might even be considered as noise. In real world scenarios however, the percentage of intrusive activities is much higher than that given in the KDD Cup or DARPA datasets (McHugh 2000). Referring back to the results, the Normal class accuracy has also not improved at all with the new modifications and thus the false alarm rate remains high at 2.68%. However, the cost per example score has reduced from 0.41 to 0.30 which is a significant improvement. Also note that UCS with imbalanced class modifications evolves significantly lesser number of rules in all the classes except Normal.

4.4.6 Class-sensitive Deletion

The deletion procedure in UCS stochastically removes less fit classifiers from the population because the number of classifiers in the population can not exceed a predefined maximum population size limit. As discussed in §2.4.3.5 the deletion of the classifiers is biased towards the larger niche sizes to keep a balance of rules in all niches. However, it is possible that some classes have smaller niche sizes despite the fact that they are more prevalent in the dataset.

In all of the experiments reported in the preceding sections, we observed that UCS evolves most number of rules for the Normal class which are far higher than the number of rules evolved for any of the other classes. To address this issue, we augmented the current deletion scheme by a class distribution factor. Before deleting a rule, we estimate a class distribution in the current rule population. Deletion of rules is then biased towards the classes with higher number of rules in the population than the other classes. The new deletion procedure becomes:

$$dv = \begin{cases} ns \cdot num \cdot \frac{\overline{F}}{F} \cdot D[cl.a] & \text{if } exp > \theta_{del} \text{ and } F < \delta\overline{F} \\ ns \cdot num \cdot D[cl.a] & \text{otherwise} \end{cases}$$

where $cl.a$ corresponds to the action or predicted label of the classifier for which the deletion vote is being calculated and D is a vector that keep current distribution of classifiers for each class. Note that the class distributive bias is in addition to the bias towards large niches. The objective of this heuristic is to maintain the population diversity in imbalanced class environments.

4.4.7   Cost-sensitive Prediction

Cost based classification is another technique that is employed to reduce generalisation error of a classifier in imbalanced class problems (Elkan 2001) (Japkowicz 2002). (Butz, Kovacs, Lanzi, and Wilson 2004b) showed, for a balanced multiplexer problem, that using a biased reward function can considerably improve the convergence rate in XCS. Given severe class imbalance in KDD Cup data we introduced a cost-sensitive prediction method in UCS in attempt to improve the accuracy on very rare classes.

Usually the cost for misclassifying classes in a particular problem is decided by domain experts. In our experiments, we used the cost matrix provided with the KDD Cup dataset (see §3.3.2) for this purpose. The cost sensitive prediction works as follows. First, a prediction array is calculated as usual from all the classifiers that match the current test example and the best class is chosen with the highest prediction value. Next, all other prediction values are normalised to the maximum prediction value. If a prediction falls within a threshold of the maximum prediction it is considered as a competing class. Finally, the class that would incur the highest misclassification cost according to the given cost matrix is chosen as the predicted label of the example. Mathematically, the function can be described as:

$$C_c = \begin{cases} \max(PA(i)) & : & PA(i) \geq \theta_c \\ \max(CM(i,j)) & : & i,j \in [1,m] \end{cases}$$

where C_c is the predicted class, PA is the prediction array, θ_c is the threshold for choosing a competing class, CM is the cost matrix and m is the number of competing classes having a prediction value under θ_c of the maximum prediction.

The results of running UCS with class-sensitive deletion and cost-sensitive prediction are given in Table 4.9. The baseline parameter settings is used for these experiments also except that the two modifications mentioned here were incorporated in the framework. The value of θ_c is set to 0.1 for these experiments.

Table 4.9: UCS Performance on KDD Cup dataset with class-sensitive deletion and cost sensitive prediction. Numbers in **bold** are significantly better and those in *italics* are significantly worse than the baseline UCS.

Class Accuracy				
Normal	Probe	DOS	U2R	R2L
97.08(0.41)	**67.27(1.32)**	**96.07(0.72)**	16.38(5.83)	**4.96(2.04)**

Number of Rules					
Normal	Probe	DOS	U2R	R2L	Overall
5027(41)	*808(15)*	*1299(37)*	*261(16)*	*389(16)*	7785(21)

Other Performance Measures			
Avg Accuracy	FA Rate	Hit Rate	CPE
91.08(0.55)	*2.92(0.42)*	**91.75(0.77)**	**0.27(0.01)**

The two modifications significantly improve the baseline UCS accuracy on all attack classes but not on the Normal class. Especially on the DOS class, we gain around 10% and on Probe class around 6% improvement. Overall, UCS achieves around 91% accuracy against 82% baseline accuracy. Also note that these results are far more stable than the baseline UCS results. The modified UCS also achieves a cost per example score of 0.27 in comparison to 0.41 baseline score. However, the false alarm rate is higher than the corresponding baseline rate.

The effect of using class-sensitive deletion can be seen by the number of rules evolved by UCS shown in the middle tabular. Note that rule allocation is much balanced than the baseline rule allocation. The number of rules for Normal class has been reduced by around 1000 rules on average and similarly all other classes get significantly higher proportion of rules.

4.5 Putting it All Together

In this section, we evaluate UCS with all the modifications proposed in the preceding sections on the KDD Cup dataset. We refer to this version of UCS as the extended UCS and shall denote it as UCSx from hereon. To summarise UCSx includes the following modifications:

- fixed covering as described in §4.2.3 with a covering interval size of 0.3,

- fitness sharing as described in §4.4.1,

- Class-distributive accuracy function as described in §4.4.2,

- local θ_{ga} adaptation as described in §4.4.3,

- class-sensitive deletion as described in §4.4.6 and

- cost-sensitive prediction as described in §4.4.7 with θ_c=0.1.

In the experiments, we use the same methodology and baseline parameter settings as described in §3.4.

Table 4.10 replicates the baseline UCS results presented in Table 3.10 for UCSx. First note that UCSx achieves significantly better accuracy on all classes except R2L where its accuracy is not significantly different than the baseline system. Overall UCSx improves the baseline accuracy by almost 10% to 92.03%. The accuracy achieved by UCSx is also better than all other systems with individual modifications except R2L where its performance is not significantly better than other systems.

UCSx also achieves a false alarm rate of 0.62% improved from a high 2.53% using the baseline system. Also note that the modified UCS produces much more stable outcome than the baseline system.

Both modified UCS and baseline systems evolved almost the same number of rules overall. Although the number of rules are better balanced class-wise in modified UCS due to the class-sensitive deletion.

Table 4.10: Extended UCS (UCSx) performance on KDD Cup dataset. The numbers in **bold** are significantly better and those in *italics* are significantly worse than the baseline UCS at 99% confidence level using a pairwise *t-test*.

Confusion Matrix

Predicted

		Normal	Probe	DOS	U2R	R2L	Accuracy
	Normal	60214.83	180.57	118.13	47.60	31.87	**99.38(0.07%)**
	Probe	757.53	3139.60	253.57	12.70	2.60	**75.36(0.76%)**
Actual	DOS	6928.20	438.50	222423.30	6.40	56.60	**96.77(0.14%)**
	U2R	48.97	1.07	0.37	15.07	4.53	**21.52(4.19%)**
	R2L	15649.30	204.83	15.37	19.13	458.37	2.80(1.67%)

Number of Rules

Normal	Probe	DOS	U2R	R2L	Overall
5384(33)	*527(17)*	*1246(27)*	*204(11)*	*259(14)*	**7620(21)**

Other Performance Measures

Overall Accuracy =	**92.03(0.14)%**
False alarm rate =	**0.62(0.07)%**
Hit rate =	**90.66(0.16)%**
Cost per example =	**0.26(0.00)**

The single-pass UCSx still lacks in achieving performance equivalent to the KDD Cup winner (see Table 3.9). However, it is much better placed in comparison to the baseline UCS. The published results provide a benchmark performance for the KDD dataset. We, however, acknowledge that a direct comparison with these results is unfair because the participants of the competition did not have access to test labels. Moreover, the number of instances for two of the classes (i.e., U2R and R2L) in our case are different from the original test set (see §3.2.2.5). Nonetheless, we emphasise that UCS is a single-pass and incremental rule-based learner. All of these characteristics are very interesting from a real time intrusion detection viewpoint. UCSx achieves competitive performance using a single-pass through the KDD data which is quite encouraging.

4.6   Summary and Way Forward

We identified several issues relating to UCS performance on the KDD Cup dataset and proposed modifications to address them individually. In particular,

- We analysed UCS performance with increasing population sizes and found that increasing the population size does not result in any significant improvement in the test set accuracy after reaching a maximum. The number of macro classifiers also stays near the maximum limit showing no sign of convergence even with larger population size limits. Increasing the population size, however, results in a linear increase in run time. We concluded that a lower population size can thus be traded off with some loss of performance.

- We analysed the effect of evolutionary and covering search operators on the system performance. It was observed that without genetic search both systems could achieve reasonable accuracy overall and thus the search methods need modifications to deal with this kind of search space. We introduced a simple heuristic to do so by using fixed covering intervals of various sizes and obtained significant improvements in performance by adapting this parameter. This is necessarily problem-dependent and time-consuming but we have both empirical evidence and theoretical justification for the heuristic of using small intervals in covering. We conclude that genetic search with this representation faces serious challenges in the type of high-dimensional real-valued space encountered here. Our optimisation of the covering interval helped somewhat but a more general and effective solution is needed. In next chapter we will introduce a new system to better control the genetic search.

- We brought to light the issue of coverage gaps in test spaces and introduced a distance-metric based technique for predicting test instances (such as novel attacks) that are not covered by evolved population of rules. The distance based technique significantly improved UCS performance in uncovered search spaces and thus overall. It also reduced high false alarm rate of baseline UCS to an acceptable level. We recommended it be adopted as the standard approach in both XCS and UCS instead of using a random prediction.

- We analysed UCS performance in the presence of imbalanced classes and comprehensively compared several strategies to deal with class imbalance issue in UCS. We also proposed a new accuracy function, techniques to adapt GA rate, class-sensitive deletion and cost-sensitive prediction techniques to better handle class imbalance in UCS. Together all these modifications significantly improved UCS performance on several key evaluation metrics when tested with the KDD Cup dataset.

The performance of the modified UCS, although not better, is competitive with the performance of KDD Cup winner. But UCS learns in a single-pass and incrementally without needing to update the entire model after seeing a new instance, a common approach in most traditional incremental learners. In addition, UCS adaptively evolves classification models that are highly expressive in the form of interpretable if-then rules. All these characteristics are ideal for real time intrusion detection and thus give UCS an edge over traditional batch learning algorithms.

We note that UCS has difficulty in converging to a smaller representation and that the genetic search needs better control. We delve into this issue in the next chapter and present an algorithm to actively retrieve generalisations learnt by UCS during its operation.

Chapter 5

Real Time Signature Extraction From UCS

5.1 Chapter Objectives

One of the key strengths of UCS is interpretability of its learned hypotheses in the form of simple if-then rules or *classifiers*. However, a large number of these rules may be needed to describe a hypothesis and this number could grow with the problem complexity. This may happen due to various reasons (e.g., representational issues of the rules and the ability of the evolutionary search to find multiple generalisations). Too many rules in turn reduce the readability of the evolved knowledge rendering it difficult to comprehend by the human experts, the potential beneficiaries of this learned knowledge in real world problems. In addition, the processing time could increase exponentially with the rise in the number of rules, which is a major issue for time critical applications like intrusion detection.

There has been some efforts recently in compacting the post training rule sets in XCS. However, many recent data mining applications, including network intrusion detection, require dealing with data as it arrives. In this chapter, we present an algorithm to extract the effective generalisations learnt by UCS in real time (i.e., during its online learning operations). The outcomes of the algorithm are a reduced set of optimal rules (that we refer to as signatures) extracted in real time (i.e., without post processing the UCS population), improved processing time, better control over evolutionary search and an auto termination mechanism for batch learning problems.

In this chapter, we first briefly summarise existing techniques for XCS rule compaction. Next, we describe the signature extraction algorithm in detail and present its pseudo-code. The empirical validation of the algorithm is provided under theoretical learning time bounds on a synthetic binary problem. The algorithm is then extended for continuous attributes and its performance is analysed in noisy and imbalanced class problems using a real-valued synthetic dataset. Mechanisms for the online adaptation of algorithm's parameters are proposed to cope with class noise and imbalance. Finally, the signature extraction system is evaluated on the KDD Cup dataset and its performance is compared with the baseline and modified UCS systems developed in the last chapter.

5.2   Related Work

In his pioneering work, (Wilson 1995) pointed to the rule set reduction as one of the potential techniques to improve XCS efficiency. He suggested two methods; first the use of generality favoured fitness function when the prediction error is below a threshold, and second condensing the population to remove unnecessary classifiers. *Condensation* is applied once the system has evolved the optimal population by switching off the mutation and crossover operators and letting the selection, subsumption and deletion operators work. Later on, (Kovacs 1997) extended this work and introduced measures for automatically triggering the condensation process and terminating the algorithm. Condensation can be quite sensitive to problem complexity and requires a long user-defined delay before it can be triggered. He also proposed a subset extraction method to obtain optimal populations from the

XCS evolved populations. However, the subset extraction may not scale well with increasing problem sizes as the number of subsets to consider for extraction (2^n) increase exponentially for the larger problems. Wilson later introduced Compact Ruleset Algorithm (CRA) for XCS (Wilson 2001a). CRA works by post processing XCS population to find a minimal set of rules that achieve close to 100% accuracy on the training set. The introduction of CRA sparked some research in this area and few variants of CRA have since been proposed. They include modified CRA (Fu and Davis 2002), CRA2 (Dixon, Corne, and Oates 2003) and modifications of CRA and CRA2 by (Wyatt, Bull, and Parmee 2004).

All of the rule reduction techniques mentioned above post process the XCS populations (i.e., XCS is run for a predefined number of iterations and then the final evolved population is pruned using the training set). The concentration of these algorithms is to find a subset of the post training rule population that performs equivalent to the actual population on the training set. Our method in contrast extracts signatures in real time as they are learnt. Almost all rule reduction algorithms reported in the literature are applied to XCS. Due to the similarity between the two systems, these algorithms could be extended to UCS. Nonetheless, our algorithm is the first, in addition of being real time, to report on signature extraction in UCS. We also extend Dixon's CRA2 algorithm to UCS for comparison with our algorithm which is discussed next.

5.3 A Real Time Signature Extraction Algorithm for UCS

Most machine learning algorithms are concerned with learning a generalised hypothesis from a sample of input space which can then be applied to accurately predict future cases. According to Wilson's *generalisation hypothesis*, the evolutionary search in XCS is responsible for providing generalisation (Wilson 1998). The same system dynamics applies to UCS as well, as it uses the same evolutionary search processes. Selection pressure drives the population towards generality while the subsumption and deletion processes counter balance this pressure and drive the system towards evolving an optimal or maximally general population (Butz, Kovacs, Lanzi, and Wilson 2004b). The end result is a compact population which contains the maximally general classifiers among others. Convergence to a smaller rule set, however, does not occur quickly and requires that the system be run for a large number of iterations even after reaching the optimal performance. Moreover, the end population is not minimal (i.e., it always contain many classifiers that are not part of the optimal population).

5.3.1 An Overview of the Algorithm

The aim of our algorithm is to automatically detect the presence of optimal classifiers as they are discovered by UCS and terminate the search process as soon as a complete maximally general solution is found. Figure 5.1 shows a block diagram of the proposed system. We will refer to this system as *UCSSE* for *UCS with real time Signature Extraction* system.

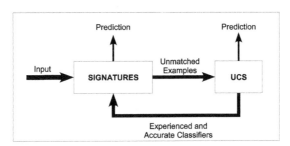

Figure 5.1: UCS with Real time *Signature* Extraction System (UCSSE).

The *signature set* [S] in UCSSE is essentially a subset of [P] consisting of optimal classifiers extracted during the operation of UCS. An input from the environment is first presented to [S] whereby [M] is generated using the current input label and the accuracy of the signatures participating in $[M]$ are updated similar to UCS (see §2.4.3.5). The discovery component of UCS (i.e., the GA) however is bypassed when the system is run through $[S]$. Thus signatures do not preserve the numerosity, fitness and nichesize parameters of UCS. An input is escalated to UCS only if no cover is available in $[S]$, in which case standard UCS takes over and runs its performance and discovery components using $[P]$ for a certain number of trials. Meanwhile, the extraction process of accurate and experienced classifiers from $[P]$ to $[S]$ is triggered periodically.

Initially $[S]$ is empty and system runs mainly through $[P]$ getting enough exploration opportunities. The operation is shifted gradually to $[S]$ as it starts getting populated. The transition completes when the system discovers the best map of the input space and the control is transferred to $[S]$ in which case the evolutionary search is completely halted and the system is made to run from $[S]$. A pruning step in $[S]$ is carried out when the average experience of the signatures in $[S]$ reaches a threshold. In the pruning step, all inaccurate and below average signatures are deleted from $[S]$. If deletion causes a covering gap, control is handed back to $[P]$ and the process is repeated until the system stabilises to run from $[S]$, at which point the learning process can be terminated. The complete pseudo-code for the algorithm is given below.

To understand the significance of the proposed system, imagine an always *"on"* intrusion detection system which identifies illegitimate activities in a production network. The signatures learned from UCS can work as a first line of defence in such an environment. As new intrusions emerge, the system could adapt by learning new signatures using the main UCS application. In a steady state condition one would expect most of the inputs being covered by signatures and the genetic search of UCS only being invoked when there is an indication of a concept change in the environment. As for offline data mining applications, there is a tradeoff between choosing a compact model with some loss of generalisation accuracy and having a large rule set which could exponentially increase processing times and reduce the comprehensibility of the model.

5.3.2 Pseudo-Code

Before presenting the pseudo-code of the algorithm we list important variables along with their descriptions.

- $N_{[P]}$: Number of standard UCS explore trials since the last extraction step.

- T_{ext} : Number of time steps since the last extraction step.

- T_{opt}: Minimum number of time steps for which control is switched to UCS when a $[M]$ through $[S]$ is found empty.

- θ_{xacc}, θ_{xexp}: Accuracy and experience thresholds for extracting a signature to $[S]$.

- C: A constant positive integer used in controlling the deletion experience threshold in $[S]$. Deletion in $[S]$ occurs when average set experience exceeds $C.\theta_{xexp}$.

- θ_{dacc}, θ_{dexp}: Accuracy and experience thresholds for deleting a signature from $[S]$.

The pseudo-code of the algorithm is given below following the convention used in (Butz and Wilson 2002).

5.3.2.1 RUN EXPERIMENT

The main routine of the algorithm is given in Procedure 1 and adds few additional steps to the main loop of the standard UCS algorithm (Butz and Wilson 2002). At each time step $[P]$ is scanned for optimal rules provided the extraction criteria are satisfied. If $[S]$ is non-empty, $[M]$ is formed out of $[S]$ as usual and signatures' parameters (i.e., *accuracy* and *experience*) are updated accordingly. In case no matching signature is found, the system runs standard UCS explore cycles for T_{opt} time steps. The Exploit or test phase works similarly except that there is no extraction or UCS learning during this phase and a class with the highest vote among the matching signatures is predicted. The vote is calculated solely on the aggregative accuracy of the matching signatures. If no matching signature is found, then the class is predicted using $[P]$ as usual (see §2.4.3.4).

Procedure 1 RUN EXPERIMENT
_____

1: **foreach** input situation σ **do**

2:     $[S] \leftarrow$ EXTRACT SIGNATURES out of $[P]$

3:     **if** $[S] \neq \emptyset$ **then**

4:        $[M] \leftarrow$ GENERATE MATCH SET out of $[S]$ using σ

5:        **if** $[M] \neq \emptyset$ **then**

6:           $act \leftarrow$ SELECT ACTION according to σ

7:           UPDATE SET $[M]$ according to act

8:        **else**

9:           switch to standard UCS for next T_{opt} time steps

10:        **end if**

11:     **else**

12:        run a standard UCS trial

13:     **end if**

14: **end for**
_____

5.3.2.2   EXTRACT SIGNATURES

The extraction from $[P]$ to $[S]$ is triggered after a sufficient number of trials since the last extraction has occurred and there has been at least one standard explore cycle during this time. This ensures that the population is not scanned unnecessarily and the extraction step takes place only when the population contains at least some newly discovered optimal classifiers. In addition, a pruning procedure in $[S]$ is invoked if the average set experience exceeds a multiple of θ_{xexp}. Procedure 2 shows the pseudo-code.

Procedure 2 EXTRACT SIGNATURES ($[P]$)

1: **if** $N_{[P]} \geq 1 \wedge T_{ext} \geq T_{opt}$ **then**

2:     **foreach** classifier cl in $[P]$ **do**

3:         **if** cl IS QUALIFIED FOR INSERTION **then**

4:             INSERT cl in SIGNATURE SET

5:         **end if**

6:     **end for**

7: **end if**

8: **if** $\overline{[S].experience} \geq C.\theta_{xexp}$ **then**

9:     PRUNE SET $[S]$

10: **end if**

5.3.2.3   IS QUALIFIED FOR INSERTION

Any classifier with experience greater than θ_{xexp} and accuracy greater than θ_{xacc} is considered qualified for insertion in $[S]$ as a *signature*. The rationale is that those classifiers matching sufficiently large number of examples without much loss of generalisation error are more likely to be maximally general and will have a better accuracy estimation. Procedure 3 shows the pseudo-code.

Procedure 3 IS QUALIFIED FOR INSERTION (cl)

1: **if** $cl.accuracy > \theta_{xacc} \wedge cl.experience > \theta_{xexp}$ **then**

2:     **return** *true*

3: **else**

4:     **return** *false*

5: **end if**

5.3.2.4 INSERT IN SIGNATURE SET

For a higher generalisation pressure, a signature is checked for either way subsumption when inserted in $[S]$. If the qualified classifier to be inserted in $[S]$ is logically subsumed by an existing member of $[S]$ (i.e., all of its condition predicates are equal to or more specific than the existing one) it is not inserted in $[S]$. On the other hand, any of the existing classifiers subsumed by the new classifier are deleted from $[S]$ and the new more general classifier is inserted in $[S]$ as a *signature*. The pseudo-code is given in Procedure 4.

Procedure 4 INSERT IN SIGNATURE SET (qcl)

1: $subsumed = false$
2: **foreach** classifier cl in $[S]$ **do**
3:   **if** cl SUBSUMES qcl **then**
4:     $subsumed = true$
5:   **else if** qcl SUBSUMES cl **then**
6:     DELETE cl
7:   **end if**
8: **end for**
9: **if** $subsumed = false$ **then**
10:   ADD qcl TO SET
11: **end if**

5.3.2.5 PRUNE SET

Since the algorithm is tuned to extract optimal classifiers as soon as they are evolved by UCS, it is likely that the rules which meet the extraction criteria but are actually slightly overgeneral or less than maximally general are extracted to $[S]$. In this case, $[S]$ can contain many rules which over time become inaccurate as they start matching more instances of other classes or the rules which are less experienced as they match fewer instances than the maximally general classifiers. To overcome this issue we can either constrict the extraction criteria by increasing extraction thresholds or introduce a periodic pruning routine which cleans $[S]$ from such classifiers. Since, the former approach can unnecessarily delay the retrieval of optimal rules we adopt the latter approach of greedy extraction and periodic pruning in $[S]$.

Procedure 5 PRUNE SET ($[S]$)

1: **foreach** classifier cl in $[S]$ **do**

2:     **if** $cl.accuracy < \theta_{dacc}$ **then**

3:         DELETE cl

4:     **end if**

5: **end for**

6: SORT $[S]$ according to experience

7: **for** $i = 1$ to $i < [S].size$ **do**

8:     $prevExperience \leftarrow S[i-1].experience$

9:     $currExperience \leftarrow S[i].experience$

10:     **if** $prevExperience/currExperience < \theta_{dexp}$ **then**

11:         $cutoff \leftarrow i$

12:     **end if**

13: **end for**

14: **for** $i = cutoff$ to $i < [S].size$ **do**

15:     DELETE classifier

16: **end for**

The pseudo-code for the pruning procedure is given in Procedure 5. During pruning all classifiers that have an accuracy below θ_{dacc} are deleted from $[S]$. Next, $[S]$ is sorted in a descending order of classifiers' experience. A ratio between the experience of each consecutive pair is then calculated. If this ratio exceeds θ_{dexp}, all remaining signatures are deleted from $[S]$. Note that every time a new classifier is extracted to $[S]$ from $[P]$, the experience of all signatures is reset to zero (not shown in Procedure 2). This ensures that all signatures are weighted equally when being considered for deletion.

Clearly, the deletion accuracy threshold used for pruning inaccurate classifiers is quite subjective and cannot be determined in advance for problems where the optimal classification accuracy is not known due to noise and other complexities. Similarly the deletion procedure for inexperienced classifiers would also bias the deletion of minority class classifiers in environments where the classes are not equally distributed. We will analyse these problems in more detail in §5.5 and will consequently present alternate mechanisms in §5.6.

5.3.3   Validation of the Algorithm

The underlying assumptions of the signature extraction algorithm are that UCS is able to evolve optimal rules during its search process and that these optimal rules or signatures can be extracted from the population successfully. Given that UCS can discover optimal rules, the decision to choose extraction time appropriately becomes critical for proper operation of the algorithm. The other important decision in the signature extraction process is that of switching from $[P]$ to $[S]$ and back at right times. That is to decide how many search opportunities should be given to LCS that will be enough to evolve an optimal representation of the problem. Both of these decisions can be controlled by the T_{opt} parameter. To reiterate, T_{opt} corresponds to the number of time steps the control is switched to the normal UCS when $[M]$ out of $[S]$ is found empty. It tries to find a balance between providing enough exploration opportunities to the classifier system using $[P]$ and switching back to $[S]$ as soon as the signatures are discovered and extracted to $[S]$. Ideally, we would like to run the search process using $[P]$ for the duration of finding at least one optimal classifier before carrying out an extraction process and switching back to $[S]$. Hence T_{opt} can be formulated as the sum of the expected time to discover an optimal classifier and the expected time it will be evaluated θ_{rexp} times. (Butz, Kovacs, Lanzi, and Wilson 2004a) provided a time bound for finding an optimal classifier by XCS using a domino convergence model. They showed that the learning time in XCS scales polynomially in problem length and exponentially in problem complexity[1]. Using their insights, we can derive the bounds for T_{opt} as follows:

Given that

$$T_{opt} = E(\text{Time to generate an optimal classifier}) +$$
$$E(\text{Time to evaluate an optimal classifier } \theta_{xexp} \text{ times})$$

(5.1)

From (Butz, Kovacs, Lanzi, and Wilson 2004a), for an equally probable input distribution, the time bound to generate an optimal classifier is given by:

$$E(\text{Time to generate an optimal classifier}) =$$
$$\frac{1}{P(\text{generation of an optimal classifier})} < \frac{n2^{o+s([P])l}}{\mu(1-\mu)^{l-1}}$$

(5.2)

where n is the number of classes, o is the schema order, $s([P])$ is the average specificity of the population, l is the length of the string and μ is the mutation rate.

Considering an equally probable distribution, the expected time that this classifier will match an input θ_{xexp} times is given by:

$$E(\text{Time to match } \theta_{xexp} \text{ times}) =$$
$$\frac{1}{P(\text{matching an input by the optimal classifier } \theta_{xexp} \text{ times})}$$
$$= \frac{N}{N/2^o} . \theta_{xexp} = 2^o \theta_{xexp}$$

(5.3)

where N is the total number of instances in the feature space.

Substituting Equation 5.3 and the adjusted time bound ($O(l2^{o+n})$) for generating an optimal classifier from (Butz, Kovacs, Lanzi, and Wilson 2004a) in Equation 5.4,

---

[1]Since evolutionary dynamics in both XCS and UCS, which are the basis for time bound computation, are similar we argue that the same bounds can be applied to both systems. Further UCS has generally been shown to converge faster than XCS, thus the derived bounds only provide an upper bound for UCS.

the expected time to generate an optimal classifier becomes:

$$E(\text{Time to generate an optimal classifier})$$

$$< \frac{n2^{o+s([P])l}}{\mu(1-\mu)^{l-1}} + 2^o\theta_{xexp} < l2^{o+n} + 2^o\theta_{xexp} \qquad (5.4)$$

$$= \gamma(l2^{o+n} + 2^o\theta_{xexp})$$

where γ is a constant between 0 and 1. To test the validity of the above expression
we experimented with the binary multiplexer problem of length 6, 11, 20 and 37.
The theoretical values of T_{opt} can be calculated by substituting the values of l and o
in Equation 5.4 for each of the above mentioned lengths of multiplexer and keeping
$\gamma=1$. This gives us values of 352, 1024, 3200 and 10752 for 6, 11, 20 and 37 bit multiplexer respectively. The experimental values are obtained by recording the actual
time when a member of the best action map (BAM) (Bernadó-Mansilla and Garrell
2003) is found with an experience equal to θ_{xexp} (set to 20 for these experiments)
for different lengths of multiplexer.

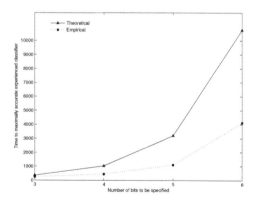

Figure 5.2: Theoretical and experimental bounds for T_{opt} in the binary multiplexer
problem.

Figure 5.2 shows a comparison between the theoretical and empirical bounds. Both
curves show a similar increasing trend, although the difference between the two

bounds increases with the increase in the number of bits to be specified or the schema order. This can be expected as we are using higher population sizes and higher $P_\#$ values for higher length multiplexer, in contrast to the theoretical bound which are derived assuming same parameter values for all lengths. The value of T_{opt} can be tuned using γ. A value of γ closer to 1 could delay the extraction process and thus increase the processing time. On the other hand, a value closer to 0 could lead to early switching to $[S]$ thereby losing important exploration opportunities to discover optimal rules.

5.3.4 Guidelines for Setting Parameters

The *signature* extraction algorithm presented in this section introduces a few new parameters that need to be set externally; namely T_{opt}, C, θ_{xacc}, θ_{dacc}, θ_{xexp}, and θ_{dexp}. In the previous section we discussed the criticality of T_{opt} and the guidelines for setting its value for binary problems with known complexity. Also the trade-off between a higher and lower value is described. More generally, Equation 5.4 suggests that the value of T_{opt} should increase linearly in problem length and exponentially in problem complexity. The parameter C as a multiple of θ_{xexp} ensures that *signatures* have been evaluated long enough before $[S]$ can be pruned. We found a value between 5 and 10 is suitable for C. θ_{dexp} refers to the threshold of ratio between the experiences of a pair of classifiers in a experience wise sorted $[S]$. To avoid a very strong deletion pressure towards specific classifiers, θ_{dexp} can be set between 0.5 to 0.7. The other three parameters (i.e., θ_{xacc}, θ_{dacc}, θ_{xexp}) are more sensitive to problem characteristics. For noise-free, equal class distribution problems these parameter could be set equal to the existing UCS parameters (i.e., acc_0 and θ_{del}). In §5.6 we will provide mechanisms for the online adaptation of these parameters.

5.3.5   Experiments with Multiplexer Problem

XCS and UCS dynamics are well studied on binary problems, especially the multiplexer problem. It is a good starting platform where we can take guidelines from
the developed theory and analyse the dynamics of our algorithm with ease. In this
section we test UCSSE with 11, 20 and 37 bit multiplexer problems.

For UCS we used the same parameter settings as described in §4.4.4 except the
population size and $P_\#$ which were varied with the problem length. The values of N
and $P_\#$ used in different experiments are given in the captions of the corresponding
plots. Also, to speed up convergence, each run was bootstrapped with a random
initial population and an initial $P_\#$ value of 0.8. For UCSSE parameters, we used
$C = 10$ and $\theta_{prun} = 0.9$. T_{opt} was calculated using the respective o and l values for
each multiplexer problem and setting $\gamma = 0.65$.

Figures 5.3(a), 5.4(a) and 5.5(a) show a comparison between UCS and UCSSE for
the three multiplexer problems. The performance (i.e., rate of correct classifica-

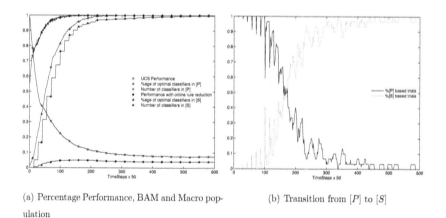

(a) Percentage Performance, BAM and Macro pop-   (b) Transition from $[P]$ to $[S]$
ulation

Figure 5.3: 11 Multiplexer with and without real time signature extraction. N=800,
$P_\#$=0.45, Trials=30000

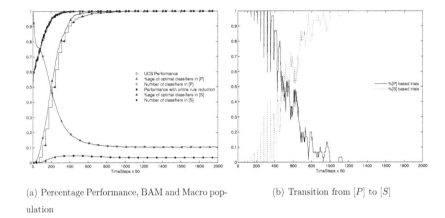

(a) Percentage Performance, BAM and Macro population

(b) Transition from $[P]$ to $[S]$

Figure 5.4: 20 Multiplexer with and without real time signature extraction. N=2000, $P_\#$=0.55, Trials=100000

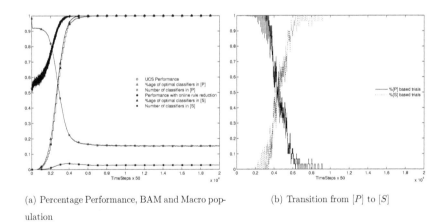

(a) Percentage Performance, BAM and Macro population

(b) Transition from $[P]$ to $[S]$

Figure 5.5: 37 Multiplexer with and without real time signature extraction. N=5000, $P_\#$=0.65, Trials=1000000

tions), Best Action Map (BAM)[2] (i.e., percentage of accurate and maximally general classifiers in the population) and macro population curves are plotted for each multiplexer. Figures 5.3(b), 5.4(b) and 5.5(b) show the corresponding transition curves for UCSSE. Y-axis shows the percentage of trials through [S] and [P] in a window of last 50 trials. Curves are averaged over 30 runs. Note that the performance curves overlap for both systems, showing no performance degradation. The BAM curves also closely follow except a small delay in the case of UCSSE. This is because UCSSE alternates between [P] and [S] based operations and since UCS with signature extraction does not get as many exploration opportunities as the standard UCS does, BAM is fully discovered a little later than the standard UCS run. Moreover, the BAM curves for UCSSE shows the stair case behaviour indicating the signature extraction steps from [P] to [S]. Also it can be seen from the transition curves that the control shifts completely to [S] as soon as all the optimal classifiers get extracted to [S].

Table 5.1: Number of rules evolved and CPU time used by UCS and UCSSE in the Multiplexer problem. Numbers in bold are significantly better at 99% significance level using a pair-wise ttest.

	Number of Rules		CPU Time (secs)	
Problem	UCS	UCSSE	UCS	UCSSE
MUX11	58.53(6.61)	**31.53(2.22)**	3.57(0.20)	**2.43(0.21)**
MUX20	201.7(9.35)	**65.73(3.97)**	46.89(2.57)	**35.43(4.28)**
MUX37	753.2(31.05)	**139.9(8.59)**	3575.35(458.07)	**2645.50(377.68)**

Table 5.1 shows the average number of rules numerically at the end of the run evolved by each system and the CPU time in seconds used by both systems along with corresponding standard deviations in parentheses. The values in bold are significantly better than the other system at a 99% significance level using a pair-

---

[2]an alternate measure of system's performance (Bernadó-Mansilla and Garrell 2003).

wise ttest. Notice that the number of rules in $[S]$ are higher than the BAM. For example, the 11 bit multiplexer can be represented by exactly 16 maximally general rules, which have only 4 specified bits, 3 of which are the address bits. However, this is considering that a unique map of the problem is available. In the case of the 11 multiplexer problem, a don't care bit can occur in one of the address bits position while two bits can be specified in the data bits and still the classifier can be as maximally general and accurate as its counterparts. The signature extraction algorithm does not distinguish between overlapping maximally general classifiers and hence extracts all maximally general classifiers discovered by the system. This in a sense is advantageous since a completely non-overlapping solution is not always desired (Kovacs 2002). Also, the CPU time results show the reduction in processing time improves with the increase in the string length. UCSSE time can be further reduced if the system is stopped when it completely switches to signature based operation.

5.4 Signature Extraction in Real Valued Problems

Unlike binary problems where search space can often be enumerated, continuous valued problems pose unprecedented search spaces and finding precise decision boundaries for even simple problems can be hard. Furthermore, the evolutionary search can produce many overlapping generalisations making the population convergence even more difficult as we saw in the case of KDD Cup dataset in the last chapter. In Wilson's own words:

"... The search processes (crossover and mutation) result in a huge number of candidate "better" classifiers, which are only very slowly either eliminated or emphasised. Furthermore, since the dataset occupies only a minuscule fraction of the input space, many different accurate generalisations are possible. They overlap only partially, so the GA and subsumption mechanisms have difficulty eliminating the less general of them. Fortunately, however, a small number of classifiers sufficient to accurately process the dataset are evolved, among all others,..." (Wilson 2001a)

This has a direct implication for UCSSE which is designed to extract all maximally general rules without distinguishing any overlap between them. Consequently, to overcome this problem we introduce two new subsumption mechanisms in an attempt to reduce overlap between signatures as they are discovered and inserted in $[S]$.

5.4.1 Modified Subsumption Operator

The first technique that we called *modified subsumption* extends the standard subsumption procedure of UCS. The modified subsumption operator is introduced in the insertion routine of signature extraction algorithm (Procedure 4). The pseudo-code for the modified subsumption operator is given below, where LB and UB correspond to the lower and upper bounds of an interval predicate respectively and cl_a refers to the subsuming classifier: The objective of the modified subsumption operator is to minimise overlap between rules by slightly relaxing the subsumption conditions. In the original subsumption operation, a classifier which is sufficiently experienced and accurate can only subsume another classifier if the subsuming classifier completely encapsulates the other classifier. The modified subsumption allows a classifier to subsume the other if overlap between them is within a range specified by $\theta_{subrange}$.

5.4.2 The Expand and Contract Operators

One of the limitations of the modified subsumption operator is that it caters only for overlapping between those signatures belonging to the same class and does not

---

Procedure 6 SUBSUMES (cl_a, cl_b)

1: **if** $cl_a.class \neq cl_b.class$ **then**

2:    **return** $false$

3: **end if**

4: **foreach** interval in cl_a **do**

5:    **if** $cl_a.LB > cl_b.LB \land cl_a.UB < cl_b.UB$ **then**

6:       **return** $false$

7:    **else if** $(cl_a.LB - cl_b.LB) > \theta_{subrange} \lor (cl_a.UB - cl_b.UB) < -\theta_{subrange}$ **then**

8:       **return** $false$

9:    **end if**

10: **end for**

11: **return** $true$

---

consider overlaps between opposite classes. Also when an overlap is found which falls in the subsumption bounds, the more specific rule is simply deleted even if this opens a covering gap in $[S]$ as we observed in the last section.

In this section, we present two new operators, *expand* and *contract*, in order to address these two issues; namely, the reduction of covering gaps and the resolution of overlap between opposing classes in signatures. These operations can be applied when inserting a new signature in $[S]$ or using other schemes (e.g., when the average experience of $[S]$ exceeds a threshold or in a matchset). Here, we present the pseudo-code and explanation of the new insert procedure along with other related functions.

5.4.2.1   INSERT IN SIGNATURE SET

Every time a new signature is found and inserted in $[S]$, it is first scanned against each signature of the opposite class in $[S]$. If an overlap is found between any two signatures, the one with lower accuracy and lower experience is *contracted* to resolve the overlap. Next the signature being inserted is scanned against each existing signature with the same class prediction. If an overlap is found which cannot be

---

Procedure 7 INSERT IN SIGNATURE SET (qcl)

1:   $subsumed = false$

2: **foreach** cl in $[S]$ **do**

3:    **if** $qcl.class \neq cl.class$ **then**

4:     **if** DOES OVERLAP (qcl, cl) **then**

5:      DISJOIN (qcl, cl)

6:     **end if**

7:    **end if**

8: **end for**

9: **foreach** cl in $[S]$ **do**

10:    **if** $qcl.class == cl.class$ **then**

11:     **if** cl SUBSUMES qcl **then**

12:      $subsumed = true$

13:      $break$

14:     **else if** qcl SUBSUMES cl **then**

15:      DELETE cl

16:      $continue$

17:     **else if** DOES OVERLAP (qcl, cl) **then**

18:      $subsumed =$ MERGE (qcl, cl)

19:      **if** $subsumed$ **then**

20:       $break$

21:      **end if**

22:     **end if**

23:    **end if**

24: **end for**

25: **if** $subsumed = false$ **then**

26:    ADD qcl TO $[S]$

27: **end if**

---

resolved by traditional subsumption operator, one of the signatures is expanded to subsume the other (see §5.4.2.4 for more details). Pseudo-code for the updated insertion procedure is given in Procedure 7.

5.4.2.2 DOES OVERLAP

The two hyperrectangles are considered overlapping if they overlap in all of their dimensions. Since the hyperrectangles represented by interval based coding of the classifier's condition are axes parallel hyperplane, finding overlap between them is much easier. Figure 5.6 shows different ways in which the two intervals can overlap (Foley 1995). The two intervals are clearly disjoint in the first two cases (Figures 5.6(a), 5.6(b)) and overlap in the later four cases (Figures 5.6(c) - 5.6(f)). Consequently this procedure returns true if all intervals of the two signatures or hyperrectangles overlap in any combination of the above mentioned four ways. (Note: if all intervals of a hyperrectangle fall within the other then it is considered a common subsumption case).

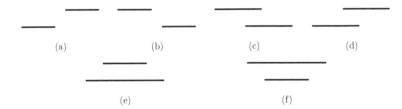

Figure 5.6: Different ways in which two intervals can overlap.

5.4.2.3 DISJOIN

This procedure is used to resolve the overlap between two signatures whose class prediction does not match. First, the rule with the lower accuracy of the two is selected for contraction. If both rules are equally accurate, then the one with lower experience is *contracted*. Next, the predicate that should be clipped is determined by sorting all dimensions according to their respective overlap distances. All interval values are first normalised so that every attribute is weighted equally regardless of its range. Then the dimension or the allele with the minimum overlap is chosen for contraction. Finally, the selected interval's upper or lower bounds are adjusted to resolve the overlap depending upon the overlap type shown in Figure 5.6(c) - 5.6(f). The overlap distance of an interval lying completely within the other interval (5.6(f), considering the lower interval belongs to the contracted condition) is set to infinity (i.e., the bounds are not clipped). In all other cases one of the bounds of the selected interval is moved in the direction of minimum change, such that no portion of the *contracted* interval lies within the bounds of the other interval.

5.4.2.4 MERGE

Two overlapping signatures predicting the same class are merged provided the overlapping volume of at least one of the hyperrectangles, formed by the *signature* conditions, with respect to its total volume exceeds a threshold (θ_{ol}). Thus, the expansion process is essentially controlled by (θ_{ol}). The higher the value of (θ_{ol}) the more conservative is the expansion operator. During merging the ratios of the overlapping volumes are first calculated. The condition which has greater portion of its volume in the overlap with respect to its total volume is merged into the other condition. In other words, the larger condition's upper and lower bounds for each interval are *expanded* to completely encapsulate the smaller one.

5.4.3 Experiments with Checkerboard

In this section, we evaluate the performance of UCSSE extended with the above mentioned operators on the checkerboard problem (see §4.4 for the description of checkerboard problem). Similar to binary multiplexer problems that facilitated validation of the algorithm, the two-dimensional checkerboard provides a test bench with real valued data where the dynamics of the algorithm with the new operators can be analysed visually by plotting the extracted signatures.

To ensure a fair comparison between UCS and UCSSE we also implemented Dixon's rule reduction algorithm (Dixon, Corne, and Oates 2003) to clean the post training rule populations evolved by UCS. This algorithm has shown to be a magnitude faster than Wilson's rule reduction algorithm (Wilson 2001a) while achieving equivalent performance in terms of test accuracy. The actual algorithm is proposed and tested for XCS but could be extended for UCS. It works in two steps; in the first step the so called *non-qualified* classifiers (i.e., rules with low experience, high prediction error and low prediction) are removed from the population. In our implementation, the prediction and prediction error parameters are replaced with the accuracy parameter in UCS. Thus the rules with low experience and low accuracy are considered non-qualified. In the second step, $[M]$ and $[C]$ are formed for each training example as in the standard explore phase of UCS. The classifier with the highest prediction in each $[C]$ is marked as *useful*. Again we used accuracy in place of prediction to identify useful classifiers in UCS. Once the whole training set is processed, the classifiers not marked as useful are removed from the population and the resultant rule set is used to predict the test cases.

For UCS the same parameter settings has been used as described in §4.4. UCSSE parameters were set as follows:

$$T_{opt} = 1200,\ C = 10,\ \theta_{xacc} = 0.99,\ \theta_{xexp} = 100,\ \theta_{dacc} = 0.97,\ \theta_{dexp} = 0.5.$$

In addition, for experiments with the modified subsumption operator, $\theta_{subrange}$ was set to 0.015 and for expand and contract operators θ_{ol} was set to 0.9. Since the relationship of Equation 5.4 cannot be directly used for real valued problems, we chose a moderate value for T_{opt} for these experiments using the general heuristics drawn in §5.3.3 and §5.3.4. The extraction thresholds are set higher in the absence of any noise to ensure only optimal classifiers are selected as signatures. The deletion thresholds are slightly relaxed so that signatures with minor overlaps are not deleted unnecessarily. Similarly, the overlap ranges are set rather conservatively to avoid excessive generalisation pressure.

For Dixon's rule reduction algorithm any classifiers with experience less than 20 and accuracy less than acc_0 is considered as non-qualified.

In the experiments, we compare the performance of three systems (i.e., UCS, UCS with Dixon's rule reduction algorithm, referred to as UCSD, and UCSSE). The results are averaged over 30 runs. Statistical significance is tested using a pair-wise *t-test* at a significance level of 99%. A ▲ is used if UCSD or any variant of UCSSE is significantly better (higher in accuracy and coverage and lower in the number of rules) than UCS. A ◆ shows that UCSD or any of the UCSSE variant is significantly better than both UCS and the other systems. Similarly a △ denotes that UCSD or UCSSE is significantly worse (lower in accuracy and coverage and higher in number of rules) than UCS. A ◇ denotes that UCSD or UCSSE is worse than the other two systems. We will use the same methodology to compare these three systems through out rest of the experiments in this chapter unless stated otherwise.

Using a *non-overlapping* representation, 16 rules are needed to represent the checkerboard problem. However, as discussed above, exact class boundaries of the form (0.000-0.250),(0.000-0.250)$\Rightarrow$ Class 0 may not be learnt by UCS. This in turns implies that at all times $[S]$ will contain classifiers which will either partially overlap with adjoining opposite classes (e.g., (0.01-0.251),(0.00-0.250) $\Rightarrow$ Class 0) or classifiers which are not exactly maximally general (e.g., (0.00-0.249),(0.00-0.250) $\Rightarrow$ Class 0). Nonetheless, UCSSE retrieves near optimal number of rules with both rule compression operators introduced above.

Table 5.2 presents a comparison of the accuracy achieved on the test set and the number of rules evolved by UCS and the rule set sizes achieved by UCSD and both versions of UCSSE on the checkerboard problem. It also shows the percentage coverage achieved by the rule set of each system on the test set. There are a few observations about these results. First, we note that both versions of UCSSE retrieve significantly less number of rules than UCS. In fact, UCSSE using expand

and contract operators, retrieves 16.10 rules on average which is almost equal to the bare minimum number of rules needed to represent this problem. The system with the modified subsumption operator also performs equivalently and retrieves significantly less number of rules than both UCS and UCSD. UCSSE with expand and contract operators also retrieves 100% test accuracy which is the same as UCS. The system with modified subsumption operator however loses some accuracy and achieves 99.03% on average which is still better than the accuracy achieved by UCSD.

Table 5.2: Comparison of test accuracy, number of rules and rule coverage between UCS, UCSD and UCSSE on checkerboard problem. MS refers to Modified Subsumption and EC refers to Expand and Contract operators used in UCSSE. See text for the explanation of notations used in the significance tests.

	System	Class 0	Class 1	Overall
Accuracy (%)	UCS	99.97(0.18)	100.00(0.00)	100.00(0.00)
	UCSD	96.06(4.15)$^\diamond$	97.32(3.51)$^\diamond$	96.67(2.72)$^\diamond$
	UCSSE(MS)	99.23(0.39)	99.29(0.22)	99.03(0.18)
	UCSSE(EC)	99.96(0.18)	100.00(0.00)	100.00(0.00)
Rules	UCS	43.83(10.23)	45.37(8.88)	89.20(13.34)
	UCSD	9.77(1.61)$^\blacktriangle$	10.70(1.93)$^\blacktriangle$	20.47(2.70)$^\blacktriangle$
	UCSSE(MS)	8.17(1.21)$^\blacktriangle$	8.40(1.47)$^\blacktriangle$	16.56(2.39)$^\blacktriangle$
	UCSSE(EC)	8.03(0.40)$^\blacklozenge$	8.07(0.36)$^\blacklozenge$	16.10(0.47)$^\blacklozenge$
Coverage (%)	UCS	99.98(0.06)	99.96(0.09)	99.97(0.06)
	UCSD	92.23(8.18)$^\diamond$	94.82(6.64)$^\diamond$	93.53(5.12)$^\diamond$
	UCSSE(MS)	98.95(1.43)$^\triangle$	99.51(0.89)$^\triangle$	99.23(1.03)$^\triangle$
	UCSSE(EC)	98.72(0.03)$^\triangle$	99.05(0.02)$^\triangle$	98.88(0.02)$^\triangle$

The decision boundaries realised by UCSSE using both compression operators are shown in Figure 5.7. The rule set obtained using *expand* and *contract* operators

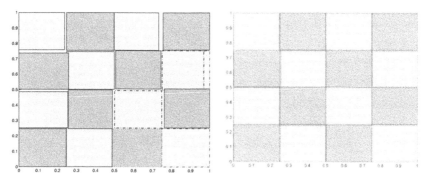

(a) Modified Subsumption operator (18 rules)   (b) Expand and Contract operators (16 rules)

Figure 5.7: Decision boundaries retrieved by UCSSE in checkerboard problem using compression operators. Solid lines represent the actual class boundaries and dashed lines show the boundaries obtained using signatures.

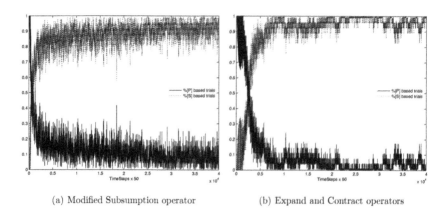

(a) Modified Subsumption operator   (b) Expand and Contract operators

Figure 5.8: Transition from [P] to [S] in checkerboard problem (2000000 training trials).

match very closely to the actual class boundaries with virtually no overlapping and covering almost the whole feature space without leaving any gaps. While the decision boundaries achieved with the modified subsumption operator are also close to optimal albeit with more covering gaps and overlap. Figure 5.8 shows the corresponding load variation on $[S]$ and $[P]$ for both operators respectively. It can be seen that using the expand and contract operators signatures almost completely take over the control around 500000 trials on average. While the load curves for the modified subsumption operator oscillate heavily showing the extract-delete cycle that occurs due to the covering gap and strong deletion pressure in the signature set.

Table 5.3 shows a comparison of average CPU time used by each system in a single run. It can be seen that UCSSE with expand and contract operators significantly performs better than all other systems. UCSD proves to be the most expensive system as it makes two passes through the data to post prune UCS population. Given its better performance, we decided to choose expand and contract operators for compression in signatures. From hereon UCSSE will refer to the system with the expand and contract operator and will be used for the rest of the experiments.

Table 5.3: Comparison of CPU time between UCS, UCSD and UCSSE on checkerboard problem. The numbers are rounded to the nearest integer. See text for the explanation of notations used in the significance tests.

Time (secs)			
UCS	UCSD	UCSSE(MS)	UCSSE(EC)
22(1)	32(1)$^{\diamond}$	17(2)$^{\blacktriangle}$	14(2)$^{\blacklozenge}$

5.5   Signature Extraction in Noisy and Imbalanced Class Environments

Noise, among other peculiarities, is a common characteristic of many real world data mining problems. It is generally defined as an unwanted distortion that affects the quality of a signal. From a classification viewpoint, noise refers to the distortion or error in attribute values or in the classification signs, i.e., the class of a data instance. In the real world, noise can be caused by various reasons such as wrong labeling by human experts or missing or wrong attribute readings due to sensor malfunctioning. Regardless, the noise can affect the predictiveness of a classification algorithm. (Quinlan 1986) showed that the noise due to classification errors is more significant than the attributive noise for the rule-based concept learning systems. Noise plays an important role in determining the performance of intrusion detection systems. Specifically, intrusion detection systems can generate a high number of false alarms in the presence of noise. In this section, we look at the effect of classification noise on the performance of UCSSE using a test problem (i.e., noisy checkerboard).

Many earlier researchers have looked into the effect of noise on machine learning algorithms and the ways of addressing this issue such as (Angluin and Laird 1988)(Aha 1992). GAs are generally considered robust in noisy environments (Miller and Goldberg 1996). Some researchers have looked at the effects of noise and its remedies in XCS such as, (Butz, Sastry, and Goldberg 2005). Nonetheless, the objective of this work is to analyse and improve the performance of the proposed signature extraction system in noisy environments.

5.5.1   Experiments with Noisy Checkerboard

The effect of noise is generally studied by simulating noise in the data (e.g., by introducing random classification errors according to some distribution (Angluin and Laird 1988)). Following this practice, we simulate noise by introducing False

Positives (FP) and False Negatives (FN) in the checkerboard problem. To create a noisy-checkerboard, the data instances are sampled online from the feature space randomly as usual and assigned a class 0 or 1 depending on their respective coordinates on the checkerboard. An FP or FN is introduced by inverting the correct class of an instance randomly based on the noise level η. Four different noisy environments are created with varying degrees of noise in one or both classes. These are listed in Tables 5.4 and 5.5. Figure 5.9 shows a dataset with 5000 instances, 20% FP rate and 20% FN rate.

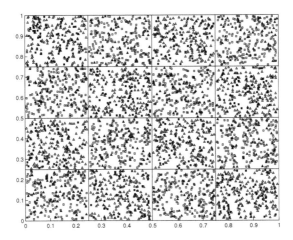

Figure 5.9: Checkerboard with 20% FP and 20% FN. ▲ shows FP and ■ shows FN.

Let us first look at the behaviour of UCS in the presence of noise. Referring to Tables 5.4 and 5.5, it can be seen that UCS performance with noisy training data is quite impressive. The test set accuracy does not degrade proportional to the increasing noise levels. Given a uniform distribution of noise, the expected accuracy on a class with 10% noise is 90% at most. However UCS performs far better thanks to its fitness weighted voting policy during prediction. Contrary to test accuracy which is not effected severely, the number of rules evolved by UCS grows quickly with increasing levels of noise.

The small accuracy degradation with noisy training data (98.24% on noisy class with 20% FP rate) can be understood by examining the post training rule population evolved by UCS. As the noise level increases in the training data, the number of rules covering the wrong labels starts increasing (see Figure 5.10).

Table 5.4: Comparison of number of rules and their test set coverage between UCS, UCSD and UCSSE on the four noisy checkerboard problems.

	N	Class 0	Class 1	Overall	%Coverage
UCS	10% FP 0% FN	100.77	63.60	164.37	99.98
	10% FP 10% FN	115.40	114.40	229.80	99.98
	20% FP 0% FN	99.83	77.57	177.40	99.98
	20% FP 20% FN	135.60	134.53	270.13	99.99
UCSD	10% FP 0% FN	1.20	10.03	11.23	47.61
	10% FP 10% FN	1.27	1.17	2.43	7.28
	20% FP 0% FN	0.33	10.03	10.37	46.75
	20% FP 20% FN	0.17	0.13	0.30	0.76
UCSSE	10% FP 0% FN	0.00	8.00	8.00	48.30
	10% FP 10% FN	0.00	0.03	0.03	0.13
	20% FP 0% FN	0.00	7.77	7.77	47.81
	20% FP 20% FN	0.00	0.00	0.00	0.00

These rules also become fitter with increasing noise level since they start matching a greater number of examples with wrong labels. On the other hand, the fitness of the most numerous rules covering the correct labels in the noisy data decreases with the increasing noise. Consequently, the rules with wrong labels start winning more often during testing thereby impairing the accuracy on the noise-free test set. Moreover, the average specificity of the rules covering the class with noise increases with the rate of noise (i.e., UCS allocates rules more conservatively in the presence of noise). This also explains the increase in the number of rules for classes with noisy

Table 5.5: Comparison of test set accuracy achieved by UCS, UCSD and UCSSE on the four noisy checkerboard problems.

	N	Class 0	Class 1	Overall
UCS	10% FP 0% FN	99.76	100.00	100.00
	10% FP 10% FN	99.89	99.83	99.97
	20% FP 0% FN	98.24	100.00	99.00
	20% FP 20% FN	99.38	99.63	99.40
UCSD	10% FP 0% FN	53.48	94.07	73.73
	10% FP 10% FN	53.58	53.67	53.57
	20% FP 0% FN	50.60	95.62	73.10
	20% FP 20% FN	50.58	50.18	50.40
UCSSE	10% FP 0% FN	99.31	100.00	99.83
	10% FP 10% FN	99.89	99.83	99.97
	20% FP 0% FN	97.45	100.00	98.77
	20% FP 20% FN	99.38	99.63	99.40

training data. When the rate of noise is the same in both classes, the fitness and generality of rules for both classes are affected equally and hence the test accuracy improves in comparison to a single class noise case.

Next, we look at the performance of UCSD and UCSSE in the presence of noise. Looking at Table 5.4, it can be seen that both UCSD and UCSSE have difficulty in preserving rules for the noisy classes[3]. To understand the reasons we again refer to the post training UCS rule populations. According to the generality hypothesis of XCS (and hence UCS), the most numerous rules are also the most consistent as well as maximally general rules. They are also the main contributors towards the test prediction. Table 5.6 shows the most numerous rules evolved by UCS at the end of

---

[3]We do not provide significance tests for these results since both systems could not retrieve a representation for the noisy classes.

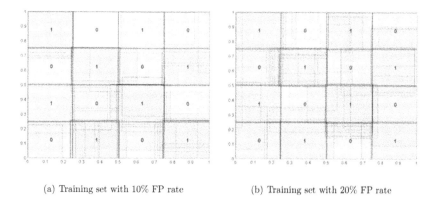

(a) Training set with 10% FP rate   (b) Training set with 20% FP rate

Figure 5.10: UCS rules covering the non-noisy data (class 1) and the FP. The space covered by rules is plotted in transparent. The strength of the shade corresponds to the level of overlapping between rules. Solid lines represent true class boundaries and dotted lines represent the boundaries realised by the rules.

a typical training run for the checkerboard with 20% FP rate. Table 5.5 shows the accuracy achieved by the three systems on the test set.

It can be seen that the accuracy of these good rules is dictated by the amount of noise in the training data. Since the extraction accuracy (θ_{xacc}) in UCSSE is set pre-hand to a very high level (99%), there would be no classifiers in the UCS population to be extracted at this high threshold level in the presence of noise in the training data. Similarly the deletion accuracy (θ_{dacc}) is set crisply to a high 97%. Even if some signatures could be extracted by lowering the extraction experience (θ_{xexp}) threshold, they will get deleted by the signature deletion routine which is invoked when the average experience in $[S]$ exceeds a threshold (see §2). UCSD has a similar problem and a high accuracy threshold for removing non-qualified classifiers removes all good rules from the population. It is not clear from the literature as to how the algorithm should be modified to handle noise in the data. In §5.6 we will present mechanisms for improving the robustness of signatures in the presence of noise in the training data with the help of online adaptation of extraction and deletion thresholds. For a fair comparison, we will also use dynamic thresholds in UCSD.

Table 5.6: The list of most numerous rules evolved by UCS in the checkerboard problem with 20% FP. I1 and I2 correspond to the two interval predicates, C to Class, A to Accuracy and N to Numerosity of the rules. Class 0 contains 20% noise in training.

I1	I2	C	A	N
[0.50492 − 0.73977]	[0.49838 − 0.74401]	0	0.811	23
[0.50449 − 0.74643]	[0.00000 − 0.25378]	0	0.787	22
[0.25257 − 0.50204]	[0.75579 − 1.00000]	0	0.871	22
[0.00000 − 0.23996]	[0.00000 − 0.24328]	0	0.825	20
[0.75051 − 0.99544]	[0.25878 − 0.49544]	0	0.822	16
[0.75051 − 1.00000]	[0.25878 − 0.49544]	0	0.846	15
[0.04894 − 0.24834]	[0.50423 − 0.75177]	0	0.800	11
[0.50449 − 0.75547]	[0.00000 − 0.25378]	0	0.782	10
[0.24684 − 0.47185]	[0.25185 − 0.50507]	0	0.831	10
[0.00000 − 0.24641]	[0.74945 − 1.00000]	1	0.999	42
[0.50366 − 0.75159]	[0.75180 − 1.00000]	1	0.994	38
[0.00000 − 0.24881]	[0.25242 − 0.49941]	1	1.000	38
[0.74711 − 1.00000]	[0.50015 − 0.74900]	1	0.992	36
[0.25240 − 0.50181]	[0.00000 − 0.24746]	1	0.992	32
[0.75159 − 1.00000]	[0.00000 − 0.24658]	1	1.000	28
[0.51020 − 0.75041]	[0.25589 − 0.48715]	1	0.997	20
[0.51020 − 0.75041]	[0.25589 − 0.49410]	1	1.000	13

The accuracy of UCSD on noisy classes is almost equal to 50%, which corresponds to the random guess used by UCSD (similar to UCS) in predicting a class when no matching rules are found in the population. Interestingly, the test set accuracy achieved by UCSSE is almost similar to that of UCS in all of the four noisy problems despite the fact that UCSSE is unable to extract signatures in the presence of noise. Recall that in UCSSE a data instance is first presented to [S] and if no match is found then the control is passed to a standard UCS which builds [M] using [P]. This scheme might undermine the model's comprehensibility if too many inputs are being processed by the UCS population. On the contrary, it provides a graceful fall back mechanism and can be advantageous in real-time intrusion detection where concepts can change over time. This is the direction towards which we are trying to drive our application (as explained in §5.3).

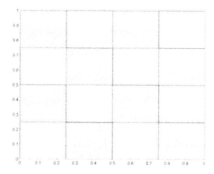

Figure 5.11: Decision boundaries realised by signatures in noisy checkerboard (10% FP rate).

The empirical evidence in this section shows that to retrieve signatures in noisy environments, the extraction and deletion accuracy thresholds of the signature extraction algorithm must be adjusted adaptively according to noise in the input signal. We will address this problem in the next section.

5.5.2 Experiments with Imbalanced Checkerboard

We studied the effect of class imbalance on the performance of UCS in the last chapter (see §4.4), and compared several strategies to deal with this problem in UCS. Intrusion detection is inherently an imbalanced class problem where rare attacks exist among the prevalent normal activities. In this section, we analyse the performance of UCSSE on the imbalanced checkerboard problem introduced in the last chapter. In these experiments, we used the class-distributive accuracy along with fitness sharing and local θ_{ga} adaptation in UCS as they showed better performance in imbalanced environments.

Tables 5.7 and 5.8 present a comparison using test accuracy, number of rules and the test set coverage between UCSD and UCSSE on imbalanced checkerboard problems. The results show that UCSD performs significantly better than UCSSE on all imbalance levels except $i = 1$. It is also getting almost the right number of minority class rules and slightly higher majority class rules on imbalance levels $i \leq 7$. On

Table 5.7: Comparison of test accuracy achieved by UCSD and UCSSE with UCS on imbalanced checkerboard problems.

	Test Accuracy (%)					
	UCSD			UCSSE		
I	Class 0	Class 1	Overall	Class 0	Class 1	Overall
1	99.69	99.63	99.63$^\diamond$	100.00	99.93	100.00
2	99.73$^\diamond$	99.46	99.73	100.00	98.44$^\diamond$	99.20$^\diamond$
3	98.92	98.89	99.00	100.00	94.55$^\diamond$	97.27$^\diamond$
4	99.01$^\diamond$	97.06$^\triangle$	98.03$^\triangle$	100.00	84.45$^\diamond$	92.27$^\diamond$
5	98.41$^\diamond$	92.75	95.60$^\triangle$	100.00	68.92$^\diamond$	84.37$^\diamond$
6	97.81$^\diamond$	78.54	88.17	99.99	46.09$^\diamond$	73.10$^\diamond$
7	97.40$^\diamond$	55.92	76.73	99.93	23.91$^\diamond$	61.87$^\diamond$
8	97.97$^\diamond$	35.56$^\blacklozenge$	66.83	100.00	1.73$^\diamond$	50.83$^\diamond$
9	97.98$^\diamond$	17.63	57.93	100.00	1.86$^\diamond$	50.93$^\diamond$

the other hand, UCSSE is still having problems in retrieving signatures and it could not retrieve any minority class rules for $i \geq 6$ and for this reason we do not conduct the test of significance for number of rules and percentage coverage. The inability of UCSSE to extract signatures at higher imbalance levels can be attributed to the fixed extraction experience threshold (θ_{xexp}). At higher imbalance levels the rules predicting the minority class become low in experience and hence they are not extracted to signatures.

This is a similar problem that we encountered for accuracy thresholds in noisy problems. In addition, the deletion procedure (Procedure 5) for removing the in-experienced classifiers from $[S]$ also biases the deletion of minority class rules as discussed before. To fix the latter issue, we modified Procedure 5 such that the rules for each class are now sorted in a decreasing order of experience independent of other classes and the pair-wise experience ratio is calculated separately for each class. In the next section, we will provide some mechanisms for the adaptation of experience and accuracy thresholds. We hope this would allow UCSSE to perform better in problems that have noise and class imbalance.

5.6 Online Adaptation of Extraction and Deletion Thresholds

In the presence of noise or imbalance class distribution in the training data, the accuracy of a classification algorithm is expected to drop, as we experienced in the last two sections for UCS. In addition, it is often not possible to determine apriori the best possible accuracy that a classification algorithm can achieve on a real world problem. For these reasons, setting the extraction and deletion thresholds manu-ally in UCSSE is not an appropriate strategy for effective signature extraction. In this section, we discuss some techniques for the online adaptation of these parame-ters. The control mechanisms together with the earlier mentioned changes improve UCSSE performance significantly in the two studied problems (i.e., noise and class imbalance).

The block diagram of UCSSE control scheme for the online adaptation of extraction

Table 5.8: Comparison of number of rules and test set coverage, achieved by UCSD and UCSSE, with UCS on imbalanced checkerboard problems.

	Number of Rules					
	UCSD			UCSSE		
I	Class 0	Class 1	Overall	Class 0	Class 1	Overall
1	8.90	8.57	17.47	7.50	7.97	15.47
2	9.73	8.63	18.37	7.63	4.13	11.77
3	10.37	8.83	19.20	7.77	2.77	10.53
4	12.03	8.93	20.97	8.60	2.30	10.90
5	13.47	9.43	22.90	10.20	0.87	11.07
6	15.57	10.47	26.03	12.47	0.63	13.10
7	15.30	8.77	24.07	11.30	0.00	11.30
8	12.93	5.63	18.57	4.43	0.00	4.43
9	10.07	2.30	12.37	7.87	0.00	7.87
	Test Set Coverage (%)					
1	99.13	99.05	99.09	92.31	98.04	95.18
2	99.43	98.87	99.15	94.06	51.15	72.61
3	97.75	98.39	98.07	88.82	37.51	63.17
4	97.94	96.46	97.20	84.67	37.65	61.16
5	96.96	93.18	95.07	80.59	33.04	56.81
6	95.58	89.50	92.54	81.90	48.05	64.98
7	95.02	89.45	92.24	85.61	64.42	75.02
8	96.05	89.27	92.66	100.00	98.10	99.05
9	96.00	92.36	94.18	100.00	97.88	98.94

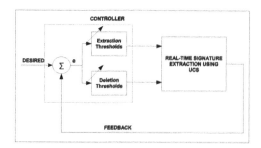

Figure 5.12: Adaptive control for extraction and deletion thresholds in UCSSE.

and deletion accuracies is shown in Figure 5.12. First, let us look at the adaptation of accuracy thresholds (i.e., θ_{xacc}, θ_{dacc}). In §5.5.1 we observed that the accuracy of optimal rules in UCS drops in proportion to the noise level in the data. Since the level of noise is not known apriori in most problems, the extraction and deletion accuracy thresholds in UCSSE should be adapted during learning. A simple procedure to adapt the extraction accuracy is given in Procedure 8.

Procedure 8 UPDATE EXTRACTION ACCURACY

1: $\theta_{xacc} \leftarrow acc_0$

2: **foreach** Class c **do**

3: $\quad \Delta = $ GET SUPPLY ACCURACY(c)

4: $\quad$ **if** $\Delta > \overline{[S]_c.accuracy}$ **then**

5: $\quad\quad \theta_{xacc}[c] = \Delta$

6: $\quad$ **end if**

7: **end for**

At each extraction step the update procedure looks for the most accurate rule in $[P]$ that has enough experience ($> \theta_{xexp}$) to be extracted as a signature. If this accuracy value (referred to as *Supply Accuracy*) is higher than the average accuracy in $[S]$ then θ_{xacc} is adjusted to the new value. Notice that the accuracy for each class is computed independently. This allows the handling of varying levels of noise in different classes. Similarly, the deletion accuracy threshold θ_{dacc} is adjusted at each deletion step as follows:

$$\theta_{dacc}(c) = \overline{[S]_c.accuracy} - \Delta_c \tag{5.5}$$

where Δ varies between $[0,\overline{[S].accuracy}]$ based on the *error* signal between the desired $[S]$ based trials and the current feedback (i.e., the number of $[S]$ based trials since the last deletion step). Note that *error* here corresponds to the set point error (as commonly used in controller notations) and it has nothing to do with the classification error. Initially, when $[S]$ is empty, all inputs are sent to the standard UCS and the error is maximum, hence Δ is set to a minimum. The error starts dropping as the signatures are extracted to $[S]$ and some of the inputs are blocked by the signatures. Accordingly, Δ is increased based on the controller response. Since we are dealing with a single independent variable, the response can be given by a simple linear relationship of the form $y = f(x)$, where y corresponds to the controlled parameter and x is the current error signal. To gain control over the rate of change of the controlled parameter, $f(x)$ can be modeled as a simple linear exponential function. Figure 5.13 shows such a response curve with $f(x) = 1/\exp^{ax}$. For an upper and lower bound of the controlled parameter the function can be written as:

$$y = y_{min} + (1/\exp^{ax} -1/\exp^{x_{max}})\frac{y_{max} - y_{min}}{\|1/\exp^{x_{max}} -1/\exp^{x_{min}}\|}$$

where y_{min} and y_{max} corresponds to the lower and upper bounds of the controlled parameter respectively and the error range is given by x_{min} and x_{max}.

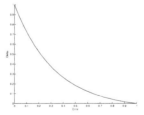

Figure 5.13: Exponential response of the controller.

Other schemes for adapting these parameters are possible and various other techniques were tried, however, the update combination mentioned above yielded the best outcome in terms of the test set accuracy and work load convergence.

Table 5.9: Comparison of performance of UCSD and UCSSE with UCS on noisy checker-board problems. UCSSE was run with accuracy thresholds adaptation and UCSD used average accuracy thresholds. N corresponds to the noise level; 1=10% FP 0% FN , 2=10% FP 10% FN, 3=20% FP 0% FN, 4=20% FP 20% FN. See text for the explanation of notations used in significance tests.

Test Accuracy (%)

	UCSD			UCSSE		
N	Class 0	Class 1	Overall	Class 0	Class 1	Overall
1	$97.10^\triangle$	$99.45^\triangle$	$98.20^\diamond$	99.36	$99.53^\triangle$	$99.53^\triangle$
2	$98.57^\diamond$	$98.83^\diamond$	$98.67^\diamond$	99.70	99.93	99.93
3	$95.92^\diamond$	$99.38^\triangle$	$97.70^\diamond$	$99.40^\blacklozenge$	$99.13^\triangle$	99.23
4	$95.43^\diamond$	$96.80^\diamond$	$96.07^\diamond$	99.14	99.26	99.17

Number of Rules

1	$33.20^\blacktriangle$	$11.20^\blacktriangle$	$44.40^\blacktriangle$	$8.67^\blacklozenge$	$8.47^\blacklozenge$	$17.13^\blacklozenge$
2	$32.27^\blacktriangle$	$32.87^\blacktriangle$	$65.13^\blacktriangle$	$8.77^\blacklozenge$	$9.10^\blacklozenge$	$17.87^\blacklozenge$
3	$33.10^\blacktriangle$	$13.57^\blacktriangle$	$46.67^\blacktriangle$	$8.63^\blacklozenge$	$8.57^\blacklozenge$	$17.20^\blacklozenge$
4	$30.13^\blacktriangle$	$32.07^\blacktriangle$	$62.20^\blacktriangle$	$9.07^\blacklozenge$	$9.33^\blacklozenge$	$18.40^\blacklozenge$

Test Set Coverage (%)

1	99.92	$99.91^\triangle$	$99.91^\triangle$	99.20	$97.50^\triangle$	98.35
2	99.94	$99.91^\triangle$	$99.93^\triangle$	98.43	$99.55^\diamond$	$98.99^\diamond$
3	99.88	$99.82^\triangle$	$99.85^\triangle$	99.16	99.05	99.10
4	$99.93^\triangle$	99.88	$99.90^\triangle$	$97.79^\diamond$	99.20	$98.49^\diamond$

Table 5.9 compares the test accuracy, number of rules and rules coverage of UCSSE run with the adaptation of the extraction and deletion accuracy thresholds and UCSD on the 4 noisy checkerboard problems. For UCSD, we computed the average accuracy for both classes independently at the end of each training run and used this for the removal of non-qualified classifiers. The comparison is made between the

performance of these two systems and UCS, as in Table 5.2, without showing the statistics for UCS. Notice that UCSSE is able to retrieve the approximately correct number of signatures in all four noisy problems which are also significantly less than both UCS and UCSD. It also achieves more than 99% accuracy in all four problems with a high test set coverage. The correctness of signatures is further verified by Figures 5.14 and 5.15, which show the decision boundaries realised by signatures and the load transition curves in the four noisy problems respectively.

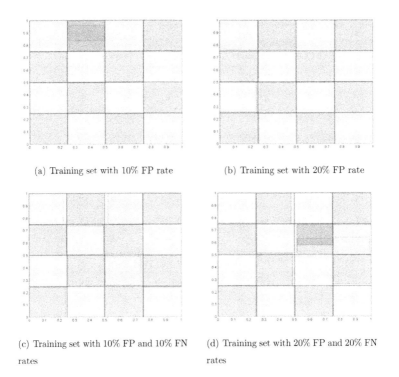

(a) Training set with 10% FP rate   (b) Training set with 20% FP rate

(c) Training set with 10% FP and 10% FN rates   (d) Training set with 20% FP and 20% FN rates

Figure 5.14: Decision boundaries obtained by signatures using adaptive online control of UCSSE parameters in noisy checkerboard problems.

Similar to the adaptation of accuracy thresholds in noisy environments, the control of extraction experience threshold is needed in the imbalanced class problems.

Since the experience of the minority class rules decrease with the increase in class

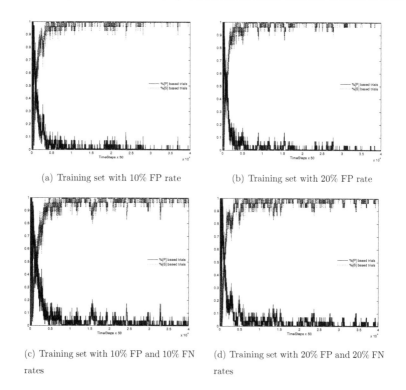

(a) Training set with 10% FP rate

(b) Training set with 20% FP rate

(c) Training set with 10% FP and 10% FN rates

(d) Training set with 20% FP and 20% FN rates

Figure 5.15: Transition from $[P]$ to $[S]$, 2000000 trials (30 runs average) using adaptive online control of UCSSE parameters.

imbalance, fixing θ_{xexp} can hinder the extraction of minority class signatures in such scenarios. Again to cater for the streaming input data, θ_{xexp} in UCSSE is adapted similar to that of global θ_{ga} adaptation in UCS (Equation 5.6), except that the rate of imbalance is measured over a window, i.e., from one extraction step to another.

$$\theta_{xexp_t} = C \cdot \theta_{xexp} \cdot \frac{I_a}{\sum_{i=1}^{C} I_i} \tag{5.6}$$

Tables 5.10 and 5.11 replicate the results of §5.5.2 with UCSSE run with both adaptive accuracy and experience controls and UCSD with the deletion accuracy threshold adjustment described above. With the help of the adaptation schemes, UCSSE extracts significantly lower number of signatures than UCS on all imbalance levels and UCSD on imbalance levels 3-5. It also improves (based on a pair-wise *t-test* at 99% confidence level) its accuracy in comparison to UCSSE without adaptive controls (Table 5.7). Although the test accuracy it achieves is less than the test accuracy achieved by UCS and UCSD for $i \geq 3$, we need to keep in mind that this can happen in real-time classification because an early extraction of a classifier over another would change the performance of the system. In comparison, an offline system such as UCSD has an advantage that it waits till the end (notice that "end" does not really exist in real time systems) before it extracts the rules. Nevertheless, the performance of UCSSE is not practically far from UCS or UCSD.

Table 5.10: Comparison of test accuracy, achieved by UCSD and UCSSE, with UCS on imbalanced checkerboard problems. UCSSE was run with accuracy and experience thresholds adaptation and UCSD used average accuracy thresholds. See text for the explanation of notations used in significance tests.

	Test Accuracy (%)					
	UCSD			UCSSE		
I	Class 0	Class 1	Overall	Class 0	Class 1	Overall
1	99.99	99.60	99.83	99.93	99.67	99.87
2	99.80	99.47	$99.70^\triangle$	99.93	$98.99^\diamond$	$99.53^\triangle$
3	99.96	98.72	99.37	99.73	$97.48^\diamond$	$98.57^\diamond$
4	99.73	$96.99^\triangle$	$98.43^\triangle$	99.83	$93.96^\diamond$	$96.77^\diamond$
5	99.50	93.42	96.30	99.43	$80.60^\diamond$	$89.97^\diamond$
6	$99.23^\triangle$	79.55	89.37	99.73	$53.72^\diamond$	$76.70^\diamond$
7	$98.07^\triangle$	$59.82^\blacklozenge$	78.90	99.30	$26.72^\diamond$	$63.03^\diamond$
8	$98.07^\triangle$	$37.16^\blacklozenge$	$67.63^\blacklozenge$	99.53	$9.09^\diamond$	$54.40^\diamond$
9	$97.75^\triangle$	18.73	58.33	99.03	$3.38^\diamond$	$51.10^\diamond$

Table 5.11: Comparison of of number of rules and test set coverage, achieved by, UCSD and UCSSE on imbalanced checkerboard problems.

	Number of Rules					
	UCSD			UCSSE		
I	Class 0	Class 1	Overall	Class 0	Class 1	Overall
1	$9.67^{\blacktriangle}$	$9.30^{\blacktriangle}$	$18.97^{\blacktriangle}$	$9.57^{\blacktriangle}$	$8.27^{\blacklozenge}$	$17.83^{\blacktriangle}$
2	$10.27^{\blacktriangle}$	$9.27^{\blacktriangle}$	$19.53^{\blacktriangle}$	$10.43^{\blacktriangle}$	$8.37^{\blacktriangle}$	$18.80^{\blacktriangle}$
3	$11.67^{\blacktriangle}$	$9.67^{\blacktriangle}$	$21.33^{\blacktriangle}$	$9.03^{\blacklozenge}$	$8.40^{\blacktriangle}$	$17.43^{\blacklozenge}$
4	$13.17^{\blacktriangle}$	$10.57^{\blacktriangle}$	$23.73^{\blacktriangle}$	$9.23^{\blacklozenge}$	$8.53^{\blacklozenge}$	$17.77^{\blacklozenge}$
5	$14.63^{\blacktriangle}$	$11.13^{\blacktriangle}$	$25.77^{\blacktriangle}$	$13.43^{\blacktriangle}$	$9.17^{\blacklozenge}$	$22.60^{\blacklozenge}$
6	$16.03^{\blacklozenge}$	$12.27^{\blacktriangle}$	$28.30^{\blacklozenge}$	$28.33^{\blacktriangle}$	$6.87^{\blacklozenge}$	$35.20^{\blacktriangle}$
7	$15.63^{\blacklozenge}$	$11.40^{\blacktriangle}$	$27.03^{\blacktriangle}$	$19.33^{\blacktriangle}$	$5.30^{\blacklozenge}$	$24.63^{\blacktriangle}$
8	$13.00^{\blacktriangle}$	$7.17^{\blacklozenge}$	$20.17^{\blacklozenge}$	$10.17^{\blacktriangle}$	$17.77^{\blacktriangle}$	$27.93^{\blacktriangle}$
9	$10.07^{\blacktriangle}$	$3.40^{\blacklozenge}$	$13.47^{\blacklozenge}$	$4.20^{\blacklozenge}$	20.93	$25.13^{\blacktriangle}$
	Test Set Coverage (%)					
1	$99.81^{\triangle}$	$99.80^{\triangle}$	$99.80^{\triangle}$	99.26	$95.79^{\triangle}$	$97.52^{\lozenge}$
2	$99.84^{\triangle}$	$99.43^{\triangle}$	$99.63^{\triangle}$	$98.45^{\lozenge}$	$93.53^{\triangle}$	$95.99^{\lozenge}$
3	$99.82^{\triangle}$	$99.09^{\triangle}$	$99.46^{\triangle}$	$97.00^{\lozenge}$	$87.54^{\lozenge}$	$92.27^{\lozenge}$
4	$99.85^{\triangle}$	$97.76^{\triangle}$	$98.81^{\triangle}$	$95.53^{\lozenge}$	$83.98^{\lozenge}$	$89.76^{\lozenge}$
5	$99.71^{\triangle}$	$95.86^{\triangle}$	$97.78^{\triangle}$	$92.28^{\lozenge}$	$76.28^{\lozenge}$	$84.28^{\lozenge}$
6	$98.53^{\triangle}$	$91.95^{\triangle}$	$95.24^{\triangle}$	$95.26^{\lozenge}$	$71.51^{\lozenge}$	$83.38^{\lozenge}$
7	$96.60^{\triangle}$	$91.68^{\triangle}$	$94.14^{\triangle}$	$90.24^{\triangle}$	$74.25^{\lozenge}$	$82.24^{\lozenge}$
8	$96.83^{\triangle}$	$91.35^{\triangle}$	$94.09^{\triangle}$	$91.44^{\triangle}$	$85.08^{\triangle}$	$88.26^{\lozenge}$
9	$96.27^{\triangle}$	$93.36^{\triangle}$	$94.82^{\triangle}$	$91.32^{\triangle}$	$89.49^{\triangle}$	$90.40^{\triangle}$

5.7 Experiments with KDD Cup Data

5.7.1 Setup

In this section, we will evaluate different versions of UCSSE, developed in this chapter, on the KDD Cup dataset and compare their performance with UCS and UCSD. Also in order to see the effect of changes made to UCS in the last chapter we run both UCSSE and UCSD with the baseline UCS setup and UCSx (Extended UCS) setup as described in §4.5. In the result tables and the following discussion, the systems run with extended setup are referred to as UCSxD and UCSxSE in order to distinguish them from those run using the baseline setup.

For UCS, the same baseline parameter settings are used as listed in §3.4 and for UCSx same as the setup described in §4.5. In UCSD per class average accuracy calculated from post training population is used to identify the unqualified classifiers in the population. And for UCSSE the two external parameters are set to $T_{opt} = 5000$ and $\theta_{ol} = 0.4$. Both of these parameters are changed to suit the increased length of the input. A higher T_{opt} value allows UCS to get increased exploration time to evolve better classifiers. A lower θ_{ol} value allows to handle major overlaps in a higher dimensional space. Also the expand and contract operators are extended for accommodating the binary and nominal variables in the KDD Cup dataset. This extension would generalise the algorithm to most real-world datasets that often are characterised by mixed attributes. Similar to Chapter 4, a single-pass through the KDD data was made to train all the systems in order to emulate a real time environment.

The results on the KDD Cup data are given in Tables 5.12 - 5.23. The numbers are averages of 30 independent runs while the corresponding standard deviations for means are shown in parenthesis. First, we compare three versions of UCSSE developed in the above sections (i.e., UCSSE without adaptive control of parameters, UCSSE+AC with adaptive control of accuracy thresholds and UCSSE+AEC with the adaptive control of both accuracy and experience thresholds). We use the same significance testing scheme for comparing these systems as used for UCS, UCSD and UCSSE in the previous experiments, except that the two adaptive versions of UCSSE are compared against the non-adaptive baseline UCSSE run without any threshold adaptation. Next, the best UCSSE version are compared with UCS and UCSD. The same set of experiments are repeated with extended UCS (UCSx) setup.

5.7.2   Experiments with Baseline UCS

Table 5.12 shows different statistics of the signatures retrieved by the three versions of UCSSE built on the baseline UCS setup. The number of signatures in the top tabular show that both UCSSE and UCSSE+AC remain unable to recover any signatures for all three rare classes. This is inline with our analysis on the checkboard problems discussed above. UCS would have difficulty in learning rules for these classes given their small representation in the population. Furthermore, the more accurate rules belonging to rare classes would tend to have lower experience. In the absence of an adaptive threshold control UCSSE will keep searching for signatures with high experience and accuracy which might not be learnt by UCS for the above mentioned reasons. The adaptation of both parameters significantly improve this situation. UCSSE+AEC retrieves a significantly higher number of signatures overall than the other two versions but it manages to extract signatures for the rare classes that provide a better coverage of the test set, presented in the middle tabular. This suggests that a tradeoff exists between the two choices. By using very high crisp values for accuracy and experience, no signatures might by obtained for rare and difficult to learn classes. On the other hand, relaxing the thresholds could raise the number of signatures in other classes.

The bottom tabular shows the average generality of signature set at the end of training runs in each system which hovers around 25% for all the classes. The generality of each rule is calculated by summing the normalised value of each predicate and then dividing by the total number of attributes. The signatures retrieved by

UCSSE+AEC show almost similar average generality for each class and the results are much more stable than the other two systems. UCSSE and UCSSE+AC have a better generalisation in the Normal class but this does not relate proportionally to the generalisation accuracy (shown in Table 5.13).

Table 5.12: Comparison of different signature statistics between adaptive and non-adaptive UCSSE versions on the KDD Cup dataset. See text for the explanation of system names.

Class	UCSSE	UCSSSE+AC	UCSSE+AEC
Number of Signatures			
Normal	193(32)	185(31)	959(122)$^\diamond$
Probe	1(2)	1(1)	342(24)$^\diamond$
DOS	157(44)	157(37)	241(94)$^\diamond$
U2R	0(0)	0(0)	32(3)$^\diamond$
R2L	0(0)	0(0)	94(15)$^\diamond$
Overall	351(48)	343(51)	1669(157)$^\diamond$
Test Set Coverage			
Normal	85.86(4.17)	85.66(4.09)	92.15(2.18)$^\blacklozenge$
Probe	1.98(1.76)	1.42(1.36)	60.26(1.35)$^\blacklozenge$
DOS	80.59(5.89)	81.98(5.20)	90.54(7.28)$^\blacklozenge$
U2R	6.91(4.80)	6.33(4.83)	29.00(6.89)$^\blacklozenge$
R2L	76.50(14.53)	77.37(15.85)	88.81(6.40)$^\blacklozenge$
Overall	80.33(4.39)	81.36(4.30)	90.34(5.23)$^\blacklozenge$
Average Generality			
Normal	27.51(0.89)	27.84(1.27)	26.07(0.44)$^\diamond$
Probe	16.40(11.46)	18.75(10.02)	24.80(0.18)
DOS	24.73(1.66)	25.93(1.41)	25.57(0.65)
U2R	0.00(0.00)	0.00(0.00)	24.66(0.60)$^\blacklozenge$
R2L	0.00(0.00)	0.00(0.00)	25.10(0.34)$^\blacklozenge$

The top tabular in Table 5.13 presents the test set accuracy achieved by different versions of UCSSE. All three versions of UCSSE achieve better overall accuracy than the baseline UCS system. UCSSE and UCSSE+AC however remain unable to retrieve any signatures as discussed above for the three minority classes (i.e., Probe, U2R and R2L). Their performance in these classes thus, can solely be attributed to the UCS population, although some coverage from other class signatures would cause the accuracy to deteriorate from that of the baseline setup. UCSSE+AEC outperforms the other two versions on all classes on average, however it only does significantly better on the Probe class and overall at 99% significance level. It is also able to retrieve signatures for all the classes including the very rare ones. These results show the usefulness of adaptive parameter control in UCSSE.

Table 5.13: Comparison of test accuracy and other performance measures between different versions of UCSSE on the KDD Cup dataset. See text for the explanation of system names.

Test Accuracy (%)

Class	UCSSE	UCSSE+AC	UCSSE+AEC
Normal	96.60(3.04)	97.31(0.40)	97.45(0.37)
Probe	55.76(10.64)	58.52(11.00)	67.80(1.02)♦
DOS	94.81(3.74)	95.02(3.51)	96.34(1.04)
U2R	15.24(5.46)	14.38(5.64)	17.67(4.51)
R2L	4.41(2.89)	3.56(2.11)	4.82(1.72)
Overall	89.87(2.87)	90.07(2.56)	91.47(0.92)♦

Other Performance Measures

Measure	UCSSE	UCSSE+AC	UCSSE+AEC
FA Rate (%)	3.40(3.10)	2.69(0.41)	2.55(0.37)
Hit Rate (%)	91.75(1.38)	91.61(1.20)	91.68(0.46)
CPE	0.28(0.05)	0.28(0.05)	0.26(0.02)

The bottom tabular in Table 5.13 shows a comparison of other key performance measures achieved by each of the three versions of UCSSE using the baseline UCS setup. The results show that UCSSE+AEC achieves lower false alarm rate and cost per example scores on average. However, the results are not statistically significant than the other two systems. But note that UCSSE performance is backed up by a much better signature coverage than the other two versions where no signatures could be retrieved for the rare classes.

Table 5.14 shows the CPU time in minutes taken by the three systems during a single training and testing pass through the KDD Cup dataset. The CPU time, in these and following experiments, is calculated using the standard Linux *times* function which does not include any time spent waiting for I/O or when some other process is running. The time spent in training a system corresponds to a single-pass through the training data while UCS works in an exploration mode (see §2.4.3), whereas the evaluation time corresponds to the exploitation phase during which each test instance is labelled using the evolved population or signatures.

Table 5.14: Comparison of CPU time in minutes between adaptive and non-adaptive UCSSE versions on the KDD Cup dataset.

Time	UCSSE	UCSSE+AC	UCSSE+AEC
Training	27.21(1.94)	22.86(6.91)	27.57(1.26)
Evaluation	10.35(2.06)	11.00(2.46)	11.62(2.35)
Total	37.56(3.08)	33.86(6.58)	39.19(2.55)

As shown almost all systems use a similar amount of CPU time during both training and testing. UCSSE+AC is the fastest, mainly because of the faster training time, among the three systems on average but the numbers are not statistically significant. Interestingly, UCSSE with online adaptive control of both accuracy and experience thresholds takes almost the same time to process the KDD data as the non-adaptive version despite the extra processing steps involved in the computation of online adaptation. This can be attributed to the better coverage of the search space achieved by the adaptive version. A higher coverage of the search space obviously allows the signature set to filter more instances and thus avoids unnecessary discovery cycles of the UCS.

Tables 5.15, 5.16 and 5.17 present a comparison between UCS, UCSD and UCSSE (with online adaptive control of both the extraction and deletion thresholds) similar to the comparison of UCSSE variants. The performance of UCSD and UCSSE is compared with the baseline UCS in these results.

Table 5.15 presents the rule statistics for the three systems. First of all note that both UCSD and UCSSE significantly reduce the number of rules on all classes than UCS. UCSD performs significantly better in terms of number of rules than both UCS and UCSSE.

Overall UCSD achieves 4 times less number of rules than UCSSE, while UCSSE retrieves almost 5 times less number of rules than the standard UCS. However, similar to the two other UCSSE variants, UCSD could not obtain any rules for U2R class. Thus the UCSD prediction for the U2R class essentially becomes a random guess since it does not have a fall back mechanism similar to UCSSE. Also note that UCSD is a post training rule processing system while UCSSE retrieves signatures in real time.

UCSSE also achieves significantly better test set coverage on the majority DOS class, Probe and overall than both other systems (although the overall improvement is not statistically significant). It however provides significantly less coverage and generality on the Normal class. UCSD also achieves significantly higher generality on the Normal class. Contrary to the expectation however, this reduces its generalisation performance on the test set (Table 5.16 discussed next). Although all the systems achieved similar mean rule set generalities, UCSSE rule sets are relatively more specific than the other two systems. But, as discussed next, both systems achieve poor performance in terms of test set accuracy and other related measures.

This indicates that the baseline UCS is lacking the right fitness pressure towards optimal generality for this dataset.

Table 5.15: Comparison of different signature statistics between UCS, UCSD and UCSSE (with adaptive parameter control) on the KDD Cup data.

Number of Rules			
Class	UCS	UCSD	UCSSE+AEC
Normal	6068(63)	342(19)$^\blacklozenge$	959(122)$^\blacktriangle$
Probe	510(24)	30(3)$^\blacklozenge$	342(24)$^\blacktriangle$
DOS	916(52)	59(7)$^\blacklozenge$	241(94)$^\blacktriangle$
U2R	105(8)	0(0)$^\blacklozenge$	32(3)$^\blacktriangle$
R2L	180(13)	8(2)$^\blacklozenge$	94(15)$^\blacktriangle$
Overall	7779(15)	439(20)$^\blacklozenge$	1669(157)$^\blacktriangle$
Test Set Coverage			
Normal	97.26(0.38)	95.10(0.53)$^\triangle$	92.15(2.18)$^\lozenge$
Probe	55.01(8.27)	48.88(10.35)$^\lozenge$	60.26(1.35)$^\blacklozenge$
DOS	84.18(9.55)	83.11(10.02)	90.54(7.28)$^\blacklozenge$
U2R	43.05(4.83)	24.10(4.28)$^\lozenge$	29.00(6.89)$^\triangle$
R2L	92.29(4.81)	88.29(5.19)$^\triangle$	88.81(6.40)
Overall	86.76(7.06)	85.25(7.47)	90.34(5.23)
Average Generality			
Normal	25.99(0.14)	27.61(0.35)$^\blacklozenge$	26.07(0.44)
Probe	24.64(0.26)	24.47(0.45)	24.80(0.18)
DOS	25.09(0.27)	25.37(0.29)	25.57(0.65)
U2R	25.30(0.28)	25.30(0.28)	24.66(0.60)$^\lozenge$
R2L	25.45(0.27)	25.08(1.30)	25.10(0.34)$^\triangle$

Figures 5.16 - 5.18 graphically present rule sets obtained by three systems at the end of a training pass. The x-axis represents the experience of rules normalised to the

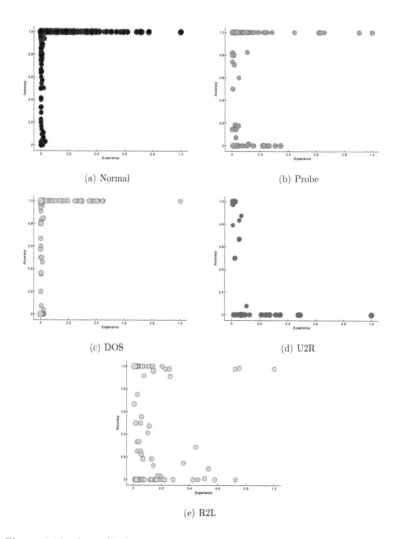

(a) Normal

(b) Probe

(c) DOS

(d) U2R

(e) R2L

Figure 5.16: A graphical representation of the rules evolved by UCS for KDD Cup dataset. Each rule in the population is represented by a circle with a radius proportional to its generality.

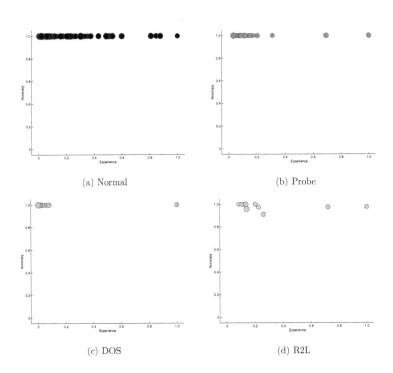

(a) Normal   (b) Probe

(c) DOS   (d) R2L

Figure 5.17: A graphical representation of the rules obtained by UCSD for KDD Cup dataset. Each rule is represented by a circle with a radius proportional to its generality. Note that UCSD was unable to recover any rule for U2R class in these experiments.

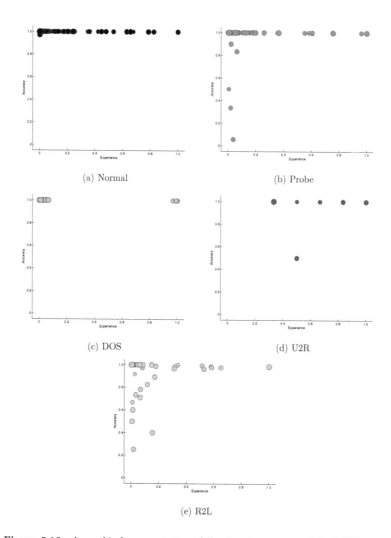

(a) Normal

(b) Probe

(c) DOS

(d) U2R

(e) R2L

Figure 5.18: A graphical representation of the signatures extracted by UCSSE using UCS as a base learner for the KDD Cup dataset. Each signature in the signature set is represented by a circle with a radius proportional to its generality.

maximum experience in the respective classes, y-axis represents the accuracy of the system and each circle on the graph represents a rule in the corresponding rule set. The thickness of the circle represents a rule's generality normalised to the maximum generality. First of all, we may notice that the UCS population contains many inexperienced classifiers at various accuracy levels. This can happen because of the minimum deletion experience threshold which allows such rules to remain in the population until they have been evaluated a sufficient number of times. For the rare classes, however, the UCS population also contains experienced rules that are highly inaccurate as well. This can happen because a single user-defined deletion threshold is applied to all the classes regardless of their distribution in the training. Both UCSD and UCSSE are able to eliminate such rules from the population. Dixon's rule reduction in UCSD is applied after completely training UCS on the dataset, thus it gets better parameter estimates for pruning. UCSSE achieves a similar effect in real time albeit with higher number of rules than UCSD. Since UCSSE is meant to work in real time, the pruning routine in UCSSE, that removes inexperienced and inaccurate signatures from the rule set, is invoked only after certain conditions are met (see §5.3) and not at the end of a training run. Further the UCSSE extraction and deletion parameters are adapted on a per class basis. The rare class signatures are evaluated far fewer times and thus are eliminated only slowly. This can be advantageous at times (for instance, UCSD did not manage to obtain any U2R rules, while UCSSE did).

The upper tabular in Table 5.16 presents a comparison using the test set accuracy achieved by UCSD and UCSSE with the baseline UCS setup on the KDD Cup dataset. UCSSE achieves significantly better accuracy on all classes than both UCS and UCSD except Normal and U2R classes where the performance is not significantly different. The lower tabular shows a comparison of other key performance measures between the three systems. Again UCSSE outperforms UCSD on all measures and UCS on all measures except false alarm rate where there is no significant difference between the two systems.

Table 5.17 shows a comparison of CPU time taken by the three systems. In addition to the training and evaluation time, time taken by UCSD to post process the UCS population is also reported. The post processing step in UCSD adds an overhead on the training time of UCS, however, this is compensated during the evaluation where UCSD processes the test set a magnitude faster than UCS. Overall UCSSE consumes around 3.5 times lower processing time than UCS and 2.8 times than UCSD. This corresponds to almost 2215 instances per second in comparison to 630 and 807 instances per second processed by UCS and UCSD respectively. This is a notable performance by UCSSE in that it improves the processing time with a better generalisation performance on the test set and with a magnitude smaller number of rules.

Table 5.16: Comparison of test accuracy and other performance measures between UCS, UCSD and UCSSE (with adaptive parameters) on the KDD Cup data.

Test Accuracy (%)

Class	UCS	UCSD	UCSSE+AEC
Normal	97.47(0.35)	95.93(0.41)$^\diamond$	97.45(0.37)
Probe	61.17(9.06)	58.21(8.64)	67.80(1.02)$^\blacklozenge$
DOS	85.13(7.76)	84.50(8.07)	96.34(1.04)$^\blacklozenge$
U2R	15.10(4.79)	15.29(4.67)	17.67(4.51)
R2L	3.10(1.56)	3.42(1.31)	4.82(1.72)$^\blacklozenge$
Overall	82.83(5.75)	82.03(5.99)	91.47(0.92)$^\blacklozenge$

Other Performance Measures

Measure	UCS	UCSD	UCSSE+AEC
FA Rate (%)	2.53(0.36)	4.07(0.42)$^\diamond$	2.55(0.37)
Hit Rate (%)	88.96(2.05)	89.05(2.04)	91.68(0.46)$^\blacklozenge$
CPE	0.41(0.10)	0.42(0.11)	0.26(0.02)$^\blacklozenge$

Table 5.17: Comparison of CPU time in minutes between UCS, UCSD and UCSSE (with adaptive parameters) on the KDD Cup dataset.

Time	UCS	UCSD	UCSSE+AEC
Training	94.73(2.26)	94.73(2.26)	27.57(1.26)$^{\blacklozenge}$
Post-processing	0.00(0.00)	10.56(0.72)$^{\diamond}$	0.00(0.00)
Evaluation	42.89(1.10)	2.27(0.13)$^{\blacklozenge}$	11.62(2.35)$^{\blacktriangle}$
Total	137.62(3.29)	107.56(2.59)$^{\blacktriangle}$	39.19(2.55)$^{\blacklozenge}$

5.7.3 Experiments with Extended UCS

In this section, we evaluate UCSSE and UCSD (referred to as UCSxSE and UCSxD) using the extended UCS setup (UCSx) developed in the last chapter. Table 5.18 compares the signature related statistics between the non-adaptive and adaptive versions of UCSxSE. As shown, all three systems significantly reduce the number of signatures retrieved in comparison to the baseline UCS setup, while achieving a better test coverage and mean generality. UCSxSE and UCSxSE+AC however are still not able to retrieve any rules for the U2R class, mainly because of very poor representation of this class in the training set (only 52 instances out of half a million records). The version with the experience threshold adaptation does a good job in retrieving signatures in this scenario.

Also notice that the average generality of signatures has improved by almost 10% without any loss of generalisation accuracy (discussed next). This is a significant improvement from previous results and indicates a better fitness pressure towards generalisation through the modifications made in the baseline UCS setup. Again the average generality for all the classes is around the same mark while UCSSE+AEC achieving slightly better generalisation in some of the classes.

Table 5.18: Comparison of different signature statistics between adaptive and non-adaptive UCSxSE versions on the KDD Cup dataset. See text for the explanation of system names.

Number of Signatures			
Class	UCSxSE	UCSxSE+AC	UCSxSE+AEC
Normal	125(12)	125(13)	$272(54)^\diamond$
Probe	3(1)	4(1)	$129(8)^\diamond$
DOS	24(6)	24(4)	$60(15)^\diamond$
U2R	0(0)	0(1)	$24(2)^\diamond$
R2L	0(0)	$2(1)^\triangle$	$25(14)^\diamond$
Overall	153(14)	155(16)	$510(63)^\diamond$
Test Set Coverage			
Normal	92.51(1.13)	92.73(1.31)	91.56(4.69)
Probe	8.65(2.52)	9.09(2.73)	$63.78(1.66)^\blacklozenge$
DOS	96.82(4.13)	95.65(5.59)	94.34(11.56)
U2R	22.52(4.69)	23.62(5.79)	$34.33(15.46)^\blacklozenge$
R2L	88.27(3.07)	$90.76(2.15)^\blacktriangle$	87.44(13.69)
Overall	94.33(3.12)	93.65(4.21)	93.01(8.43)
Average Generality			
Normal	35.94(0.32)	36.08(0.21)	35.68(0.29)
Probe	33.39(1.81)	33.47(1.78)	34.32(0.31)
DOS	35.95(1.06)	36.33(0.85)	35.81(0.66)
U2R	0.00(0.00)	3.70(11.70)	$33.91(0.51)^\blacklozenge$
R2L	6.90(14.56)	$34.33(1.29)^\blacktriangle$	$35.19(0.47)^\blacktriangle$

Table 5.19 replicates the results of Table 5.13 with the UCSx setup. The top tabular shows a comparison of test accuracy while the bottom tabular shows a comparison of other performance measures. In these experiments all three versions of UCSxSE achieve similar accuracy on all classes. The performance of UCSxSE+AEC has im-

proved significantly from the previous one and it achieves a better overall accuracy with more than 3 times less number of signatures than its predecessor (i.e., the one run with the baseline UCS setup). Again these results show the advantage of adaptive control of parameters in UCSSE. In addition, the better UCSxSE performance indicate that UCSx is discovering more effective generalisations than baseline UCS.

The bottom tabular presents the corresponding additional performance measures. Similar to the results with the baseline UCS setup, there is no significant difference between all measures achieved by the three systems except the false alarm rate where both adaptive versions of UCSxSE perform worse than the non-adaptive version.

Table 5.19: Comparison of test accuracy, number of rules and rule coverage between different versions of UCSxSE on the KDD Cup dataset. See text for the explanation of system names.

Test Accuracy (%)

Class	UCSxSE	UCSxSE+AC	UCSxSE+AEC
Normal	99.39(0.25)	$99.09(0.36)^{\triangle}$	$99.16(0.26)^{\triangle}$
Probe	75.04(1.06)	75.03(1.20)	75.54(0.81)
DOS	96.73(0.04)	96.73(0.03)	96.73(0.06)
U2R	21.43(5.24)	20.62(3.68)	21.33(4.96)
R2L	3.18(1.81)	4.24(1.82)	2.59(1.94)
Overall	92.00(0.00)	92.00(0.00)	92.00(0.00)

Other Performance Measures

Measure	UCSxSE	UCSxSE+AC	UCSxSE+AEC
FA Rate (%)	0.61(0.25)	$0.91(0.36)^{\triangle}$	$0.84(0.26)^{\triangle}$
Hit Rate (%)	90.66(0.13)	90.74(0.13)	90.68(0.16)
CPE	0.26(0.00)	0.25(0.00)	0.26(0.00)

Table 5.20 shows the CPU time used by the three UCSxSE versions. Similar to

the results with baseline UCS setup there is no significant difference between the processing time utilised by these systems. However, note that the processing time of these systems has significantly improved (around 1.5 times) from the versions run with baseline UCS setup. The main reduction in the time has come through improvement in the training time. This shows that an improvement in the generalisation ability of the base learner would further reduce the time for learning the signatures.

Table 5.20: Comparison of CPU Time between different versions of UCSxSE on the KDD Cup dataset.

Time	UCSxSE	UCSxSE+AC	UCSxSE+AEC
Training	13.34(0.80)	12.87(1.29)	13.36(0.68)
Evaluation	10.67(1.38)	10.92(1.82)	12.02(3.03)
Total	24.01(1.49)	23.79(2.71)	25.38(2.98)

Finally, we compare the performance of the extended UCS with that of UCSxD and UCSxSE with adaptive parameters control. Table 5.21 shows a comparison of post training rule statistics in the three systems. First, note that UCSxSE retrieves almost same number of signatures as those obtained by UCSxD and thus achieves almost 15 times reduction in UCSx rule set sizes. This is a significant improvement by UCSxSE from UCSSE, where UCSD obtained 4 times better compaction than UCSSE. The number of rules for UCSxD has actually increased than UCSD given better generalisation of UCSx. This shows the advantage of having the expand and contract operators in the signature extraction systems. UCSD on the other hand does not have any subsumption mechanism and would tend to obtain higher number of rules with improved UCS performance.

The test set coverage of all three systems has also improved significantly from the baseline versions. UCSx covers more than 98% of the test cases in comparison to 85% covered by UCS. Furthermore, the higher test set coverage has actually improved the test set accuracy for all three systems (discussed next). The average generality of post training rule sets has also improved by almost 10% in all systems. UCSxSE achieves a significantly better average generalisation in all classes in contrast to UCSSE that retrieved more specific signatures than the other two systems. This shows that UCSSE adapts well to the generalisation ability of the base learner.

Table 5.21: Comparison of different rule statistics between UCSx, UCSxD and UCSxSE (with adaptive parameter control) on the KDD Cup data.

Class	UCSx	UCSxD	UCSxSE+AEC
Number of Rules			
Normal	5384(33)	386(12)▲	272(54)◆
Probe	527(17)	43(2)◆	129(8)▲
DOS	1246(27)	61(3)▲	60(15)▲
U2R	204(11)	4(1)◆	24(2)▲
R2L	259(14)	13(2)◆	25(14)▲
Overall	7620(21)	508(12)▲	510(63)▲
Test Set Coverage			
Normal	99.12(0.26)	97.14(0.33)△	91.56(4.69)◇
Probe	65.59(1.00)	61.64(0.86)◇	63.78(1.66)△
DOS	98.82(0.48)	98.48(0.58)	94.34(11.56)
U2R	60.19(3.17)	40.76(4.33)△	34.33(15.46)△
R2L	97.64(1.03)	94.75(2.61)△	87.44(13.69)◇
Overall	98.36(0.39)	97.52(0.47)△	93.01(8.43)◇
Average Generality			
Normal	34.62(0.10)	35.22(0.21)▲	35.68(0.29)◆
Probe	33.81(0.12)	33.65(0.38)	34.32(0.31)◆
DOS	34.01(0.31)	34.66(0.58)▲	35.81(0.66)◆
U2R	34.25(0.15)	33.48(1.03)	33.91(0.51)
R2L	34.17(0.33)	33.89(1.04)	35.19(0.47)◆

Figures 5.19 - 5.21 graphically represent the rule sets obtained by the three systems at the end of typical training runs, similar to Figures 5.16 - 5.18. As can be seen UCSx evolves much higher number of rules for the rare classes as compared to the baseline UCS. Also note that for Probe and R2L classes, there are almost no rules with high experience and very low accuracy as was the case with UCS. For U2R class, although the number of accurate rules has increased but there are still too many experienced and inaccurate classifiers in the population. As pointed out earlier, given only 52 training instances, this class becomes very hard for evolving effective rules. The graphs for UCSxD and UCSxSE show similar trends as UCSD and UCSSE. Note that UCSxD is able to obtain rules for the U2R class from UCSx. The higher generalisation in the signature set allows UCSSE to achieve better compactness as more optimally general rules could subsume the specific ones.

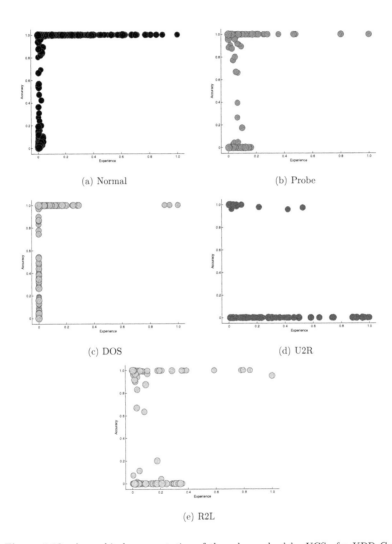

(a) Normal

(b) Probe

(c) DOS

(d) U2R

(e) R2L

Figure 5.19: A graphical representation of the rules evolved by UCSx for KDD Cup dataset. Each rule in the population is represented by a circle with a radius proportional to rule's generality.

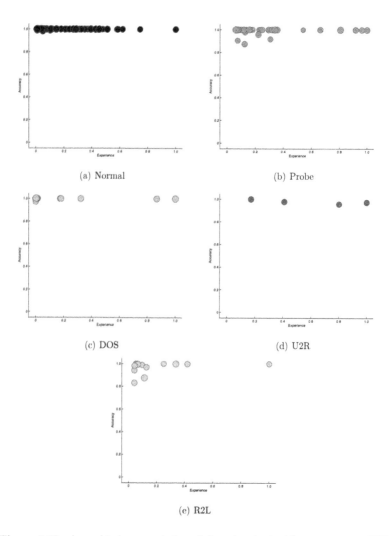

(a) Normal

(b) Probe

(c) DOS

(d) U2R

(e) R2L

Figure 5.20: A graphical representation of the rules obtained by post pruning UCSx population using Dixon's rule reduction algorithm for KDD Cup dataset. Each rule in the pruned population is represented by a circle with a radius proportional to rule's generality.

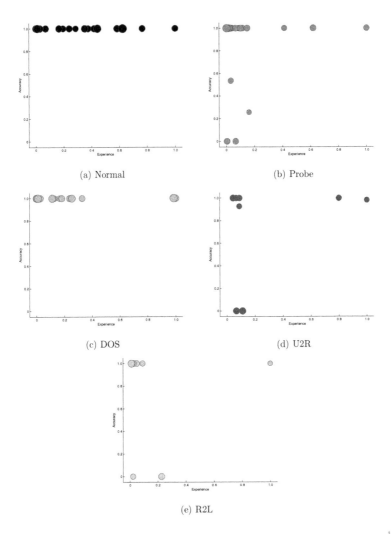

(a) Normal   (b) Probe

(c) DOS   (d) U2R

(e) R2L

Figure 5.21: A graphical representation of the signatures extracted online by UCSxSE using UCSx as a base learner for KDD Cup dataset. Each signature in the signature set is represented by a circle with a radius proportional to rule's generality.

Table 5.22 replicates the results of Table 5.16 for UCSx setup. In contrast to the results with the baseline UCS setup, there is no significant difference between the performance of these three systems in terms of test accuracy (upper tabular). This is still a positive outcome since both UCSxD and UCSxSE achieve that with almost 15 times less number of rules than UCSx. Note that as the UCS confidence builds up with all the modifications, UCSxSE starts retrieving better and compact representations. The bottom tabular presents a comparison of other performance measures achieved by the three systems using UCSx setup. All systems perform at par on hit rate and CPE score metrics. Both UCSxD and UCSxSE, however, produce significantly higher numbers of false alarms than UCSx, with UCSxD producing the worst figures.

Table 5.22: Comparison of test accuracy, number of rules and rule coverage between UCSx, UCSxD and UCSxSE (with adaptive parameters) on the KDD Cup data.

Test Accuracy (%)			
Class	UCSx	UCSxD	UCSxSE+AEC
Normal	99.38(0.07)	98.63(0.36)$^\diamond$	99.16(0.26)$^\triangle$
Probe	75.36(0.74)	75.81(1.42)	75.54(0.81)
DOS	96.77(0.14)	96.95(0.06)$^\blacklozenge$	96.73(0.06)
U2R	21.52(4.12)	7.43(5.04)$^\diamond$	21.33(4.96)
R2L	2.80(1.64)	2.55(1.84)	2.59(1.94)
Overall	92.00(0.00)	92.00(0.00)	92.00(0.00)

Other Performance Measures			
Measure	UCSx	UCSxD	UCSxSE+AEC
FA Rate (%)	0.62(0.07)	1.37(0.37)$^\diamond$	0.84(0.26)
Hit Rate (%)	90.66(0.16)	90.72(0.15)	90.68(0.16)
CPE	0.26(0.00)	0.26(0.00)	0.26(0.00)

Table 5.23 replicates the results of Table 5.17 for the UCSx setup. UCSxSE improves the margin on processing time among the three systems as it reduces the processing time by almost 5 and 3.5 times than UCSx and UCSxD respectively. This corresponds to almost 3421 instances processed per second. Also note that the processing times of both UCSx and UCSxD has improved from that of the baseline setup which now can process around 700 and 938 instances per second respectively. Note that the savings in computational time is achieved with the help of smaller rule sets and avoiding unnecessary discovery cycles. As the coverage of signatures improve over time, we could expect more savings in the computational time. UCSSE, as well as UCS, can still benefit from better implementation techniques such as rule indexing and hashing in further improving the processing time for real time deployment.

Table 5.23: Comparison of CPU time between UCSx, UCSxD and UCSxSE on the KDD Cup dataset.

Time	UCSx	UCSxD	UCSxSE+AEC
Training	71.54(2.46)	71.47(2.37)	13.36(0.68)♦
Post-Processing	0.00(0.00)	17.62(0.56)◇	0.00(0.00)
Evaluation	52.58(2.90)	3.48(0.18)♦	12.02(3.03)▲
Total	124.12(4.84)	92.57(2.74)▲	25.38(2.98)♦

Empirical evidences in this section demonstrate the usefulness of the signature extraction system for the intrusion detection problem. UCSSE with extended UCS setup is able to retrieve almost 1500% lesser number of rules with greater generality in real time. This allows almost 500% savings in the processing time which could improve over time. The results also implicate the adaptation of extraction and deletion thresholds for the proper operation of UCSSE. More sophisticated adaptive operators could lead to further improvement in the performance of UCSSE. Also note that the Dixon's rule reduction algorithm is applied after completely training the UCS population and hence is expected to perform better than UCSSE. UCSSE despite operating in real time performs competitively.

5.8   Comparison with Published Results

In this section, we compare the results of UCSx and UCSxSE with some representative results published in literature on the 1999 KDD Cup dataset. The results of nine machine learning techniques, along with UCSx and UCSxSE, are presented in Table 5.24. The first two rows refer to techniques used by the winner and runners up of the 1999 KDD Cup respectively. The next seven techniques are published after the contest and are considered among the best in their respective fields. Although many other approaches exist in the literature that have used the KDD Cup dataset for their evaluation, there are few that have reported their results on the full test dataset.

All evaluation metrics are reported for the methods that have provided the resultant confusion matrices. In all other cases, results are extracted directly from the given references. A "-" is placed where the results are not available. One of the methods mapped the problem as a binary classification task (GP Ensemble), while another reported only the false alarm rate and hit rate (Fuzzy Classifier + GA). All techniques are also compared on four salient features that are relevant to our algorithms. A hybrid detection type means that models for both Normal and attack classes are learnt by the system.

As can be seen there is no single technique that performs the best in all of the evaluation criteria and a tradeoff seems inevitable among different performance measures. Both UCSx and UCSxSE show comparable, even competitive, performance in all measures, especially when compared with the genetic based systems. The main differentiator in terms of the applicability of these methods in real world settings is their ability to process data streams without the requirement of storing the data for batch learning. In this respect, UCSx and UCSxSE stand out as the only methods that are capable of processing the data in a single-pass.

Table 5.24: A comparison of UCSx and UCSxSE with the published results.

Techniques	Detection Type	Features			Test Accuracy(%)						Other Measures		
		Rule Based	Genetic Based	Single Pass	Normal	Probe	DOS	U2R	R2L	Overall	FA Rate	Hit Rate	CPE
Bagged Boosting[a]	Misuse	-	-	-	99.45	83.32	97.12	13.16	8.40	92.71	0.55	91.81	0.23
Kernel Miner[b]	Misuse	-	-	-	99.42	84.52	97.47	11.84	7.32	92.92	0.58	91.53	0.24
Multi Classifier[c]	Misuse	-	-	-	88.70		97.30	29.80	9.60	-			0.23
NaiveBayes[d]	Hybrid	-	-	-	96.64	78.18	96.38	11.84	7.11	91.47	3.36	-	0.23
Three-tier IDS[e]	Hybrid	Mixed	-	-	96.20	92.87	97.48	3.51	28.65	93.52	3.80	94.35	0.18
PNRule[f]	Hybrid	✓	-	-	99.54	73.02	96.96	6.58	10.69	92.59	0.46	91.08	0.24
RSS-DSS GP[g]	Hybrid	-	-	-	98.60	96.70	85.70	59.20	9.30	84.36	1.30	91.40	-
GP Ensemble[h]	Hybrid	-	✓	-	73.59	-	-	-	-	90.55	26.41	94.65	-
Fuzzy Classifier + GA[i]	Hybrid	-	✓	-	-	-	-	-	-	-	10.63	95.47	-
UCSx	Hybrid	✓	✓	-	99.38	75.36	96.77	21.52	2.8	92.03	0.62	90.66	0.26
UCSSE	Hybrid	✓	✓	✓	99.16	75.54	96.73	21.33	2.59	92.00	0.84	90.68	0.26

[a] KDD Cup Winner - (Pfahringer 2000)
[b] KDD Cup Runner Up - (Levin 2000)
[c] (Sabhnani and Serpen 2003)
[d] (Amor, Benferhat, and Elouedi 2004)
[e] (Hwang, Lee, and Lee 2007)
[f] (Ramesh and Mahesh 2001)
[g] (Song, Heywood, and Zincir-Heywood 2005)
[h] (Zhang and Bhattacharyya 2004)
[i] (Gomez and Dasgupta 2002b)

5.9 Summary and Way Forward

In this chapter, we have have attempted to address the issue of compression in the UCS rule sets. Our approach is fundamentally different than existing approaches and our aim is to retrieve optimal generalisations learnt by UCS in real time (i.e., during its discovery operation). An algorithm is presented for real time signature extraction in UCS, named UCSSE. The signature extraction mechanism is implemented on top of the existing UCS framework. This allows the system to use the extracted signatures during its operation and the evolutionary search is invoked only when no signatures are found for an input. Thus providing a better control over evolutionary search, faster processing times and considerably compact rule sets.

The validity of the algorithm is verified using the learning time bound theory of XCS and the algorithm is tested on two benchmark test problems used in LCS research. On the binary multiplexer and real-valued checkerboard problems, the algorithm is able to retrieve all optimal generalisations in real time.

To minimise redundancy among the retrieved signatures, two new operators are introduced that can handle major overlaps between the same class and opposite class rules. The analysis of the algorithm is extended to noisy and imbalanced class problems and subsequently control mechanisms for online adaptation of signature extraction thresholds are provided. With the adaptive threshold control of accuracy parameters, UCSSE is able to retrieve near optimal decision boundaries for noisy checkerboard problems.

Finally, different versions of UCSSE are evaluated on the KDD Cup dataset based on the baseline and extended UCS setups developed in the last chapter. In all cases, UCSSE with adaptive parameter control achieves test set accuracy which is at par or better than UCS. It does so with a significantly fewer number of rules. When run with the extended UCS it reduces the rule set size by 15 times than the original algorithm, without any degradation in test accuracy and consumes 5 times lesser CPU time.

We also extended a recent rule reduction algorithm for XCS to UCS and compared its performance with UCSSE. The rule reduction algorithm suffers when there is noise in the data because it also uses preselected fixed thresholds to prune post training rule sets. To fix this problem thresholds are replaced with per class average rule set accuracy. In noisy checkerboard problems, UCSSE performs better than both UCS and UCSD in the number of rules while achieving equivalent test set accuracy. In imbalanced checkerboard problems, UCSD performs better than UCSSE and achieves higher accuracy. UCSSE still faced some difficulties in retrieving signatures at higher imbalance levels. On the KDD Cup data UCSD achieves significantly fewer number of rules than UCSSE when run with baseline UCS, however it does so at the cost of some accuracy loss. The modified UCSSE catches up with UCSD and there is no significant difference in the performance of both systems. It is important to note that UCSD has an edge since it post prunes the trained UCS population whereas UCSSE works in real time (i.e., as the rules are being discovered) and still provides competitive performance overall.

At the end, the performance of both UCS and UCSSE with extended setup are compared with some of the most representative published results.

In conclusion, UCSSE provides a framework for the active retrieval of generalisations, outputs compact representations and provides faster processing times than the standard UCS. It also provides a mean to control the evolutionary search process in UCS. Although the system is built on top of UCS, which is the focus of this thesis, it can easily be extended to XCS and possibly other LCS. The framework is developed while keeping in view the requirements of real time intrusion detection and thus can be prototyped into an intrusion detection system with some extensions (e.g., by incorporating active learning mechanisms with a security supervisor's feedback).

In the next chapter, we will evaluate the signature extraction system developed in this chapter along with the standard and extended UCS developed in the last chapter with real network traffic. We will also develop tools to automate the processing of real network traffic into the representation suitable for UCS and UCSSE systems.

Chapter 6

Evaluation with Real Network Traffic

6.1 Chapter Objectives

In the last two chapters we used the 1999 KDD Cup datasets for the evaluation of UCS and UCSSE respectively. As mentioned, these datasets are derived from several weeks of network traffic dumps and host logs which were obtained by simulating background traffic and attacks in an isolated networking environment as part of the 1998 DARPA IDEVAL program. Traditionally, the computer security research community has used the DARPA datasets for the evaluation of their systems whereas the KDD research community interested in the evaluation of their techniques for intrusion detection problem has concentrated on the KDD Cup datasets.

Despite their usefulness the DARPA datasets have been shown to contain simulation artefacts and other problems by some researchers (Mahoney and Chan 2003a; McHugh 2000). Likewise, some researchers have argued the inappropriateness of training machine learning algorithms with the KDD Cup dataset (Sabhnani and Serpen 2004). It is unknown, however, what effect could these artefacts have on the KDD Cup datasets as most of the fields causing these artefacts in DARPA datasets are packet header values (e.g., IP Time To Live (TTL) or source IP addresses) and are not directly used in the KDD Cup datasets. The DARPA datasets are also considered somewhat outdated because of the developments in the networking technologies and the evolution of attacks in response to these improvement, since the dataset was created.

Furthermore, a major limitation in using the KDD Cup datasets is the inaccessibility to the actual logged data. KDD Cup datasets were built by applying association rule mining algorithms that were tuned to extract certain features which the authors of these datasets considered useful for the detection of intrusions in the DARPA datasets. Subsequently, the intrusion detection techniques that used these datasets for their evaluation had to stick with the provided feature set and at best could minimise the number of features, in the given set, that would maximise information gain. This might suffice for the general classification tasks where the main concern for machine learning algorithms is to improve their prediction accuracy on the given test set. But for the systems that intend to address the intrusion detection problem in general and not limited to this dataset, it poses an inherent limitation which must be overcome by developing tools that can independently preprocess network data in the required format for the detection engine or learning algorithms.

Consequently, in this chapter we develop our own methodology to address these issues and evaluate the systems presented in the last chapters with real network data. To overcome the problem of staleness and simulation artefacts in the above mentioned datasets, we capture real background traffic on a university departmental server over several weeks. We simulate hundreds of modern day attacks that trigger Snort, a state-of-the art intrusion detection system, signatures.

Another hurdle in preparing datasets from raw network data is the preprocessing step. Most machine learning algorithms accept data in the form of feature vectors. Furthermore, supervised learning algorithms require that data is labelled to train and subsequently evaluate their performance. We develop tools to extract features from these packet traces and perform a packet to feature vector translation. We show the effectiveness of these features empirically using several subsets of the main dataset. We used Snort intrusion detection system to label the feature vectors extracted from these datasets.

Although the presented methodology is used for testing UCS and the signature extraction system presented in the last chapters, it can be used for the evaluation of any other machine learning systems that require feature vector representation.

Eventually, we evaluate the systems developed in the previous chapters on the new dataset and provide a detailed analysis of results. Our objective is to show the effectiveness of UCS and UCSSE in automatically learning signatures from real data that can potentially be replaced by the manually created signatures in the signature-based intrusion detection systems. The methodology developed for collecting and preprocessing the network data complements our learning algorithms in building a prototype intrusion detection system based on evolutionary learning classifier systems.

6.2 Related Work

Due to the limitations posed by a few publicly available intrusion detection evaluation benchmark datasets, many alternative approaches have been proposed for evaluating intrusion detection techniques, especially for network based intrusion detection systems (NIDS). Broadly these techniques can be classified into three categories based on the method of traffic generation; those that simulate or emulate legitimate and malicious traffic or the ones that replay captured traces mixing them with simulated attack traffic. Below is a brief summary of some of the works that used such techniques.

(Mahoney 2003) collected live network traffic on a university departmental server for several weeks and later mixed it with the DARPA traffic dumps, by modifying the timestamps, to test his network anomaly detection system. Some other researchers have used Mahoney's tools to mix DARPA traffic with the background traffic collected from their own private networks (Hwang, Cai, Chen, and Qin 2007). (Jung, Paxson, Berger, and Balakrishnan 2004) collected traces from two qualitatively different sites to evaluate their Threshold Random Walk algorithm for detecting fast network port scans. (Luo and Marin 2004) collected background traffic traces from a university departmental server and then built statistical models of several TCP based application level protocols from the captured traces. They simulated background traffic using these statistical models in a network simulator. (Sommers, Yegneswaran, and Barford 2005) created a tool named *Trident* which can simulate realistic traffic in a laboratory environment by replacing the payloads and other characteristics of simulated traffic with realistic values from collected traces. Realistic traces were collected from a gateway router. They also augmented their tool for simulating malicious traffic by replaying the attack traffic in DARPA datasets. (Antonatos, Anagnostakis, and Markatos 2004) developed a traffic generation tool that could emulate background traffic with several application protocols with a control on detail levels. (Massicotte, Gagnon, Labiche, Briand, and Couture 2006) emulated a network environment using virtual network infrastructure and used several publicly available exploit tools and mutants to build a fully documented dataset consisting of thousands of attacks. The dataset did not however contain any background traffic. Some researchers have also opted to use data collected at white hat hackers conferences, such as DefCon (Almgren and Jonsson 2004).

The focus of most of these techniques is to evaluate existing open source (and in some cases commercial) industry standard NIDS by generating customised workloads. These intrusion detection systems, such as Snort and Bro, are designed to work with raw network traffic and integrate tools like network sniffers in their frameworks. Consequently, the testbeds developed to evaluate these systems have concentrated on effective traffic generation methods without worrying about the representation or labelling issues. Machine learning techniques on the other hand generally require data in a structured format. Our approach, presented in this chapter, is thus to extend these methodologies to generate intrusion detection datasets in machine learning suitable format.

6.3 A Methodology to Build Intrusion Detection Dataset

The main steps in the proposed methodology are depicted in Figure 6.1 that involve obtaining background traffic from a real active network, obtaining attack traffic through simulation and feature extraction and assignment of labels by replaying the collected traces through an existing NIDS and customised tools to construct feature vectors from the raw network packets. Each of the steps is discussed in the following sections.

6.3.1 Collection of Real Background Traffic

The background traffic is needed to learn normal behaviour of the protected system so that any future anomalous activities can be detected. On the other hand, misuse detection algorithms are generally only concerned with learning the attack patterns. Nonetheless, inclusion of background traffic is important for two reasons; first, the patterns of illegitimate activities cannot be learnt in isolation as they are embedded in the normal traffic and second, the algorithms that learn attack patterns can complement their strengths by learning patterns of normal activities and in turn providing anomaly detection.

The advantage of collecting such traffic in a controlled environment, such as that used by DARPA IDEval program, is that normal activities can easily be labelled, as the intent and timing of each activity is known in advance. Such an exercise, however, is expensive and does come with unwanted side effects (such as those found in DARPA dataset). Thus it is preferable to collect real background traffic from a private network using commonly available network sniffers. This however should not be a limitation in principle as some real network traces are publicly available through the Internet, such as `http://ita.ee.lbl.gov/html/traces.html` and `https://www.openpacket.org/`. It is important to note that the collection of real background traffic poses its own privacy and security concerns and always carries the risk of wrong labelling.

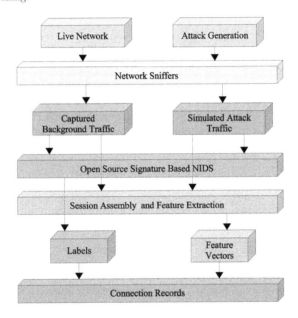

Figure 6.1: Steps involved in building a labelled intrusion detection dataset.

6.3.2 Simulation of Attacks

The next step in the phase of preparing the dataset is the induction of modern day attacks in the background traffic. In the DARPA IDEval program, the attack generation process was carried out by using publicly available hacking tools and developing new attack scripts for several known exploits. To simplify this task, IDS penetration testing tools can be used to generate attacks locally (i.e., without the need of simulating the attacks on a stand-alone network). This is a far cheaper and safer method of executing the attack traffic without the need for disrupting the live network traffic or physically building a network for the emulation of attacks.

Many such open source tools exist, such as Mucus (Mutz, Vigna, and Kemmerer 2003), FTester (Barisani 2003) and fpg (Geschke 2004). The purpose of these tools is to generate attack packets that trigger alerts using a signature based IDS, such as Snort. Other exploitation tools that can simulate a wider variety of attacks, such as Metasploit (Team 2006), can also be used. However, there is less flexibility in the latter case as the detection of all types of attacks may not be guaranteed. Another possibility is to use online available repositories of attack traces, such as `http://lobster.ics.forth.gr/traces/`. Although in order to mix well, these traces will need to be modified according to the setup where the background traffic is collected.

6.3.3 Feature Extraction

Feature extraction is an additional step in the processing of raw network traffic or audit data in order to apply data mining techniques to it. Most machine learning algorithms are designed to process data in a feature vector format, where each record consists of a set of feature values and possibly a label for training purposes.

The choice of representation can have a significant impact on learning algorithms (Filippone, Camastra, Masulli, and Rovetta 2008). Careful feature selection is thus critical for improving the performance of machine learning algorithms. Direct access to raw network data and developing customised feature extraction tools allow incorporating domain knowledge and choosing an appropriate representation for a particular algorithm.

Signature based IDS, such as Snort, mainly use two types of features in their signatures; namely, payload and non-payload based features. The non-payload features are primarily extracted directly from the packet headers such as destination service or indirectly such as state of a connection or direction of traffic flow. The payload features include unique strings in ASCII or hexadecimal, regular expressions and other supporting features to locate the position of a pattern in the payload. These signatures are created manually by the domain experts who may take several hours to days before coming up with effective intrusion patterns.

To automate the process of feature extraction several factors need consideration, such as the type of attacks to be detected and processing time. Several open source tools exist that can process binary data into human readable format (e.g., Unix based utility ipsumdump). However, these tools need to be extended for feature extraction process. Generally, the packet based features can be extracted relatively easily by parsing the packet header and using other techniques such as reassembling. It is much more challenging, however, to extract payload features that would lead to intelligent learning of similar patterns as used in the hand-made signatures. Besides, this would require an intense processing that may not be feasible for real time operation of a learning algorithm. Nevertheless, other more general payload based features such as byte frequency distribution (Wang and Stolfo 2004) could be used for payload modelling. In addition, frequency and time based features, such as those used in the KDD Cup dataset, may also be calculated by replaying the traffic on the actual capture timescale using tools like TCPReplay (Turner and Bing 2005).

6.3.4 Labelling

The final step in the preparation of the dataset is record labelling. Labelling is required for training and evaluation of supervised learning algorithms. Manually labelling large volumes of network data is next to impossible and thus a major hurdle in building intrusion detection datasets.

In DARPA's IDEval program, the participants were provided with a list of time stamps pointing to exactly when a particular attack commenced in the simulated traffic and the length of time it lasted. Since all other traffic was simulated in a controlled environment, it was considered benign. Subsequently the labels used in the KDD Cup data were assigned using these time stamps.

Since attacks in the adopted methodology are simulated using existing IDS signatures; labelling attack traffic is straight forward and requires matching given alert messages in the signatures with the IDS generated log. To ensure the correctness of attacks, records corresponding to unsuccessful detections could be discarded. The background traffic could be labelled similarly by replaying the captured trace through a signature based IDS using the most up-to-date signature bases. The traces could be replayed using the actual time stamps or in a fast mode. Since the intrusion detection systems log only the intrusive activities detected through their signatures, default rules can be added to the signature chains to log every normal transaction as well. The feature vector output from the reassembling and feature extraction module can then be assigned labels by comparing time stamps or other session IDs from the IDS logs.

6.4 A Data Building Exercise

In this section we build a dataset using the methodology described in the last section.

6.4.1 Background Traffic Collection

Ideally, we would like to collect university wide network traffic on large university servers. Due to administrative reasons and privacy and security concerns, however, we had to limit the collection of traffic to one of the School of ITEE servers at our university. The server named Seal can be accessed via `http://www.itee.adfa.edu.au`, is wired on a 10 MB local Ethernet network and is connected to the outside world via a university gateway router. Seal runs a few well-known services including Web, Mail, SSH, DNS and SQL servers on a Sun Microsystems platform (Please refer to 7.4 for an explanation of abbreviations). The web server hosts hundreds of web pages linked through the school website and it is the main source of attracting outside traffic. The mail server runs SMTP and POP3 protocols and provides remote access to a few mail accounts through the POP3 server. The other two services, especially SQL, are rarely accessed from outside the network.

We collected traffic on Seal over the whole month of March of 2008 and the first week of April, excluding the weekends and public holidays during which data collection was not available. Packet capturing was limited to a maximum of 200,000 packets per day due to space limitations on the server. Since all simulated attacks (described later) were directed to the Seal server from external networks, we filtered out all local and non-IP traffic including the broadcast and multicast packets using tcpdump's capture filters.

The size of the captured network traffic amounted to almost 3 gigabytes with around 3.8 million packets captured in total. Table 6.1 below provides the detailed breakdown of the captured packets according to their respective transport and application layer protocols.

The statistics clearly show that the majority of traffic belong to TCP with Web service constituting the bulk of the log. Among the other TCP based services SMTP and POP3 are the only two protocols that have some notable activities. This is expected given the server is hosting Web and Mail servers. Also, almost no DNS traffic is observed as we filtered out all inside traffic to the server. The limited SSH activities also show that there are not many users accessing their accounts from the external network. The traffic to other services can be considered suspicious or unwanted (e.g., Seal does not host an FTP server and thus attempts of FTP connections are most likely part of a scanning activity). Further, there is only a very small percentage of UDP and ICMP based traffic in comparison to the TCP traffic.

Note that the traffic statistics shown in Table 6.1 are for the complete capture. To build the connection records we used various filtering techniques, discussed in

Section 6.4.3, which reduced the size of the data.

Table 6.1: Protocol-wise breakdown of the traffic captured on Seal

Protocol	Service	Packets	Percentage
TCP		3780991	99.505
	FTP	1092	0.029
	SSH	1468	0.039
	SMTP	82682	2.176
	DNS	19	0.001
	HTTP	3693141	97.193
	POP3	2325	0.061
	Others	264	0.007
UDP		14390	0.379
	DNS	14256	0.375
	Others	134	0.003
ICMP		4426	0.116
Total		3799807	

6.4.2 Simulation of Attacks

The attack simulation task is carried out using a Snort penetration testing tool, Mucus (Mutz, Vigna, and Kemmerer 2003). Below we provide a brief introduction to Snort and Mucus.

6.4.2.1 Snort

Snort is an open source signature based intrusion detection system that is used in production networks around the Globe. Snort signatures are developed by domain experts when new attacks or exploits are discovered. Currently, Snort rule base consists of more than 8000 rules that look for thousands of attacks or their variations. In addition, Snort uses several pre-processor modules that detect various packet level anomalies.

Snort rules are created following a simple, lightweight rule description language. Figure 6.2 shows the Snort rule syntax with an example rule. This rule matches any packet that is sent from any IP address not belonging to the protected network and is destined to port 0 on the protected machine regardless of the state of the connection. An alert is generated if this rule gets fired and a bad traffic message is logged.

[Action] [Protocol] [IP_Address] [Port] [Direction Operator] [IP_Address] [Port]
([message string]; [A list of keyword-value pairs separated by ;])

alert tcp $EXTERNAL_NET any -> $HOME_NET 0 (msg:"Bad-Traffic"; flow:stateless;
classtype:misc-activity; sid:524; rev:8;)

Figure 6.2: Syntax of Snort signatures

Snort uses around 40 main features in its rules whose values can be specified by Snort keywords. The features are of two types: payload and non-payload based features. Payload features look for specified patterns in the data portion of the packets; for example, the *content* feature specify an ASCII or hexadecimal string to be searched in the payload and *depth* specifies the number of bytes to be searched for a given content pattern. The non-payload features specify the header values and other connection related information; for example, the *dsize* feature allows matching a specified length of the packet payload and *flow* specifies the state and direction of a connection. Some of the features additionally use modifiers or operators to further identify certain conditions to match.

6.4.2.2 Mucus

Mucus is a Unix/Linux based tool written in Perl[1]. Mucus simulates attack traffic by parsing the Snort intrusion detection signatures and then generating customised network packets that match Snort signatures and eventually trigger Snort alerts. Multiple instances of the same attack can also be generated whereby Mucus randomises the source/destination IP addresses and other packet fields not specified in the rule or that have *don't care* values (e.g., port *any*). Mucus can translate most of the Snort keywords successfully, however, it does have certain limitations when parsing more complex rules such as those rules with high number of mixed conditions. Consequently in our simulation, each attack generated by Mucus was tested syntactically using the Snort's detection engine for its correctness. Another advantage of Mucus is that it can simulate stateful TCP attacks. The stateful intrusion detection systems, such as Snort, can simply ignore the out-of-band attacks. The stateful attacks require that a connection via the TCP three-way handshake is established between the attacking and targeted machines before the actual attack packets can be transferred between the two hosts. Mucus can be configured to simulate such attacks, thus ensuring that those Snort rules with the *flow* keyword are activated.

To simulate attacks, Mucus was configured to send packets through the local network adapter to the Seal's IP address. Snort was turned on with its default configuration with all the relevant rule bases and preprocessors. At the completion of the simulation, the alerts generated by Snort are compared with the rules used to generate these attacks. To ensure the validity of the attacks, the rules that did not trigger an alert are excluded from the simulation list. Finally, the attacks are regenerated using the corrected list of rules and the resultant network traffic generated by this activity was captured using the tcpdump program.

---

[1]The original Mucus code was written in 2004 and did not support most new Snort keywords. We used an updated version hosted under the Bleeding Threat project (Gregory 2005)

6.4.2.3 The Attacks

After filtering the traffic captured on Seal, the only two active TCP services left in the data are HTTP and POP3. Hence we selected rules relating to these two services from the Snort rule base for generating attacks. In particular, rules from web-cgi, web-php, web-misc and pop3 rule bases of Snort were selected. It makes sense, since injecting other attacks could lead to a simulation artefact where the attacks not belonging to these two services could easily be identified based on a single distinguishing feature (e.g., the destination service).

There is only very little UDP activity on Seal as shown by Table 6.1. Thus, there was not much choice for UDP based attacks that can be injected into the Seal traffic. Therefore, we chose UDP attacks that can be directed towards any service and modified the attack rules to generate traffic directed towards the destination ports seen in our collected trace. The ICMP based attacks were chosen similar to UDP attacks.

About 500 Snort rules were used to generate the attacks. Only a single instance of attack was generated per rule. Although multiple instances per attack can be generated, this could reduce the covertness of the attacks making it easier for the algorithm to detect. Almost all of the simulated attacks are content based attacks and can be classified under the DOS, U2R or R2L categories used in the KDD Cup datasets. The flooding type DOS attacks, such as smurf and syn-flood, that aim to consume target host or network bandwidth were not simulated. Once launched, there is little intrusion detection systems can do about such attacks other than silently discarding packets to a certain extent. In addition, slow probing, or scanning, attacks that require keeping statistics for connections on host or service levels are also not included. These attacks cannot be simulated using tools like Mucus and require mixing up with real background traffic. They are also hard to label, since Snort uses various thresholds that need to be tuned to detect such attacks.

6.4.3 Feature Extraction

Most of the features in the KDD Cup data were built using the association rule mining algorithms. These features are aimed at detecting the attacks found in the DARPA datasets. For instance, to detect flooding type DOS attacks, time based features were extracted on host and service levels that captured the intensity of traffic on target hosts in a given time window. Similarly, statistical features were extracted that captured possible reconnaissance activities on target hosts. Since most of simulated attacks are content based and are specifically tailored to trigger Snort alerts, similar features as used by Snort rules in detecting these attacks should be extracted ideally. This is not a problem for the non-payload based features which can either be extracted directly from packet headers or by reassembling the sessions between communicating hosts. Payload based features, however, need improvisation as Snort is a pattern matching system whereas machine learning algorithms work on feature spaces to learn generalised hypotheses.

We extended Mahoney's *tcpdump extraction* program (Mahoney 2003), used in the first stage of ALAD, to extract features from attack and background traffic trace files, stored in a tcpdump format. The program sequentially reads each binary file, reassembles TCP sessions and extracts packet level information including packet header and payload in a human readable ASCII format. We modified the original code written for DARPA IDEVAL traffic dumps to handle the Seal traffic in the correct byte order. Further, the original code restricted the payload extraction to the first 1000 bytes, which was also removed. Finally, functions to handle UDP and ICMP traffic and calculate the payload based features on the fly were added.

Since all the attacks are directed from external networks to the server, the tool filters out all out going packets from Seal. It also filters out traffic to non well-known services (i.e., the packets with a destination port greater than 1023). Further, to extract connection related features, the TCP sessions are reassembled and the state of each connection is tracked. Only the TCP data packets that belong to an established stream are used in building the records, while the UDP and ICMP

Table 6.2: Payload features extracted from real background traffic and simulated attacks.

Feature Name	Description
WCount	Number of complete words in the payload separated by whitespace or other special characters
HotWords	Number of hot words in the payload given a list of words (e.g., root, login)
MaxWLen	Length of the longest word in the payload
LowAlpha	Percentage of upper case letters in the payload
UppAlpha	Percentage of lower case letters in the payload
Numeric	Percentage of digits in the payload
WSpc	Percentage of white spaces in the payload
Control	Percentage of control characters in the payload such as line feed and carriage return
Reserve	Percentage of reserved characters such as @, $
Unsafe	Percentage of unsafe (URI) characters in the payload such as %,
NonPrint	Percentage of non-printable (> ASCII 0x7E) characters in the payload
Others	Percentage of other characters in the payload that do not fall into one of the above categories

packets are logged regardless of the direction of flow or the state of the connection. Next, the summarised packet information is converted to a feature vector format by extracting feature values from the packet summary.

The extended tool is able to extract tcpdump time stamp, all of the IP header fields as well as the fields from the TCP, UDP and ICMP headers, including TCP flags, sequence/acknowledgement numbers, source/destination port numbers and the ICMP ID, type, code and sequence numbers. A flow feature is added in each record, similar to Snort, that tells the direction of a connection (i.e., from internal to external network or vice-versa). In addition, 12 other features are extracted from the payload section of the packets listed in Table 6.2.

As can be seen all of the attributes correspond essentially to the percentages of ASCII characters categorised under different features. Most payload based attacks attempt to exploit buffer overflows in software using various techniques, such as illegal characters in URL, long strings or a specific combination of unsafe characters. Therefore, we expect these features to provide good information gain against such attacks. Some further analysis on the relationship between these features and the obtained labels is provided in §6.4.5.

Although additional features could be built such as those used in the KDD Cup datasets, our primary objective is to demonstrate the usefulness of the methodology and develop extensible tools that can complement in evaluating our systems. Besides the presented features can be easily calculated on the fly without needing to revisit the data or spending long time in the pre-processing. This could be beneficial, especially, for the algorithms that aim to detect and learn intrusion patterns online (i.e., in single-pass or real time), such as those developed in the last two chapters.

6.4.4 Labelling

In order to label background traffic collected through Seal, Snort was run in the read mode with all of its detection modules and rule bases turned on. Specifically, we turned on Snort's Stream 5 pre-processor that can rebuild and keep track of TCP streams to detect stateful attacks. Since Snort only alerts on attack traffic, we introduced a set of default rules at the end of Snort rule chains. Thus if a packet did not trigger any attack alerts it was logged as *Normal*. The default rules match only the data packets which belonged to an established TCP stream. Control packets such as those used in TCP connection establishment and termination were not logged. The UDP and ICMP packets were logged independent of the state of the connection. This matched the configuration used in the feature extraction module described above. Finally, the feature vectors generated from the background traffic were labelled by comparing the time stamps and packet IDs from both the Snort alert logs and the feature vectors.

The attack vectors were labelled in a similar way to the labelling of the background traffic. Snort alert logs were compared with the alert messages specified in the rules used for generating the attacks. In some cases, Snort generated multiple alerts for a single attack. In other cases, Snort did not raise an alarm because the signatures generated by Mucus were malformed and attacks did not launch successfully. In the former case, we chose the alert messages specified in the rule to be the label while the traffic that did not trigger alerts was simply removed from the trace. Stateful TCP attacks were labelled using the same procedure as described above for the background traffic. The first word of each alert message was used as the label names, this essentially corresponds to the name of rule base used for the generation of attacks (e.g., DOS, DNS, WEB-CGI).

6.4.5 Putting it All Together

The overall process of data preparation is depicted in Figure 6.3. Several weeks of real traffic captured on a university departmental server is replayed using Snort IDS as well as a feature extraction program. The feature extraction program performs the reassembling of TCP streams and transforms the binary data from the network packet structure to a readable text format. Features are extracted from this summarised information and connection records are converted to the feature vector format. The feature vectors are labelled using the Snort alert logs and added to the data corpus.

The attacks are simulated using Mucus which generates attack traffic tailored to

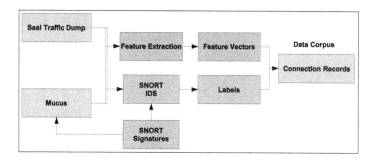

Figure 6.3: Overview of data preparation

activate Snort intrusion detection rules. The attack traffic is processed to labelled feature vectors in a similar fashion as we described for the background traffic. The attack records are then added to the same data corpus.

The final dataset consists of almost 100,000 records including more than 3000 attack records. The difference in the number of captured packets and the number of records is mainly due to the filtering out of the TCP control packets and limiting the detection to the inbound traffic. Table 6.3 provides the complete class distribution in the final dataset.

As can be seen, most records (97.26%) built from the traffic collected at Seal expectedly belongs to the normal traffic. The background traffic however is not completely clean. Out of the remaining instances, 0.5% are flagged by the Snort preprocessor modules labelled as *DECODER* in the above table. Preprocessor alerts are triggered normally due to protocol anomalies among other reasons and can produce unwanted alerts generated because of protocols implementation related issues. The highest number of Snort alerts are triggered by the WEB-MISC rule base which includes signatures for various potentially dangerous Web activities such as those related to the crawlers used by search engines. Also note that almost all of the Snort alerts correspond to the TCP based packets with no UDP related alerts and only 21 ICMP related alerts. There could be more attacks in the normal traffic which are not detected by Snort (e.g., we observed many ICMP packets which are most likely

Table 6.3: Class distribution in the dataset built from captured traffic and simulated attacks.

Label	Seal	Mucus	Total	Percentage
DNS	0	5	5	0.005
DOS	0	3	3	0.003
DECODER	507	4	511	0.525
EXPLOIT	0	13	13	0.013
ICMP	21	17	38	0.039
NORMAL	94250	0	94250	96.771
POP3	0	21	21	0.022
RPC	0	77	77	0.079
SCAN	0	4	4	0.004
WEB-CGI	38	172	210	0.216
WEB-MISC	2031	149	2180	2.238
WEB-PHP	51	32	83	0.085
Total	96898	497	97395	

a part of some scanning activities and are not flagged by Snort). Conversely, Snort could have also falsely labelled a normal packet as an attack (e.g., as in the case of WEB-MISC alerts).

In our experiments later in this chapter, we used only TCP based records which account for more than 99% of the data. The UDP related records are removed because there are not many simulated UDP attacks and the few attacks could be detected because of the destination port artefact. The ICMP records are removed since many of its connections labelled as normal by Snort were suspicious. Note that the removal of non-TCP records is a data collection constraint and not a limitation of the methodology to generate the dataset. We will refer to this as TCP dataset. The TCP dataset consists of five classes (i.e., NORMAL, POP3, WEB-CGI, WEB-MISC and WEB-PHP) and amounted to around 90,000 records. Each record consisted of 20 features which include 8 features extracted from the packet headers (namely, IP header length, IP datagram length, fragment id, TTL, source and destination port numbers, TCP sequence and acknowledgement numbers and the length of data portion in the packet) and 12 payload based features listed in Table 6.2 above. Note that there were 13 more non-payload based features in the full dataset, but they were removed either because their values remained constant over the whole dataset or they contained sensitive information such as the IP addresses.

6.5   Comparison with the KDD Cup dataset

The network dump used for constructing the KDD Cup dataset consisted of both internal and external traffic and involved more than one internal host. This allowed many short duration communication sessions between host. The Seal dataset is built from the traffic captured on a single server with many long duration connection sessions. This is also the reason for the difference in the number of services used in both datasets.

The KDD Cup dataset has 41 features many of which were constructed offline using data mining techniques. The Seal dataset contains 33 features, all of which can be built online and do not require any windowing techniques. It, however, does require session tracking which is an essential part of modern intrusion detection systems.

The KDD Cup dataset contains 38 attacks in total all of which can be categorised under 4 categories. The Seal dataset contains a wide variety of attacks, around 500 in total, which are classified under 11 different categories. Most of the attacks in the Seal dataset are payload based and are targeted towards end host applications. The KDD Cup dataset, in contrast, contains very few payload based attacks.

The KDD Cup dataset is characterised with high class imbalance and two of the attack classes are extremely rare. However, there is apparently no sign of noise in the data except minor labelling inconsistencies which can be rectified. The Seal dataset also contains very high class imbalance. In fact, all of its attack classes are extremely rare in the dataset. Also note that in the KDD dataset, DOS attacks are the majority class in training whereas in the Seal dataset, the Normal class is the majority class. We believe this is more appropriate and nearer to real situations where normal activities are predominant and attacks are usually rare. Although not definitive, the Seal dataset may contain noise due to labelling errors.

Finally, the KDD Cup dataset was developed in 1999 with a 1998 simulated traffic dump whereas the Seal dataset is built in 2008. Although, we do not claim that our dataset is better suited to study intrusion detection problems, there are some advantages in using the methodology developed to build the dataset.

6.6 Evaluation

In this section, we evaluate the performance of the baseline UCS, UCSx developed in Chapter 4 and UCSSE with adaptive parameter control developed in Chapter 5 on the TCP dataset described above.

6.6.1 Methodology

In the experiments conducted in the last two chapters we had access to separate training and test datasets provided during the KDD Cup competition. In these experiments, we used a standard cross-validation technique for evaluating the systems. The performance of each system on the TCP dataset described above is measured using a 5-fold cross-validation test. The dataset was divided into 5 stratified and disjoint train/validate samples. Then each system was trained and tested on every fold using 6 different seeds. Thus all the results are averages of 30 independent runs. Notice, however, that a single training pass is used still to train all the systems in order to simulate a real time environment. The rest of the setup including parameter settings is the same as that used in the experiments of Chapter 5. The UCSSE results correspond to the fully adaptive version developed in the last chapter (i.e., with both accuracy and experience threshold controls).

In the result tables, each of the two systems (i.e., UCSD and UCSSE) are compared against UCS. Similar to Chapter 5, two sets of experiments are conducted: one with the baseline UCS setup and the other with the extended UCS setup (i.e., UCSx). The results are also presented in a similar manner as in Chapter 5. First, statistics related to the rule sets of each system are shown along with the rule generalisation figures used to graphically represent the rule sets. Then per class and overall test accuracy, false alarm rate and hit rate for each system are reported. The cost per example score (CPE) is not reported in these results as no cost matrix was defined for these problems. Consequently, the cost based prediction technique introduced in Chatper 4 is not used in the UCS setups. The significance testing scheme is also the same as that used in previous chapters (i.e., the performance of UCSD and UCSSE is compared with that of UCS and the significantly better or worse systems are highlighted).

6.6.2 Experiments

Table 6.4 shows statistics related to rule sets obtained by UCS, UCSD and UCSSE for the TCP dataset. Similar to the baseline UCS results for the KDD Cup dataset, UCS nearly uses the maximum population size limit and evolves more than 7000 rules. The number of rules evolved are proportional to the class distribution in the training set. Both UCSD and UCSSE achieve significant reduction in the number of rules and obtain more than 31 and 27 times smaller rule sets than UCS respectively. UCSD, however, could not obtain any rule for the POP3 class. UCSSE on the other hand retrieves signatures for all the classes. However its overall coverage of the validation set is significantly lower than the other two systems. The bottom tabular shows the average generality of the rule sets obtained by each system. Both UCSD and UCSSE show a similar trend and obtain significantly higher generalised rule for the two majority classes (i.e., NORMAL and WEB-MISC classes), while retrieving significantly specific rules for the other classes.

Table 6.4: Comparison of different signature statistics between UCS, UCSD and UCSSE (with adaptive parameter control) the TCP dataset.

Number of Rules			
Class	UCS	UCSD	UCSSE
NORMAL	5373(115)	192(22)▲	86(16)◆
POP3	90(6)	0(0)◆	14(1)▲
WEB-CGI	273(11)	7(3)◆	42(7)▲
WEB-MISC	1305(90)	27(5)◆	103(78)▲
WEB-PHP	141(10)	1(1)◆	20(7)▲
Overall	7181(35)	226(23)◆	265(81)▲
Test Set Coverage			
NORMAL	99.74(0.06)	97.79(0.99)△	87.24(4.63)◇
POP3	44.17(23.88)	1.67(6.24)◇	48.33(23.21)
WEB-CGI	97.30(2.86)	82.06(7.00)◇	87.22(3.34)△
WEB-MISC	99.25(0.43)	86.03(11.15)△	75.82(11.62)◇
WEB-PHP	94.09(6.44)	79.91(14.16)△	80.86(12.84)△
Overall	99.70(0.05)	97.42(1.09)△	86.94(4.72)◇
Average Generality			
NORMAL	40.43(0.40)	44.09(0.74)▲	45.82(1.06)◆
POP3	37.01(0.69)	37.01(0.69)	32.05(1.12)◇
WEB-CGI	35.54(0.85)	34.61(1.61)△	34.07(0.84)△
WEB-MISC	39.47(1.22)	41.78(2.75)▲	40.81(2.53)▲
WEB-PHP	36.47(0.58)	36.33(3.12)	33.47(0.99)◇

Figures 6.4 - 6.6 graphically show the post training rule sets obtained by the three systems. Generally, all three systems get rules with higher generality for better

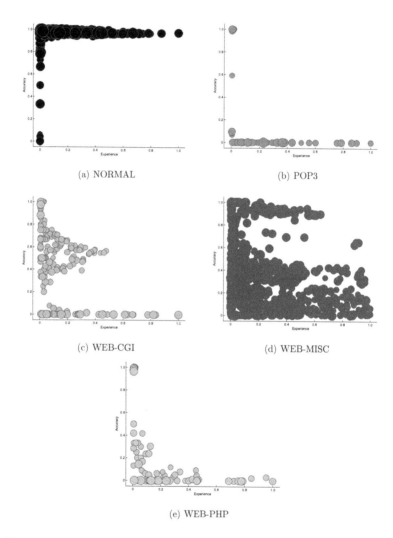

(a) NORMAL

(b) POP3

(c) WEB-CGI

(d) WEB-MISC

(e) WEB-PHP

Figure 6.4: A graphical representation of the rules evolved by UCS for the TCP dataset. Each rule in the population is represented by a circle with a radius proportional to rule's generality.

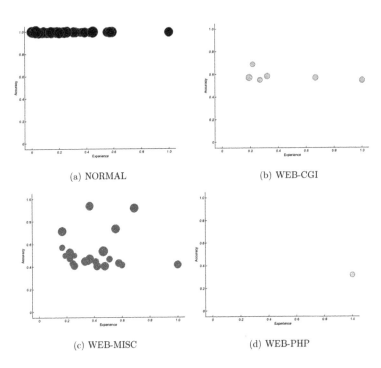

(a) NORMAL (b) WEB-CGI

(c) WEB-MISC (d) WEB-PHP

Figure 6.5: A graphical representation of the rules obtained by UCSD for the TCP dataset. Each rule in the pruned population is represented by a circle with a radius proportional to rule's generality. Note that UCSD was unable to recover any rule for POP3 class in these experiments.

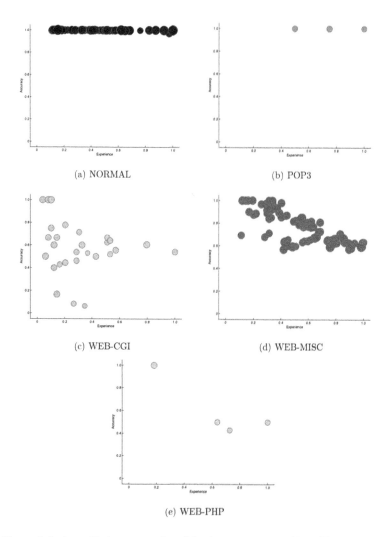

(a) NORMAL

(b) POP3

(c) WEB-CGI

(d) WEB-MISC

(e) WEB-PHP

Figure 6.6: A graphical representation of the signatures extracted by UCSSE using UCS as a base learner for the TCP dataset. Each signature in the signature set is represented by a circle with a radius proportional to rule's generality.

represented classes in the training data. This can be expected given the opportunity based reproduction scheme used in UCS. UCS evolves most number of rules for the NORMAL class (Figure 6.4(a)) and with the highest generality among all classes. The majority of these rules, however, are very low in experience. Moreover, the accuracy of NORMAL class rules might not reflect their overgenerality as the number of attack class instances are highly rare in the dataset. For instance, a rule matching a high number of NORMAL class instances with HTTP destination service may still be highly accurate if it also covered all of the WEB-PHP attack instances. Nevertheless, UCS does evolve some highly experienced and accurate rules for the NORMAL class. For the second most prevalent class in the dataset (i.e., WEB-MISC), UCS evolves a high number of rules as well. Unlike NORMAL class rules, however, the majority of the WEB-MISC rules have low accuracy (Figure 6.4(d)) and there are a fewer rules with high experience and high accuracy. The quality of rules for the rest of the three classes (i.e., POP3, WEB-CGI and WEB-PHP) is quite poor. For POP3 and WEB-PHP, almost all high experience rules have very low accuracies, while for the WEB-CGI class, there are a few rules with average experience and accuracy.

Figure 6.5 shows a typical rule set obtained after pruning the post training population of UCS using Dixon's rule set reduction algorithm. As expected, UCSD retains classifiers that have above average accuracies and sufficient experience. It could not obtain any POP3 rules as UCS faces difficulties in learning optimal rules for this most rare class in the dataset. On the other hand, UCSSE is able to retrieve a few accurate and experienced rules for the POP3 class. This shows another advantage of real time signature extraction; i.e., it can avoid the forgetting problem by extracting good rules to a signature base as soon as they are discovered and before being replaced by overgeneral rules of the prevalent classes. Likewise, UCSSE is able to retrieve good rules in all other classes. Further the signatures extracted by UCSSE are relatively more general and higher in experience in comparison to the rules obtained by UCSD in all classes.

Table 6.5 shows a comparison of UCS, UCSD and UCSSE run with the baseline UCS setup on the TCP dataset. As can be seen, UCSSE achieves significantly better accuracy than UCS on all attack classes except POP3 attacks where the mean accuracy is better than UCS but is not statistically significant. In fact, UCSSE also performs better than UCSD on three of the four attack classes (i.e., POP3, WEB-MISC and WEB-PHP). It, however, performs poorer than both the systems on the NORMAL class and thus overall because of the sheer majority of NORMAL instances in the dataset.

The lower tabular shows the false alarm and hit rates for the three systems. Both UCSD and UCSSE achieve significantly higher hit rates but only at the cost of significantly higher rates of false alarms than the baseline UCS, highlighting a tradeoff between the size of rule sets and the generalisation accuracy.

Table 6.5: Comparison of test accuracy and other performance measures between UCS, UCSD and UCSSE (with adaptive parameters) on the TCP dataset.

Test Accuracy (%)

Class	UCS	UCSD	UCSSE
NORMAL	99.97(0.08)	97.87(1.17)$^\triangle$	96.25(2.50)$^\diamond$
POP3	50.83(26.21)	19.17(23.88)$^\diamond$	56.67(21.34)
WEB-CGI	34.42(20.06)	55.03(9.49)$^\blacktriangle$	54.68(16.71)$^\blacktriangle$
WEB-MISC	1.05(0.67)	30.90(18.59)$^\blacktriangle$	45.14(19.95)$^\blacklozenge$
WEB-PHP	3.79(4.50)	5.25(6.37)	12.03(8.99)$^\blacklozenge$
Overall	97.00(0.00)	95.97(0.80)$^\triangle$	94.77(1.91)$^\diamond$

Other Performance Measures

Measure	UCS	UCSD	UCSSE
FA Rate (%)	0.21(0.04)	2.20(1.16)$^\triangle$	4.25(3.77)$^\diamond$
Hit Rate (%)	8.94(4.38)	46.50(18.23)$^\blacktriangle$	53.47(14.71)$^\blacktriangle$

Table 6.6 presents a comparison of average CPU time in minutes used by the three systems on the TCP dataset. These experiments are also run on the same high performance computing machines as the KDD Cup experiments. Similar to KDD Cup results, UCSSE achieves significant reduction in training and thus overall CPU time. However, the margin of reduction is not as big as for the KDD Cup data. This is mainly because of the difference in the two dataset sizes both in terms of number of records and features. A similar behaviour was observed in §5.3.5 where the difference in CPU time consumed by UCSSE and UCS improved with the increase in input length.

UCSSE took around 14.5 minutes on average to process the whole dataset. This corresponds to more than 6000 records per minute. Recall that the raw data captured from the Seal server and generated by Mucus amounted to around 3 gigabytes or 24 gigabits. The tool that we developed to preprocess the raw data into feature vector format took around 6 minutes to translate this data into connection records on a Pentium-IV machine with a processor speed of 1.70 GHz, 512 MB RAM and running Linux (kernel 2.6) operating system. This corresponds to around 66 megabits of binary packet data per second. UCSSE processed the same data in 14.5 minutes which correspond to around 27 megabits of binary data per second[2]. This is still faster than the 10 megabit Ethernet where the background data is captured. Although the bandwidth utilisation on local area networks varies from organisation to organisation, it has been shown that the average network bandwidth utilisation on the Internet is around 40-50% (TeleGeography 2008). Taking these figures as a general guideline and the above mention estimation of the time bounds, UCSSE should be able to handle network traffic with 50 megabits per second. This capacity can be improved easily by optimising the current experimental implementation of the tools and incorporating hashing based rule matching algorithms. However, the performance of the systems would need to be tested in a real environment for guaranteeing the estimated rates.

---

[2]Note that UCSSE was run on a much faster machine in comparison to the preprocessing tool.

Table 6.6: Comparison of CPU time in minutes between between UCS, UCSD and UCSSE on the TCP dataset.

Time	UCS	UCSD	UCSSE
Training	18.10(0.78)	18.10(0.64)	14.01(1.53)$^\blacklozenge$
Post Process	0.00(0.00)	2.70(0.34)$^\diamond$	0.00(0.00)
Evaluation	2.85(0.12)	0.10(0.01)$^\blacklozenge$	0.49(0.16)$^\blacktriangle$
Total	20.95(0.88)	20.86(0.88)	14.49(1.63)$^\blacklozenge$

The next set of tables (Tables 6.7 - 6.9) present the results of the experiments run with the extended UCS setup referred to as UCSx on the TCP dataset. The results are tabulated using the same format as for the above set of experiments except that the performance of UCSx is compared with that of UCSxD and UCSxSE.

Table 6.7 compares the rule set statistics of the three systems. Note that UCSx evolves a higher number of rules overall but balances the rule allocation between different classes better than UCS. This is in line with the results on the KDD Cup dataset. UCSxSE retrieves almost half the number of signatures than UCSxD. This is in contrast to the previous results where UCSD obtained smaller rule sets on average than UCSSE. UCSxD obtains almost double the number of rules than UCSD as it extracts higher number of rules for both NORMAL and WEB-MISC classes. This shows that UCSx is achieving better estimates for the rule parameters of these two classes in comparison to UCS. However, UCSx achieves a lower test accuracy (Table 6.8, discussed later in this section) on the NORMAL class than UCS. It suggests that UCSx evolves more overgeneral rules for the NORMAL class than UCS. UCSxD similar to UCSD also fails to recover any POP3 rules. UCSxSE retrieves more than 34 times less number of rules than UCSx and thus improves its reduction from UCSSE. But the reduction in rule has only come at the cost of significantly lower test coverage on almost all classes.

The average rule set generality, shown in the bottom tabular, for all three systems

Table 6.7: Comparison of different rule statistics between UCSx, UCSxD and UCSxSE on the TCP dataset.

Class	UCSx	UCSxD	UCSxSE
Number of Rules			
NORMAL	4826(82)	421(44)▲	88(30)♦
POP3	231(14)	0(0)♦	13(1)▲
WEB-CGI	408(18)	16(3)♦	51(13)▲
WEB-MISC	1584(76)	106(22)▲	54(38)♦
WEB-PHP	278(15)	9(2)▲	9(7)▲
Overall	7328(23)	552(52)▲	215(51)♦
Test Set Coverage			
NORMAL	99.61(0.06)	98.19(0.26)△	81.12(5.30)◇
POP3	41.67(26.87)	2.50(7.50)◇	47.50(31.19)
WEB-CGI	97.06(2.43)	85.16(5.69)△	84.13(5.68)△
WEB-MISC	99.22(0.41)	95.05(1.75)△	51.61(13.86)◇
WEB-PHP	93.09(6.97)	79.41(12.33)△	72.09(14.78)△
Overall	99.57(0.06)	98.04(0.26)△	80.39(5.32)◇
Average Generality			
NORMAL	39.50(0.37)	43.16(0.70)▲	45.18(1.24)♦
POP3	38.58(0.37)	38.58(0.37)	31.60(1.03)◇
WEB-CGI	36.67(0.59)	35.43(1.03)△	34.04(1.03)◇
WEB-MISC	37.10(0.64)	38.30(1.02)▲	37.85(1.60)▲
WEB-PHP	37.84(0.40)	36.72(1.35)△	34.90(2.47)◇

follow the same trend as in the case of baseline UCS setup except that the rule sets with the UCSx setup are slightly more specific.

Figures 6.7 - 6.9 graphically show the rule sets obtained by each system for different classes. Starting with the UCSx rule sets, it can be seen that UCSx is evolving much

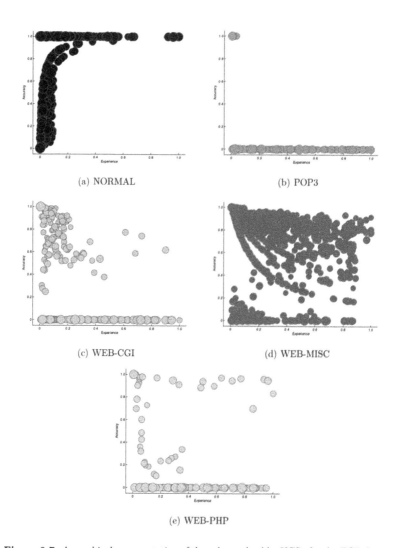

(a) NORMAL   (b) POP3

(c) WEB-CGI   (d) WEB-MISC

(e) WEB-PHP

Figure 6.7: A graphical representation of the rules evolved by UCSx for the TCP dataset. Each rule in the population is represented by a circle with a radius proportional to rule's generality.

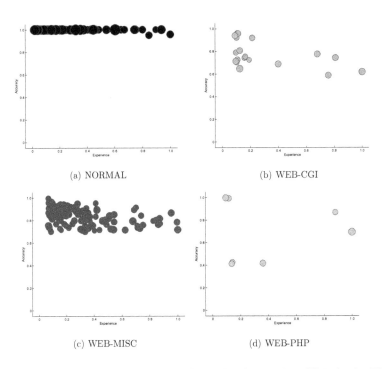

(a) NORMAL   (b) WEB-CGI

(c) WEB-MISC   (d) WEB-PHP

Figure 6.8: A graphical representation of the rules obtained by UCSxD for the TCP dataset. Each rule in the pruned population is represented by a circle with a radius proportional to rule's generality. Note that UCSxD was unable to recover any rule for POP3 class in these experiments.

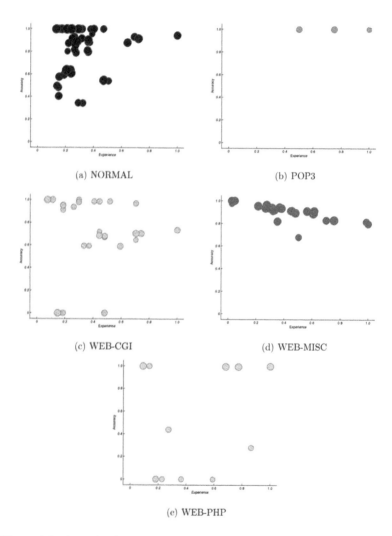

(a) NORMAL   (b) POP3

(c) WEB-CGI   (d) WEB-MISC

(e) WEB-PHP

Figure 6.9: A graphical representation of the signatures extracted by UCSxSE using UCSx as a base learner for the TCP dataset. Each signature in the signature set is represented by a circle with a radius proportional to rule's generality.

higher number of rules with better accuracy and higher experience than the baseline UCS (see Figure 6.4) for all classes except POP3 where the results are not different from UCS. A significant improvement can be seen especially for all the attack classes. For instance, UCS could not evolve any highly experienced and accurate rules for WEB-PHP but UCSx evolves quite a few such rules. Similarly, most of WEB-MISC rules in UCS were low in experience and accuracy. This situation has almost reversed in UCSx rule sets. UCSxD and UCSxSE rule sets are improved accordingly as both systems now obtain a higher number of accurate and experienced rules. UCSxD could not obtain any rules for the POP3 class as UCSD. This can be understood as UCS or UCSx both do not contain any accurate and experienced rules for these two classes in their post training populations. UCSxSE retrieves rules for all the classes including POP3 similar to UCSSE. However UCSxSE achieves a much lower test coverage. We hypothesise that this occurs because of the higher generalisation pressure caused by the deletion operation in the signature set. As the rule estimates in UCS population improve, this drives the adaptive deletion thresholds to higher values, consequently deleting more signatures and opening covering gaps.

Table 6.8 presents a comparison of test set accuracy and other performance measures achieved by UCSx, UCSxD and UCSxSE. First, notice that the test accuracy of all UCSx based systems has improved significantly on all of the attack classes except UCSxD which performs worst on the POP3 class. But the accuracy on the majority NORMAL class has dropped up to 2 to 3% in all systems in comparison to the UCS based systems. One of the reasons for this loss of accuracy could be an effect of the modified accuracy function introduced in Chapter 4, which is biased towards the minority class instances but might deteriorate majority class performance when there is noise in the data. In the KDD Cup data there was no sign of explicit noise and thus the extended UCS performed better overall than the baseline UCS. Nonetheless, it is encouraging that the accuracy on the minority or attack classes have significantly improved. The performance of UCSxSE seems to be coherent with the previous results except that it only performs significantly better on the WEB-CGI, class whereas on other attack classes the mean accuracies are better than the other two systems but these numbers are not statistically significant.

Table 6.8: Comparison of test accuracy and other performance measures between UCS, UCSD and UCSSE (with adaptive parameters) on the TCP dataset.

Test Accuracy (%)			
Class	UCSx	UCSxD	UCSxSE
NORMAL	97.65(0.55)	97.39(0.76)	93.30(3.55)$^\diamond$
POP3	75.00(19.36)	0.00(0.00)$^\diamond$	81.67(19.29)
WEB-CGI	44.12(14.11)	57.34(13.62)$^\blacktriangle$	72.20(6.77)$^\blacklozenge$
WEB-MISC	62.46(6.20)	58.46(7.71)	60.04(7.60)
WEB-PHP	14.98(10.32)	19.88(13.39)	19.86(10.49)
Overall	96.53(0.50)	96.23(0.67)	92.57(3.29)$^\diamond$

Other Performance Measures			
Measure	UCSx	UCSxD	UCSxSE
FA Rate (%)	2.37(0.48)	2.66(0.77)	6.60(3.62)$^\diamond$
Hit Rate (%)	68.03(5.39)	65.56(7.20)	69.20(6.72)

The bottom tabular shows a comparison on two other performance measures. Although UCSxSE achieves a higher mean hit rate than the other two systems, the numbers are not statistically significant. All of the systems, however, have achieved significantly improved hit rates than the baseline versions, especially UCSx which improves the hit rate by almost 60%. On the other hand, the false alarm rate has worsened in all the systems suggesting that a tradeoff exists between the two performance measures. In summary, UCSxSE performs equivalent to both other systems with a 34 times reduction in the rule set size achieved in real time.

Table 6.9 shows a comparison of average CPU time, in minutes, taken by the three systems on the TCP dataset. Again UCSxSE uses significantly less amount of time than the other two systems. In comparison to the baseline UCS based systems the

Table 6.9: Comparison of CPU time between UCSx, UCSxD and UCSxSE (with adaptive parameters) on the TCP dataset.

Time	UCSx	UCSxD	UCSxSE
Training	20.31(1.87)	20.38(1.81)	16.64(2.12)$^\blacklozenge$
Post Process	0.00(0.00)	2.35(0.19)$^\diamond$	0.00(0.00)
Evaluation	2.54(0.14)	0.19(0.02)$^\blacklozenge$	0.62(0.13)$^\blacktriangle$
Total	22.85(2.00)	22.92(0.90)	17.26(2.22)$^\blacklozenge$

processing time has increased in all the systems. This is contrary to the KDD Cup results where UCSx based systems significantly improved the processing times from the baseline systems. This can be expected as UCSx evolves around 200 more rules than the baseline UCS for the TCP dataset. UCSxSE uses more computation time since it achieves poorer coverage than UCSSE on this dataset and thus has to shift to UCSx rule sets, more often increasing the processing cost.

Nonetheless, using the same time calculations as discussed for the baseline results UCSxSE can process 23 megabits of raw data per second. This is 4 megabits per second less than UCSSE, but with a significant improvement in the detection of all attack classes.

Tables 6.10 and 6.11 show some of the experienced and accurate signatures learnt by UCSSE and UCSxSE respectively from the TCP dataset. In these tables, the actual interveral sizes for attributes with large numerical values such as tcpack and tcpseq are rounded for better readability. Closely looking at these rules suggest that they overlap in several attributes, however the ranges for each attributes differ for different classes. For instance, Normal class rules have destination port ranges in 80s and 90s whereas for POP3 these ranges reach to 110 which is the destination port number for this service. There might have been some artefacts introduced by Mucus attack traffic. For instance, all of the WEB-MISC rules show a ttl range of 30 to 141 and quite low ttl values in other cases. Moreover, the rules evolved by

UCSxSE seem more specific than UCSSE rules.

Also note that almost 500 Snort signatures are used to generate the attacks in the dataset. In addition, Snort used more signatures to label suspicious activities in the background traffic. Both UCSSE and UCSxSE learnt 179 and 127 signatures on average for all attack classes (265 and 215 including the NORMAL class signatures) respectively, which are almost half of Snort signatures. Both systems achieved an average hit rate of 53.47% and 69.20% respectively.

Table 6.10: Signatures obtained by UCSSE from TCP dataset. Condition corresponds to rule's antecedent, Class corresponds to rule consequent and A stands for Accuracy. Attributes with large numbers, such as *tcpack* and *tcpseq*, are rounded for better readability.

Condition	Class	A
(iplen *leq* 708) and (3620 *leq* fragid *geq* 65500) and (30 *leq* ttl *geq* 144) and (29000 *leq* src_port *geq* 65500) and (dest_port *leq* 110) and (tcpack *geq* 1090000000.00) and (payloadlen *leq* 782) and (wcount *leq* 149) and (maxwordl *leq* 122) and (0.28 *leq* lalpha *geq* 0.88) and (ualpha *leq* 0.45) and (numeric *leq* 0.26) and (wspc *leq* 0.12) and (cont *leq* 0.21) and (0.09 *leq* resv *geq* 0.32) and (unsafe *leq* 0.25) and (nonprint *leq* 0.28) and (others *leq* 0.09)	NORMAL	1
(iplen *leq* 1017) and (30 *leq* ttl *geq* 168) and (dest_port *leq* 84) and (tcpseq *leq* 3720000000.00) and (tcpack *geq* 873000000.00) and (payloadlen *leq* 782) and (wcount *leq* 195) and (maxwordl *leq* 82) and (0.36 *leq* lalpha *geq* 0.89) and (0.03 *leq* ualpha *geq* 0.39) and (numeric *leq* 0.40) and (wspc *leq* 0.15) and (cont *leq* 0.08) and (0.02 *leq* resv *geq* 0.14) and (unsafe *leq* 0.19) and (nonprint *leq* 0.00) and (others *leq* 0.22)	NORMAL	1
(iplen *leq* 1168) and (fragid *leq* 27300) and (39 *leq* ttl *geq* 135) and (dest_port *leq* 85) and (873000000.00 *leq* tcpack *geq* 3330000000.00) and (payloadlen *leq* 965) and (wcount *leq* 145) and (maxwordl *leq* 78) and (0.29 *leq* lalpha *geq* 0.92) and (ualpha *leq* 0.38) and (numeric *leq* 0.34) and (wspc *leq* 0.31) and (cont *leq* 0.08) and (0.05 *leq* resv *geq* 0.42) and (unsafe *leq* 0.14) and (nonprint *leq* 0.19) and (others *leq* 0.54)	NORMAL	1
(iplen *leq* 1017) and (30 *leq* ttl *geq* 144) and (29000 *leq* src_port *geq* 65500) and (dest_port *leq* 98) and (tcpseq *geq* 469000000.00) and (tcpack *geq* 1090000000.00) and (payloadlen *leq* 1279) and (wcount *leq* 144) and (maxwordl *leq* 95) and (0.36 *leq* lalpha *geq* 0.89) and (ualpha *leq* 0.45) and (numeric *leq* 0.26) and (wspc *leq* 0.26) and (cont *leq* 0.07) and (resv *leq* 0.23) and (unsafe *leq* 0.36) and (nonprint *leq* 0.28) and (others *leq* 0.36)	NORMAL	1
(iplen *leq* 776) and (fragid *leq* 46500) and (30 *leq* ttl *geq* 168) and (dest_port *leq* 84) and (tcpseq *geq* 1550000000.00) and (payloadlen *leq* 1047) and (wcount *leq* 216) and (maxwordl *leq* 112) and (0.23 *leq* lalpha *geq* 0.75) and (ualpha *leq* 0.19) and (0.02 *leq* numeric *geq* 0.40) and (wspc *leq* 0.16) and (cont *leq* 0.19) and (resv *leq* 0.15) and (unsafe *leq* 0.17) and (nonprint *leq* 0.29) and (others *leq* 0.24)	NORMAL	1
Continued on next page		

Table 6.10 – continued from previous page		
Condition	Class	A
(iplen *leq* 624) and (fragid *leq* 12500) and (ttl *leq* 10) and (23900 *leq* src_port *geq* 65500) and (dest_port *leq* 110) and (tcpseq *leq* 196000000.00) and (tcpack *leq* 917000000.00) and (payloadlen *leq* 298) and (wcount *leq* 111) and (maxwordl *leq* 160) and (0.08 *leq* lalpha *geq* 0.23) and (0.04 *leq* ualpha *geq* 0.37) and (numeric *leq* 0.09) and (wspc *leq* 0.19) and (cont *leq* 0.31) and (resv *leq* 0.41) and (unsafe leq 0.35) and (0.14 *leq* nonprint *geq* 0.64) and (others *leq* 0.27)	POP3	1
(iplen *leq* 967) and (fragid *leq* 19000) and (ttl *leq* 55) and (36500 *leq* src_port *geq* 63400) and (dest_port *leq* 110) and (tcpseq *leq* 1450000000.00) and (tcpack *leq* 790000000.00) and (payloadlen *leq* 908) and (wcount *leq* 161) and (maxwordl *leq* 147) and (0.03 *leq* lalpha *geq* 0.48) and (ualpha *leq* 0.29) and (numeric *leq* 0.33) and (wspc *leq* 0.20) and (cont *leq* 0.48) and (resv *leq* 0.12) and (unsafe *leq* 0.17) and (0.42 *leq* nonprint *geq* 0.79) and (others *leq* 0.09)	POP3	1
(iplen *leq* 149) and (fragid *leq* 12600) and (ttl *leq* 26) and (25600 *leq* src_port *geq* 65500) and (dest_port *leq* 110) and (tcpseq *leq* 212000000.00) and (tcpack *leq* 854000000.00) and (payloadlen *leq* 459) and (wcount *leq* 133) and (maxwordl *leq* 53) and (lalpha *leq* 0.47) and (ualpha *leq* 0.30) and (numeric *leq* 0.15) and (wspc *leq* 0.03) and (cont *leq* 0.27) and (resv *leq* 0.38) and (0.02 *leq* unsafe *geq* 0.17) and (0.47 *leq* nonprint *geq* 0.73) and (others *leq* 0.29)	POP3	1
(iplen *leq* 191) and (fragid *leq* 11400) and (ttl *leq* 60) and (36000 *leq* src_port *geq* 65500) and (dest_port *leq* 82) and (tcpseq *leq* 970000000.00) and (tcpack *leq* 1140000000.00) and (payloadlen *leq* 69) and (wcount *leq* 135) and (maxwordl *leq* 139) and (lalpha *leq* 0.37) and (ualpha *leq* 0.38) and (0.21 *leq* numeric *geq* 0.49) and (wspc *leq* 0.31) and (cont *leq* 0.18) and (resv *leq* 0.30) and (unsafe *leq* 0.25) and (nonprint *leq* 0.58) and (others *leq* 0.03)	WEB-CGI	0.68
(iplen *leq* 191) and (fragid *leq* 11400) and (ttl *leq* 60) and (36000 *leq* src_port *geq* 65500) and (dest_port *leq* 82) and (tcpseq *leq* 970000000.00) and (tcpack *leq* 1140000000.00) and (payloadlen *leq* 351) and (wcount *leq* 135) and (maxwordl *leq* 139) and (lalpha *leq* 0.32) and (ualpha *leq* 0.38) and (0.21 *leq* numeric *geq* 0.49) and (wspc *leq* 0.31) and (cont *leq* 0.18) and (resv *leq* 0.30) and (unsafe *leq* 0.25) and (nonprint *leq* 0.33) and (others *leq* 0.02)	WEB-CGI	0.74
(iplen *leq* 191) and (fragid *leq* 11400) and (ttl *leq* 60) and (36000 *leq* src_port *geq* 65500) and (dest_port *leq* 82) and (tcpseq *leq* 970000000.00) and (tcpack *leq* 1140000000.00) and (payloadlen *leq* 69) and (wcount *leq* 135) and (maxwordl *leq* 139) and (lalpha *leq* 0.32) and (ualpha *leq* 0.38) and (0.21 *leq* numeric *geq* 0.49) and (wspc *leq* 0.31) and (cont *leq* 0.18) and (resv *leq* 0.30) and (unsafe *leq* 0.25) and (nonprint *leq* 0.33) and (others *leq* 0.02)	WEB-CGI	0.63
Continued on next page		

Condition	Class	A
Table 6.10 – continued from previous page		
(iplen *leq* 191) and (fragid *leq* 11400) and (ttl *leq* 60) and (36000 *leq* src_port *geq* 65500) and (dest_port *leq* 82) and (tcpseq *leq* 970000000.00) and (tcpack *leq* 1140000000.00) and (payloadlen *leq* 351) and (wcount *leq* 135) and (maxwordl *leq* 139) and (lalpha *leq* 0.32) and (ualpha *leq* 0.38) and (0.21 *leq* numeric *geq* 0.49) and (wspc *leq* 0.31) and (cont *leq* 0.18) and (resv *leq* 0.30) and (unsafe *leq* 0.25) and (nonprint *leq* 0.33)	WEB-CGI	0.69
(iplen *leq* 254) and (fragid *leq* 56000) and (30 *leq* ttl *geq* 141) and (10600 *leq* src_port *geq* 65500) and (dest_port *leq* 84) and (tcpseq *geq* 755000000.00) and (payloadlen *leq* 782) and (wcount *leq* 187) and (maxwordl *leq* 147) and (0.41 *leq* alpha *geq* 0.74) and (0.08 *leq* ualpha *geq* 0.26) and (numeric *leq* 0.44) and (wspc *leq* 0.43) and (cont *leq* 0.31) and (resv *leq* 0.32) and (nonprint *leq* 0.03) and (others *leq* 0.33)	WEB-MISC	0.54
(iplen *leq* 254) and (30 *leq* ttl *geq* 141) and (dest_port *leq* 84) and (tcpseq *geq* 1450000000.00) and (tcpack *geq* 298000000.00) and (payloadlen *leq* 782) and (wcount *leq* 187) and (maxwordl *leq* 147) and (0.60 *leq* lalpha *geq* 0.74) and (ualpha *leq* 0.26) and (numeric *leq* 0.44) and (wspc *leq* 0.43) and (cont *leq* 0.31) and (resv *leq* 0.32) and (nonprint *leq* 0.03) and (others *leq* 0.33)	WEB-MISC	0.54
(iplen *leq* 254) and (fragid *leq* 56000) and (30 *leq* ttl *geq* 141) and (dest_port *leq* 84) and (tcpseq *geq* 1450000000.00) and (tcpack *geq* 298000000.00) and (payloadlen *leq* 782) and (wcount *leq* 187) and (maxwordl *leq* 147) and (0.60 *leq* lalpha *geq* 0.74) and (ualpha *leq* 0.26) and (numeric *leq* 0.44) and (wspc *leq* 0.43) and (cont *leq* 0.49) and (resv *leq* 0.32) and (nonprint *leq* 0.03) and (others *leq* 0.33)	WEB-MISC	0.58
(iplen *leq* 254) and (30 *leq* ttl *geq* 141) and (src_port *leq* 48200) and (dest_port *leq* 84) and (tcpseq *geq* 755000000.00) and (tcpack *geq* 299000000.00) and (payloadlen *leq* 782) and (wcount *leq* 187) and (maxwordl *leq* 147) and (0.55 *leq* lalpha *geq* 0.74) and (ualpha *leq* 0.26) and (numeric *leq* 0.44) and (wspc *leq* 0.43) and (cont *leq* 0.31) and (resv *leq* 0.32) and (nonprint *leq* 0.03) and (others *leq* 0.17)	WEB-MISC	0.56
(iplen *leq* 254) and (fragid *leq* 56000) and (30 *leq* ttl *geq* 141) and (dest_port *leq* 84) and (tcpseq *geq* 1450000000.00) and (tcpack *geq* 298000000.00) and (payloadlen *leq* 782) and (wcount *leq* 187) and (maxwordl *leq* 147) and (0.60 *leq* lalpha *geq* 0.74) and (ualpha *leq* 0.26) and (numeric *leq* 0.44) and (wspc *leq* 0.43) and (cont *leq* 0.49) and (resv *leq* 0.32) and (nonprint *leq* 0.09) and (others *leq* 0.33)	WEB-MISC	0.57
Continued on next page		

Table 6.10 – continued from previous page		
Condition	Class	A
(iplen *leq* 491) and (fragid *leq* 15800) and (ttl *leq* 3) and (16300 *leq* src_port *geq* 40800) and (dest_port *leq* 92) and (tcpseq *leq* 712000000.00) and (tcpack *leq* 682000000.00) and (payloadlen *leq* 205) and (wcount *leq* 79) and (maxwordl *leq* 31) and (0.09 *leq* lalpha *geq* 0.49) and (0.15 *leq* ualpha *geq* 0.42) and (0.07 *leq* numeric *geq* 0.38) and (wspc *leq* 0.07) and (cont *leq* 0.30) and (0.03 *leq* resv *geq* 0.26) and (unsafe *leq* 0.15) and (nonprint *leq* 0.19) and (others *leq* 0.18)	WEB-PHP	0.31
(iplen *leq* 491) and (fragid *leq* 15800) and (16300 *leq* src_port *geq* 43600) and (dest_port *leq* 83) and (tcpseq *leq* 712000000.00) and (tcpack *leq* 682000000.00) and (payloadlen *leq* 205) and (wcount *leq* 79) and (maxwordl *leq* 31) and (0.09 *leq* lalpha *geq* 0.49) and (0.15 *leq* ualpha *geq* 0.42) and (0.07 *leq* numeric *geq* 0.38) and (wspc *leq* 0.07) and (cont *leq* 0.30) and (0.03 *leq* resv *geq* 0.26) and (unsafe *leq* 0.15) and (nonprint *leq* 0.19) and (others *leq* 0.18)	WEB-PHP	0.24
(iplen *leq* 222) and (fragid *leq* 4077) and (ttl *leq* 27) and (39600 *leq* src_port *geq* 60900) and (dest_port *leq* 110) and (tcpseq *leq* 1100000000.00) and (tcpack *leq* 83100000.00) and (payloadlen *leq* 613) and (wcount *leq* 66) and (maxwordl *leq* 45) and (0.18 *leq* lalpha *geq* 0.28) and (ualpha *leq* 0.52) and (numeric *leq* 0.50) and (wspc *leq* 0.45) and (cont *leq* 0.46) and (resv *leq* 0.15) and (unsafe *leq* 0.35) and (nonprint *leq* 0.04) and (others *leq* 0.17)	WEB-PHP	0.22
(iplen *leq* 610) and (fragid *leq* 8965) and (ttl *leq* 46) and (49300 *leq* src_port *geq* 65500) and (dest_port *leq* 99) and (tcpseq *leq* 1700000000.00) and (tcpack *leq* 1430000000.00) and (payloadlen *leq* 384) and (wcount *leq* 137) and (maxwordl *leq* 67) and (0.06 *leq* lalpha *geq* 0.38) and (0.15 *leq* ualpha *geq* 0.38) and (numeric *leq* 0.31) and (wspc *leq* 0.36) and (0.02 *leq* cont *geq* 0.40) and (resv *leq* 0.26) and (unsafe *leq* 0.24) and (nonprint *leq* 0.38) and (others *leq* 0.09)	WEB-PHP	0.5

Table 6.11: Signatures obtained by UCSxSE from TCP dataset. A stands for Accuracy.

Condition	Class	A
(iplen *leq* 777) and (ttl *leq* 189) and (5328 *leq* src_port *geq* 56000) and (dest_port *leq* 110) and (tcpseq *geq* 646000000.00) and (payloadlen *leq* 897) and (wcount *leq* 130) and (maxwordl *leq* 65) and (0.29 *leq* lalpha *geq* 0.92) and (ualpha *leq* 0.40) and (numeric *leq* 0.33) and (wspc *leq* 0.15) and (cont *leq* 0.12) and (0.11 *leq* resv *geq* 0.15) and (unsafe *leq* 0.37) and (nonprint *leq* 0.33) and (others *leq* 0.34)	NORMAL	0.88
(iplen *leq* 777) and (ttl *leq* 189) and (5328 *leq* src_port *geq* 56000) and (dest_port *leq* 110) and (tcpseq *leq* 3330000000.00) and (tcpack *geq* 1150000000.00) and (payloadlen *leq* 897) and (wcount *leq* 130) and (maxwordl *leq* 65) and (0.29 *leq* lalpha *geq* 0.92) and (ualpha *leq* 0.40) and (numeric *leq* 0.33) and (wspc *leq* 0.15) and (cont *leq* 0.12) and (0.11 *leq* resv *geq* 0.15) and (unsafe *leq* 0.37) and (nonprint *leq* 0.33) and (others *leq* 0.34)	NORMAL	0.71
(iplen *leq* 639) and (39 *leq* ttl *geq* 141) and (15100 *leq* src_port *geq* 63200) and (dest_port *leq* 110) and (1210000000.00 *leq* tcpseq *geq* 3840000000.00) and (1500000000.00 *leq* tcpack *geq* 4100000000.00) and (payloadlen *leq* 744) and (wcount *leq* 193) and (maxwordl *leq* 73) and (0.32 *leq* lalpha *geq* 0.80) and (0.09 *leq* ualpha *geq* 0.64) and (numeric *leq* 0.26) and (wspc *leq* 0.30) and (cont *leq* 0.26) and (resv *leq* 0.16) and (unsafe *leq* 0.31) and (nonprint *leq* 0.03) and (others *leq* 0.41)	NORMAL	0.93
(iplen *leq* 455) and (fragid *leq* 29400) and (fragfollows: 0) and (37 *leq* ttl *geq* 139) and (37600 *leq* src_port *geq* 65500) and (dest_port *leq* 85) and (75900000.00 *leq* tcpseq *geq* 4010000000.00) and (tcpack *leq* 2590000000.00) and (payloadlen *leq* 744) and (wcount *leq* 178) and (maxwordl *leq* 24) and (0.36 *leq* lalpha *geq* 0.69) and (ualpha *leq* 0.44) and (numeric *leq* 0.08) and (0.02 *leq* wspc *geq* 0.20) and (0.01 *leq* cont *geq* 0.11) and (resv *leq* 0.36) and (unsafe *leq* 0.20) and (nonprint *leq* 0.32) and (others *leq* 0.34)	NORMAL	0.76
(iplen *leq* 639) and (ttl *leq* 189) and (src_port *leq* 33500) and (dest_port *leq* 110) and (tcpack *leq* 2840000000.00) and (payloadlen *leq* 696) and (wcount *leq* 130) and (maxwordl *leq* 92) and (0.21 *leq* lalpha *geq* 0.78) and (ualpha *leq* 0.44) and (0.03 *leq* numeric *geq* 0.40) and (wspc *leq* 0.15) and (cont *leq* 0.38) and (resv *leq* 0.15) and (unsafe *leq* 0.26) and (nonprint *leq* 0.08) and (others *leq* 0.39)	NORMAL	1
(iplen *leq* 291) and (fragid *leq* 15500) and (fragfollows: 0) and (ttl *leq* 76) and (37400 *leq* src_port *geq* 65500) and (dest_port *leq* 110) and (tcpseq *leq* 1620000000.00) and (tcpack *leq* 1460000000.00) and (payloadlen *leq* 106) and (wcount *leq* 122) and (maxwordl *leq* 111) and (lalpha *leq* 0.35) and (ualpha *leq* 0.17) and (numeric *leq* 0.25) and (wspc *leq* 0.34) and (cont *leq* 0.20) and (resv *leq* 0.33) and (unsafe *leq* 0.31) and (0.36 *leq* nonprint *geq* 0.81) and (others *leq* 0.40)	POP3	1
	Continued on next page	

Table 6.11 – continued from previous page		
Condition	Class	A
(iplen *leq* 92) and (fragid *leq* 22000) and (ttl *leq* 58) and (35200 *leq* src_port *geq* 60300) and (dest_port *leq* 110) and (tcpseq *leq* 1430000000.00) and (tcpack *leq* 161000000.00) and (payloadlen *leq* 151) and (wcount *leq* 84) and (maxwordl *leq* 111) and (lalpha *leq* 0.20) and (ualpha *leq* 0.58) and (numeric *leq* 0.24) and (wspc *leq* 0.10) and (cont *leq* 0.22) and (resv *leq* 0.13) and (unsafe *leq* 0.30) and (0.04 *leq* nonprint *geq* 0.65) and (others *leq* 0.19)	POP3	1
(iplen *leq* 288) and (fragid *leq* 6406) and (ttl *leq* 51) and (35200 *leq* src_port *geq* 61600) and (dest_port *leq* 110) and (tcpseq *leq* 581000000.00) and (tcpack *leq* 461000000.00) and (payloadlen *leq* 627) and (wcount *leq* 119) and (maxwordl *leq* 133) and (lalpha *leq* 0.51) and (ualpha *leq* 0.43) and (0.10 *leq* numeric *geq* 0.60) and (wspc *leq* 0.37) and (cont *leq* 0.41) and (0.03 *leq* resv *geq* 0.16) and (0.03 *leq* unsafe *geq* 0.33) and (nonprint *leq* 0.26) and (others *leq* 0.10)	WEB-CGI	0.74
(iplen *leq* 102) and (fragid *leq* 322) and (ttl *leq* 80) and (src_port *leq* 29700) and (dest_port *leq* 107) and (tcpseq *leq* 1670000000.00) and (tcpack *leq* 682000000.00) and (payloadlen *leq* 114) and (wcount *leq* 137) and (maxwordl *leq* 139) and (lalpha *leq* 0.51) and (0.09 *leq* ualpha *geq* 0.38) and (numeric *leq* 0.27) and (wspc *leq* 0.24) and (cont *leq* 0.25) and (resv *leq* 0.37) and (unsafe *leq* 0.14) and (nonprint *leq* 0.32) and (others *leq* 0.21)	WEB-CGI	0.7
(iplen *leq* 623) and (fragid *leq* 15100) and (fragfollows: 0) and (ttl *leq* 17) and (34300 *leq* src_port *geq* 61100) and (dest_port *leq* 106) and (tcpseq *leq* 71100000.00) and (tcpack *leq* 1500000000.00) and (payloadlen *leq* 177) and (wcount *leq* 148) and (maxwordl *leq* 88) and (0.06 *leq* lalpha *geq* 0.22) and (ualpha *leq* 0.51) and (0.06 *leq* numeric *geq* 0.57) and (wspc *leq* 0.15) and (cont *leq* 0.43) and (resv *leq* 0.42) and (unsafe *leq* 0.13) and (nonprint *leq* 0.24) and (others *leq* 0.26)	WEB-CGI	0.97
(iplen *leq* 623) and (fragid *leq* 17600) and (fragfollows: 0) and (ttl *leq* 17) and (34300 *leq* src_port *geq* 61100) and (dest_port *leq* 106) and (tcpseq *leq* 71100000.00) and (tcpack *leq* 1500000000.00) and (payloadlen *leq* 177) and (wcount *leq* 148) and (maxwordl *leq* 33) and (0.06 *leq* lalpha *geq* 0.22) and (ualpha *leq* 0.51) and (0.06 *leq* numeric *geq* 0.57) and (wspc *leq* 0.15) and (cont *leq* 0.43) and (resv *leq* 0.42) and (unsafe *leq* 0.13) and (nonprint *leq* 0.24) and (others *leq* 0.26)	WEB-CGI	0.97
(iplen *leq* 317) and (25600 *leq* fragid *geq* 56400) and (fragfollows: 0) and (11 *leq* ttl *geq* 103) and (35800 *leq* src_port *geq* 65500) and (dest_port *leq* 94) and (tcpseq *geq* 1740000000.00) and (tcpack *leq* 1900000000.00) and (payloadlen *leq* 270) and (wcount *leq* 38) and (maxwordl *leq* 25) and (0.58 *leq* lalpha *geq* 0.78) and (0.02 *leq* ualpha *geq* 0.19) and (numeric *leq* 0.48) and (wspc *leq* 0.08) and (cont *leq* 0.09) and (resv *leq* 0.30) and (unsafe *leq* 0.33) and (nonprint *leq* 0.38) and (others *leq* 0.32)	WEB-MISC	0.66
Continued on next page		

Table 6.11 – continued from previous page		
Condition	Class	A
(iplen *leq* 277) and (18800 *leq* fragid *geq* 56400) and (fragfollows: 0) and (11 *leq* ttl *geq* 112) and (35800 *leq* src_port *geq* 65500) and (dest_port *leq* 94) and (tcpseq *geq* 1740000000.00) and (444000000.00 *leq* tcpack *geq* 2640000000.00) and (payloadlen *leq* 270) and (wcount *leq* 82) and (maxwordl *leq* 25) and (0.58 *leq* lalpha *geq* 0.78) and (0.02 *leq* ualpha *geq* 0.19) and (numeric *leq* 0.33) and (wspc *leq* 0.08) and (cont *leq* 0.09) and (resv *leq* 0.30) and (unsafe *leq* 0.33) and (nonprint *leq* 0.38) and (others *leq* 0.25)	WEB-MISC	0.74
(iplen *leq* 852) and (fragid *leq* 34800) and (fragfollows: 0) and (67 *leq* ttl *geq* 124) and (6938 *leq* src_port *geq* 62100) and (dest_port *leq* 98) and (910000000.00 *leq* tcpseq *geq* 2490000000.00) and (322000000.00 *leq* tcpack *geq* 3050000000.00) and (payloadlen *leq* 569) and (wcount *leq* 51) and (maxwordl *leq* 143) and (0.25 *leq* lalpha *geq* 0.85) and (ualpha *leq* 0.20) and (0.02 *leq* numeric *geq* 0.27) and (wspc *leq* 0.35) and (cont *leq* 0.33) and (0.02 *leq* resv *geq* 0.33) and (unsafe *leq* 0.03) and (nonprint *leq* 0.30) and (others *leq* 0.10)	WEB-MISC	0.9
(iplen *leq* 563) and (31700 *leq* fragid *geq* 65500) and (38 *leq* ttl *geq* 56) and (45100 *leq* src_port *geq* 65500) and (dest_port *leq* 96) and (426000000.00 *leq* tcpseq *geq* 1370000000.00) and (804000000.00 *leq* tcpack *geq* 1870000000.00) and (payloadlen *leq* 274) and (wcount *leq* 38) and (maxwordl *leq* 139) and (0.32 *leq* lalpha *geq* 0.70) and (ualpha *leq* 0.30) and (numeric *leq* 0.16) and (wspc *leq* 0.13) and (0.04 *leq* cont *geq* 0.26) and (0.02 *leq* resv *geq* 0.32) and (unsafe *leq* 0.19) and (nonprint *leq* 0.33) and (others *leq* 0.30)	WEB-MISC	0.86
(iplen *leq* 650) and (fragid *leq* 15800) and (fragfollows: 0) and (ttl *leq* 43) and (16100 *leq* src_port *geq* 50300) and (dest_port *leq* 86) and (tcpseq *leq* 186000000.00) and (tcpack *leq* 185000000.00) and (payloadlen *leq* 292) and (wcount *leq* 89) and (maxwordl *leq* 113) and (lalpha *leq* 0.57) and (0.21 *leq* ualpha *geq* 0.36) and (0.02 *leq* numeric *geq* 0.23) and (0.01 *leq* wspc *geq* 0.28) and (cont *leq* 0.46) and (resv *leq* 0.28) and (unsafe *leq* 0.44) and (nonprint *leq* 0.08) and (others *leq* 0.21)	WEB-PHP	0.45
(iplen *leq* 220) and (fragid *leq* 9264) and (ttl *leq* 1) and (9117 *leq* src_port *geq* 57000) and (dest_port *leq* 80) and (tcpseq *leq* 297000000.00) and (tcpack *leq* 151000000.00) and (payloadlen *leq* 63) and (wcount *leq* 81) and (maxwordl *leq* 54) and (0.30 *leq* lalpha *geq* 0.53) and (ualpha *leq* 0.27) and (numeric *leq* 0.27) and (0.02 *leq* wspc *geq* 0.34) and (cont *leq* 0.31) and (resv *leq* 0.27) and (unsafe *leq* 0.11) and (nonprint *leq* 0.11) and (others *leq* 0.05)	WEB-PHP	0.83

6.7 Chapter Summary

In this chapter, UCS, its variants and the signature extraction system developed in the previous chapters are evaluated with real network traffic data mixed with simulated attacks. We highlighted several difficulties in evaluating supervised machine learning algorithms for intrusion detection with real data and subsequently devised a methodology for the evaluation of our algorithms.

The dataset is built by capturing real network traffic on a university departmental server over several weeks, mixing it with attack traffic simulated in a controlled environment, processing the raw network traffic into session records, extracting packet level information to represent the data in the feature vector format and assigning labels to each record using an up-to-date signature-based intrusion detection system. After filtering, the final dataset consisted of nearly 100,000 fully labelled records obtained from processing 3 gigabytes of raw network traffic and included several hundred attack vectors categorised under 4 attack types.

Finally, three systems (i.e., UCS, UCSD and UCSSE) with both the baseline and extended UCS setups are evaluated on the preprocessed dataset and the corresponding results are presented. Using the baseline UCS setup, UCSSE achieves 27 times reduction in the rule set size and extracts around 265 signatures on average including both normal and attack traffic rules. UCSSE also significantly improves the hit rate from around 9% achieved by UCS to 54%. However, UCSSE generates significantly higher false alarms than the baseline UCS. The time calculation shows that UCSSE can handle a traffic of around 27 megabits per second. Using the extended UCS setup UCSSE further improves and achieves around 34 times reduction on average in UCS rule sets. It also improves the hit rate to almost 70% albeit the much higher false alarm rate. Thus there seems to be a tradeoff between the attack detection rate and the false alarm rate using UCSSE.

The methodology adopted in this chapter to evaluate the developed algorithms provides good estimation of the performance of the algorithms. However, it is desirable to evaluate the system with much larger datasets collected from busier networks. In addition, we note that although the dataset used in this testing is built from real network traffic, the evaluation is done offline. A human in the loop strategy could be adopted to deploy these algorithms in operational networks that are often monitored by security supervisors.

Chapter 7

Conclusions

The detection of intrusions in network traffic flows and host activities is a challenging task. The nature of intrusive behaviour is co-evolving with the pervasiveness of computing technologies and our growing reliance on their use. In order to deal with inherent challenges, such as the ever changing environment and increasing levels of threats, we clearly need different perspectives and alternative approaches to secure our systems - the approaches that can adapt to drifting concepts and provide resilience when the systems are targeted.

In this thesis, we attempt to address the problem of dynamic and adaptive signature learning for intrusion detection from live network traffic. We use a nature-inspired machine learning approach to address this problem. The highly complex systems found in nature are extremely robust and resilient systems that can adapt to environmental changes and constantly evolve their states for their betterment. Nature inspired computational techniques borrow concepts from these systems and try to provide robust and adaptive solutions to hard problems like intrusion detection.

We have developed a system to extract signatures in real time discovered by a genetic-based machine learning system, UCS, which works as a base learner in the framework. We have independently analysed the performance of UCS with intrusion data built from simulated network traffic and attacks, and subsequently proposed several modifications to extend the standard UCS algorithm that have significantly improved the quality of the evolved rule sets. Our framework allows for both anomaly and misuse based intrusion detection using a signature based approach. The signatures for both normal and intrusive events are learnt dynamically and adaptively. We have also devised a methodology to generate labelled data from a combination of real network traffic and simulated attacks that can be used to evaluate supervised learning algorithms, such as UCS, aimed at the problem of intrusion detection.

Below we provide a summary of contributions in this thesis and the future work that stems from this work.

7.1 Summary of Contributions

This thesis contributed to two fields: intrusion detection and genetic based machine learning. This section provides a summary of these contributions.

- **Analysis and extension of UCS for intrusion detection** - We started by studying the effect of several key UCS parameters on its performance using a publicly available benchmark intrusion detection dataset. We experimented with increasingly large population sizes and established that a compromise could be made by choosing lower population sizes for only a small loss in system performance.

  We looked at the effect of genetic operators on system performance and noted that genetic search has difficulties in finding optimal solutions. The UCS performance is analysed by alternatively deactivating crossover and mutation operators and it was observed that the system with mutation alone performed worst of all. The reasonable performance of UCS without the genetic search suggested that the search operators need modifications when dealing with multi-dimensional real-valued spaces posed by the intrusion data.

A simple heuristic for fixing covering interval sizes is introduced for real-valued attributes that significantly improved UCS performance on the KDD Cup dataset. The heuristic is tested empirically with varying interval sizes and it is found that an optimal range of covering intervals exist that can provide a better starting point for genetic search in UCS.

Distance-metric based prediction - The problem of coverage gaps in test feature spaces is highlighted and a distance-metric based approach is introduced for predicting uncovered test cases in UCS. The distance based technique significantly improved UCS performance on the test data and reduced the number of false alarms generated by UCS to a reasonable level. We recommend it be adopted as the standard approach in both XCS and UCS replacing the current purely random prediction approach used for such cases.

Strategies to deal with imbalance class distribution - The performance of UCS under imbalanced and noisy training data is analysed using synthetic datasets. Both of these problems exists in the data to be classified for intrusions and thus it is critical to deal with them to improve the effectiveness of UCS for intrusion detection. We introduced techniques to address these problems and comprehensively compared them with existing techniques. In particular, a new accuracy function, techniques for adapting the application of the GA rate, a class-sensitive deletion technique and cost-sensitive prediction are introduced in UCS. The class distribution in these techniques is calculated and updated online. We showed that our techniques perform better than existing techniques on synthetic imbalanced class problems.

Altogether, the fixed covering heuristic, distance metric based prediction and new strategies to deal with class imbalance significantly improved the UCS accuracy on the KDD Cup dataset. They also significantly reduced the false alarm rate to a reasonable range.

- **A framework for real-time signature extraction** - We developed a new algorithm to extract optimal rules learnt by UCS during its adaptive discovery process. The signature extraction mechanism is implemented on top of the existing UCS framework. This allows the system to use the extracted signatures during its operation and the evolutionary search is invoked only when no signatures are found for an input.

Furthermore, novel subsumption operators are introduced to resolve overlapping and redundancies among the signatures. The new operators provide better signature coverage and more compact signature sets.

Adaptive tuning of the signature extraction algorithm's parameters for noisy and imbalance class problems - The performance of the signature extraction algorithm is analysed in the presence of noise and class imbalance in the data similar to the analysis carried out with UCS. Subsequently, mechanisms were introduced to adapt crucial algorithm parameters according to noise and imbalance levels in the data calculated online from the streaming data. The adaptive tuning of the parameters significantly improves the performance of the algorithm.

The signature extraction algorithm allows better control over evolutionary search in UCS, faster processing times and considerably more compact rule sets. The framework also provides a means to practically implement UCS in a real-time IDS setting.

The signature extraction system is evaluated on the KDD Cup dataset and provides a magnitude smaller rule sets than the standard UCS. We also compared its performance with another state-of-the art offline rule reduction algorithm. Our algorithm, despite being single-pass, performs competitively. The performance of the algorithm further improves when it is run using the extended UCS that we developed during our analysis.

- **A methodology to build intrusion data for supervised learning algorithms** - In order to evaluate UCS and the signature extraction algorithms with real intrusion data, a new methodology is devised to build otherwise scarce evaluation data for intrusion detection systems. This is done by capturing real network traffic on a university departmental server over a whole month and mixing it with attack traffic that is generated in a simulated environment.

Tools are developed to process the raw network traffic into feature vectors by reassembling protocol sessions, extracting information from the packet payload sections and assigning labels to them using the Snort intrusion detection system.

Finally, the algorithms developed for learning signatures are evaluated on this dataset and insights into the resultant rules and their performance are provided.

7.2 Limitations

There are a number of limitations in our work.

- The rule learning systems developed in this thesis do not provide feature learning or feature selection procedures and rely on features provided to them through domain knowledge or other means. Consequently the quality of rules learnt by these systems could be biased by the quality of the provided features. Nonetheless, the extended UCS and signature extraction systems performed well on the realistic dataset, developed in Chapter 6, with some basic features extracted from the packet payloads.

- Although the system is aimed at learning signatures in real-time, its testing has been done offline. Testing in a real environment is prohibitive due to security and privacy concerns or can prove expensive in case of building a stand alone environment for emulation. Nonetheless, the datasets used during evaluation have been built from the real network traffic traces. We cannot, however, claim that the performance of our system will be the same when deployed in real networks.

- The real traffic collected for the evaluation of our systems is not representative of large scale computer networks. But we were constrained in collecting this data due to security and privacy concerns and unavailability of large scale traffic collection infrastructure.

- Although we have attempted to take care of any induced biases when simulating attacks, it can not be guaranteed absolutely.

7.3 Future Work

This is a first attempt in applying learning classifier systems to the intrusion detection domain. Several directions can be taken to extend this work. Further, there are still open questions with regards to improving LCS performance for this and other related domains.

- The next logical step is to integrate the developed signature extraction system with existing open-source signature based intrusion sensors such as Snort. This requires developing an interface between the signature extraction system and Snort that would unify the signature language between the two systems, integrate feature extraction procedures with Snort, escalate unmatched traffic patterns to the signature learning system and automatically update Snort's signature bases.

- The number and quality of features play an important role in learning effective signatures. The current feature set can be extended to improve detection accuracy and the coverage of signatures. Furthermore, the search space can be minimised by selecting only those relevant features that are effective in detecting certain types of attacks. A distributed multi-agent system based approach can be taken to model the system where each agent could learn signatures locally for a specific type of activity (e.g., a particular protocol or host activities running on a particular operating system) or specialise on a particular subset of features. Furthermore, the response of the security supervisor on generated alerts can be fed back into the signature learning system to reduce reliance on labelled training data. An architecture of such a system was proposed in (Shafi, Abbass, and Zhu 2006).

- A related issue that needs further work is the processing speed of learning classifier systems. Since the rule matching process in LCS accounts for most of its run time, state-of-the art rule matching algorithms, such as those used in (Llorà and Sastry 2006), can be implemented in LCS to further improve its processing speeds.

- In this thesis, we have concentrated on learning signatures from network traffic. This can be extended to learn rules from security logs and other host based activities. It would be nice to evaluate the developed systems with data collected from such sources (e.g., system call traces).

- There has been a great deal of research in the field of genetic algorithms recently and many improved algorithms and new genetic operators have been proposed (Goldberg 2002). The performance of the base learner system for signature extraction can benefit from these advances in the research. The ideas can also be borrowed from other related evolutionary algorithm fields such as evolutionary strategies to better guide the search operators used in current LCS.

- Our analysis of the covering operator and the use of a fixed covering intervals heuristic suggested that an appropriate initialisation of covering classifiers can have a significant impact on directing the search for better rules in UCS. In the future, we intend to investigate and incorporate a problem independent way to adapt this parameter in UCS. One way to approach this problem is by calculating the entropy of the data stream for every attribute and then choosing the initial covering intervals based on the relative entropy values among different attributes.

- In this work, we have focused our research on UCS. The signature extraction system is easily extendable to XCS and to other classifier systems. In fact, the concept of real time signature extraction presented here can be extended to many concept learning systems not only limited to rule learners. For example, it can be extended to extract the generalisations learnt from an ensemble of neural networks during learning.

7.4   Closing Remarks

Like many other real-world problems, there is no silver bullet for intrusion detection problems (Humphries, Ragsdale, Carver Jr, Hill, and Pooch 2000). In this thesis, we have concentrated on an important class of problems in the intrusion detection domain; that is, the adaptive learning of normal and intrusive behaviour signatures from a network traffic flow. We have proposed and implemented a framework for automatic and adaptive discovery of signatures from network activities using nature-inspired computational techniques. We do not pretend to have solved this problem but built a platform that can provide such capabilities. Extensive reevaluation and refinement of the proposed methods would lead to an autonomous and fully operational intrusion detection system. We believe this work will provide interesting insights for future research in this field.

Appendix

Table 1: Abbreviations for various network protocols seen in the real traffic.

IP	Internet Protocol
ICMP	Internet Control Message Protocol
IMAP	Internet Mail Access Protocol
TCP	Transmission Control Protocol
UDP	User Datagram Protocol
DNS	Domain Name Service
FTP	File Transfer Protocol
HTTP	Hyper Text Transfer Protocol
HTTPS	Hypertext Transfer Protocol over Secure Socket Layer
POP3	Post Office Protocol
NetBios	Network Basic Input/Output System
SMTP	Simple Mail Transfer Protocol
SSH	Secure Shell

Bibliography

Abbass, H. (2002). An evolutionary artificial neural networks approach for breast cancer diagnosis. *Artificial Intelligence In Medicine 25*(3), 265–281.

Agrawal, R. and R. Srikant (1994). Fast algorithms for mining association rules. In *Proceedings of the 20th International Conference on Very Large Data Bases*, pp. 487–499.

Aha, D. (1992). Tolerating noisy, irrelevant and novel attributes in instance-based learning algorithms. *International Journal of Man-Machine Studies 36*(2), 267–287.

Aickelin, U., P. Bentley, S. Cayzer, J. Kim, and J. McLeod (2003). Danger theory: The link between AIS and IDS. In *Proceedings of the Second Internation Conference on Artificial Immune Systems (ICARIS-03)*, pp. 147–155. Springer.

Aickelin, U., J. Greensmith, and J. Twycross (2004). Immune System Approaches to Intrusion Detection-A Review. In *Proceedings of the Second Internation Conference on Artificial Immune Systems (ICARIS-03)*, pp. 316–329. Springer.

Almgren, M. and E. Jonsson (2004). Using Active Learning in Intrusion Detection. In *Proceedings of the 17th IEEE Computer Security Foundations Workshop (CSFW'04)*, pp. 88–98. IEEE Computer Society.

Amor, N., S. Benferhat, and Z. Elouedi (2004). Naive Bayes vs decision trees in intrusion detection systems. In *Proceedings of the 2004 ACM symposium on Applied computing*, pp. 420–424. ACM New York, NY, USA.

Anderson, D., T. Frivold, and A. Valdes (1995). Next-generation Intrusion Detection Expert System (NIDES): A Summary. Technical Report SRI-CSL-95-07.

Anderson, J. (1980). Computer security threat monitoring and surveillance. Washington, PA, James P. Anderson Co.

Angluin, D. and P. Laird (1988). Learning from noisy examples. *Machine Learning 2*(4), 343–370.

Antonatos, S., K. Anagnostakis, and E. Markatos (2004). Generating realistic workloads for network intrusion detection systems. *ACM SIGSOFT Software Engineering Notes 29*(1), 207–215.

Axelsson, S. (2000). Intrusion Detection Systems: A Survey and Taxonomy. Technical Report 99-15, Chalmers University of Technology, Dept. of Computer Engineering, Göteborg, Sweden.

Bacardit, J. and M. V. Butz (2004). Data Mining in Learning Classifier Systems: Comparing XCS with GAssist. In *Seventh International Workshop on Learning Classifier Systems (IWLCS-2004)*. Springer.

Bace, R. and P. Mell (2001). Intrusion Detection Systems: A Survey and Taxonomy. Technical Report 800-31, National Institute of Standards and Technology.

Barbara, D., N. Wu, and S. Jajodia (2001). Detecting Novel Network Intrusions Using Bayes Estimators. In *Proceedings of the First SIAM Conference on Data Mining*.

Barisani, A. (2003). Testing Firewalls and IDS with FTester. *TISC Insight Newsletter 5*(6), 2–4.

Bernadó-Mansilla, E. (2002). *Contributions to Genetic Based Classifier Systems*. Phd thesis, Enginyeria i Arquitectura La Salle, Ramon Llull University, Barcelona, Spain.

Bernadó-Mansilla, E. and J. M. Garrell (2003). Accuracy-Based Learning Classifier Systems: Models, Analysis and Applications to Classification Tasks. *Evolutionary Computation 11*(3), 209–238.

Bernadó-Mansilla, E. and T. Ho (2005). Domain of competence of XCS classifier system in complexity measurement space. *IEEE Transactions on Evolutionary Computation 9*(1), 82–104.

Bernadó-Mansilla, E., X. Llorà, and J. M. G. Guiu (2002). XCS and GALE: A Comparative Study of Two Learning Classifier Systems on Data Mining. In *IWLCS '01: Revised Papers from the 4th International Workshop on Advances in Learning Classifier Systems*, London, UK, pp. 115–132. Springer.

Bonarini, A. (1996). Evolutionary learning of fuzzy rules: competition and cooperation. In W. Pedrycz (Ed.), *Fuzzy Modelling: Paradigms and Practice*, pp. 265–284. Norwell, MA: Kluwer Academic Press.

Booker, L., D. Goldberg, and J. Holland (1990). Classifier systems and genetic algorithms. *Artificial Intelligence 40*(1-3), 235–282.

Bruneau, G. (2001). The history and evolution of intrusion detection. available from, `http://www.sans.org/rr/whitepapers/detection/344.php`, Accessed on August 2005.

Bull, L. and J. Hurst (2002). ZCS Redux. *Evolutionary Computation 10*(2), 185–205.

Burges, C. (1996). Simplified support vector decision rules. In *Proceedings of the 13th International Conference on Machine Learning*, Volume 1112, pp. 71–77. Morgan Kaufmann.

Butz, M. (2005). Kernel-based, ellipsoidal conditions in the real-valued XCS classifier system. In *Proceedings of the Seventh Conference on Genetic and Evolutionary Computation*, pp. 1835–1842. ACM Press New York, NY, USA.

Butz, M. V. (2004). *Rule-Based Evolutionary Online Learning Systems: Learning Bounds, Classification, and Prediction*. Ph. D. thesis, University of Illinois at Urbana-Champaign.

Butz, M. V. and D. E. Goldberg (2003). Bounding the population size in XCS to ensure reproductive opportunities. In *Proceedings of the Fifth Genetic and Evolutionary Computation Conference*, pp. 1844–1856. Springer.

Butz, M. V., T. Kovacs, P. Lanzi, and S. W. Wilson (2004a). Bounding Learning Time in XCS. In *Proceedings of the Genetic and Evolutionary Computation Conference*, pp. 739–750. Springer, Berlin.

Butz, M. V., T. Kovacs, P. Lanzi, and S. W. Wilson (2004b). Toward a theory of generalization and learning in XCS. *IEEE Transactions on Evolutionary Computation 8*(1), 28–46.

Butz, M. V., K. Sastry, and D. E. Goldberg (2005). Strong, Stable, and Reliable Fitness Pressure in XCS due to Tournament Selection. *Genetic Programming and Evolvable Machines 6*(1), 53–77.

Butz, M. V. and S. W. Wilson (2002). An algorithmic description of XCS. *Soft Computing-A Fusion of Foundations, Methodologies and Applications 6*(3), 144–153.

Camp, J. S. and P. B. Deblois (2007). The Eight Annual EDUCAUSE Current Issues Survey Report. EDUCAUSE Quarterly.

Cantu-Paz, E. and C. Kamath (2003). Inducing oblique decision trees with evolutionary algorithms. *IEEE Transactions on Evolutionary Computation 7*(1), 54–68.

CERT Coordination Center (2003). CERT Advisory CA-2003-20 W32/Blaster worm.

CERT Coordination Center (2005). CERT/CC Statistics 1988-2005.

Chittur, A. (2002). Model generation for an intrusion detection system using genetic algorithms. High school honors thesis, NY Ossining.

Chiu, C. and P. Hsu (2005). A constraint-based genetic algorithm approach for mining classification rules. *IEEE Transactions on Systems, Man and Cybernetics, Part C 35*(2), 205–220.

Clark, P. and T. Niblett (1989). The CN2 induction algorithm. *Machine Learning 3*(4), 261–283.

Cohen, W. W. (1995). Fast effective rule induction. In *Proceedings of the Twelfth International Conference on Machine Learning*, pp. 115–123.

Dam, H., H. Abbass, C. Lokan, and X. Yao (2008). Neural-Based Learning Classifier Systems. *Transactions on Knowledge and Data Engineering 20*(1), 26–39.

Dam, H. H., H. A. Abbass, and C. Lokan (2005). Be real! XCS with continuous valued inputs. In *Proceedings of Eighth International Workshop on Learning Classifier Systems*, Washington D.C.

Dasgupta, D. (1998). *Artificial Immune Systems and Their Applications*. Springer-Verlag New York, Inc. Secaucus, NJ, USA.

Dasgupta, D. (1999). Immunity-Based Intrusion Detection System: A General Framework. In *Proceedings of the 22nd National Information Systems Security Conference*, pp. 147–160. Crystal City: NIST Publishers.

De Jong, K. and W. Spears (1991). Learning concept classification rules using genetic algorithms. In *Proceedings of the International Joint Conference on Artificial Intelligence*, pp. 651–656.

Denning, D. (1987). An intrusion-detection model. *IEEE Transactions on Software Engineering 13*(2), 222–232.

Dixon, P., D. Corne, and M. Oates (2003). A Ruleset Reduction Algorithm for the XCS Learning Classifier System. In *Proceedings of the 5th International Workshop on Learning Classifier Systems, Revised Papers*, pp. 20–29. Springer.

Domingos, P. (1995). Rule induction and instance-based learning: A unified approach. In *Proceeding of the International Joint Conference on Artificial Intelligence*, pp. 1226–1232.

Dozier, G., D. Brown, J. Hurley, and K. Cain (2004). Vulnerability analysis of AIS-based intrusion detection systems via genetic and particle swarm red teams. In *Proceedings of the 2004 IEEE Congress on Evolutionary Computation*, Volume 1, pp. 111–116.

Drummond, C. and R. Holte (2003). C4.5, class imbalance, and cost sensitivity: why under-sampling beats over-sampling. In *Workshop on Learning from Imbalanced Data Sets II*.

Elkan, C. (2000). Results of the KDD'99 classifier learning. *SIGKDD Explor. Newsl. 1*(2), 63–64.

Elkan, C. (2001). The foundations of cost-sensitive learning. In *Proceedings of the Seventeenth International Joint Conference on Artificial Intelligence*, Volume 17, pp. 973–978.

Ertoz, L., E. Eilertson, A. Lazarevic, P. N. Tan, V. Kumar, J. Srivastava, and P. Dokas (2004). MINDS-Minnesota Intrusion Detection System. In *Next Generation Data Mining*. MIT Press.

Ertoz, L., M. Steinbach, and V. Kumar (2002). A new shared nearest neighbor clustering algorithm and its applications. In *SIAM Data Mining Workshop on Clustering High Dimensional Data and its Applications at 2nd SIAM International Conference on Data Mining*.

Filippone, M., F. Camastra, F. Masulli, and S. Rovetta (2008). A survey of kernel and spectral methods for clustering. *Pattern Recognition 41*(1), 176–190.

Fogel, L. (1964). *On the organization of intellect*. Ph. D. thesis, UCLA - Engineering.

Foley, J. (1995). *Computer Graphics: Principles and Practice in C*. Addison-Wesley Professional.

Forrest, S. and S. Hofmeyr (1999). John Hollands Invisible Hand: An Artificial Immune System. Presented at the Festschrift held in honor of John Holland.

Forrest, S., S. Hofmeyr, A. Somayaji, T. Longstaff, et al. (1996). A sense of self for Unix processes. In *Proceedings of the 1996 IEEE Symposium on Security and Privacy, Oakland, CA, 6-8 May, 1996*, pp. 120–128.

Foukia, N. (2005). IDReAM: Intrusion Detection and Response executed with Agent Mobility. In *Proceedings of the International Conference on Autonomous Agents and Multi-Agent Systems (AAMAS05)*, pp. 264–270. Springer.

Foukia, N. and S. Hassas (2004). Managing Computer Networks Security through Self-Organization: A Complex System Perspective. In *Engineering Self-Organizing Systems, Nature-Inspired Approaches to Software Engineering (Lecture Notes in Artificial Intelligence, 2977)*, pp. 124–138. Springer.

Freitas, A. (1999). A genetic algorithm for generalized rule induction. In *Advances in Soft Computing - Engineering Design and Manufacturing*, pp. 340–353. Springer.

Fu, C. and L. Davis (2002). A modified classifier system compaction algorithm. In *Proceedings of the Genetic and Evolutionary Computation Conference (GECCO 2002)*, pp. 920–925. Morgan Kaufmann.

Furnkranz, J. and G. Widmer (1994). Incremental reduced error pruning. In *Proceedings of the Eleventh International Conference on Machine Learning*, pp. 70–77.

Geschke, D. (2004). FLoP - Fast Logging Project for Snort. available from, `http://www.geschke-online.de/FLoP/`.

Giacinto, G., F. Roli, and L. Didaci (2003). A modular multiple classifier system for the detection of intrusions in computer networks. In *4th International Workshop on Multiple Classifier Systems (MCS 2003), LNCS 2709*, pp. 346–355. Springer.

Goldberg, D. (2002). *The Design of Innovation: Lessons from and for Competent Genetic Algorithms*. Kluwer Academic Publishers.

Goldberg, D. and K. Deb (1991). A comparative analysis of selection schemes used in genetic algorithms. *Foundations of Genetic Algorithms 1*, 69–93.

Goldberg, D. E. (1989). *Genetic Algorithms in Search, Optimization, and Machine Learning*. Addision-Wesley Publishing Company, Inc.

Gomez, J. and D. Dasgupta (2002a). Evolving Fuzzy Classifiers for Intrusion Detection. In *Proceedings of the 2002 IEEE Workshop on Information Assurance*, Volume 6, pp. 321–323. New York: IEEE Computer Press.

Gomez, J. and D. Dasgupta (2002b). Evolving Fuzzy Classifiers for Intrusion Detection. In *Proceedings of the 2002 IEEE Workshop on Information Assurance*,
pp. 321–323. New York: IEEE Computer Press.

Gordon, L. A., M. P. Loeb, W. Lucyshyn, and R. Richardson (2006). 11th Annual
CSI/FBI Computer Crime and Security Survey, Computer Security Institute
(CSI).

Gregory, J. (2005). Mucus - Traffic generator for IDS Simulation. available from,
http://www.bleedingthreats.net/.

Haines, J. W., R. P. Lippmann, D. J. Fried, E. Tran, S. Boswell, and M. A.
Zissman (2001). 1999 DARPA Intrusion Detection System Evaluation: Design
and Procedures. Technical report, MIT Lincoln Laboratory.

Heady, R., G. Luger, A. Maccabe, and M. Servilla (1990). The architecture of a
network level intrusion detection system. Technical Report LA-SUB–93-219,
New Mexico Univ., Albuquerque.

Helmer, G., J. Wong, V. Honavar, and L. Miller (2002). Automated discovery
of concise predictive rules for intrusion detection. *The Journal of Systems &
Software 60*(3), 165–175.

Hettich, S. and S. D. Bay (1999). The UCI KDD Archive. available from, http:
//kdd.ics.uci.edu/databases/kddcup99/kddcup99.html.

Hoffmeyer, J. (1994). The swarming body. In *Proceedings of the Fifth Congress
of the International Association for Semiotic Studies*, pp. 937–940.

Hofmeyr, S. and S. Forrest (1999). Immunity by Design: An Artificial Immune
System. In *Proceedings of the Genetic and Evolutionary Computation Conference*, Volume 2, pp. 1289–1296. Morgan Kaufmann.

Holland, J., L. Booker, M. Colombetti, M. Dorigo, D. E. Goldberg, S. Forrest,
R. Riolo, R. Smith, P. Lanzi, W. Stolzmann, et al. (2000). What is a learning
classifier system. *Learning Classifier Systems: From Foundations to Applications 1813*, 3–32.

Holland, J. H. (1975). *Adaptation in Natural and Artificial Systems.* Ann Arbor: University of Michigan Press. Republished by the MIT press, 1992.

Holland, J. H. and J. S. Reitman (1978). Cognitive systems based on adaptive algorithms. In D. A. Waterman and F. Hayes-Roth (Eds.), *Pattern-directed Inference Systems.* New York: Academic Press. Reprinted in: Evolutionary Computation. The Fossil Record. David B. Fogel (Ed.) IEEE Press, 1998.

Humphries, J., D. Ragsdale, C. Carver Jr, J. Hill, and U. Pooch (2000). No Silver Bullet: Inherent Limitations of Computer Security Technologies. In *Proceedings of the 4th World MultiConference on Systemics, Cybernetics, and Informatics,* pp. 245–250.

Hwang, K., M. Cai, Y. Chen, and M. Qin (2007). Hybrid Intrusion Detection with Weighted Signature Generation over Anomalous Internet Episodes. *IEEE Transactions on Dependable and Secure Computing 4*(1), 41–55.

Hwang, T., T. Lee, and Y. Lee (2007). A three-tier IDS via data mining approach. In *Proceedings of the 3rd annual ACM workshop on Mining network data,* pp. 1–6. ACM Press New York, NY, USA.

Jacobson, V., C. Leres, and S. McCanne (1989). tcpdump. available via anonymous ftp to, `ftp://ee.lbl.gov`.

Japkowicz, N. (2002). The class imbalance problem: A systematic study. *Intelligent Data Analysis 6*(5), 429–449.

Jones, G. (1998). Genetic and evolutionary algorithms. *Encyclopedia of Computational Chemistry. John Wiley & Sons, Ltd., September.*

Joshi, M., V. Kumar, and R. Agarwal (2001). Evaluating Boosting Algorithms to Classify Rare Classes: Comparison and Improvements. In *Proceedings of the First IEEE International Conference on Data Mining,* pp. 257–264.

Jung, J., V. Paxson, A. Berger, and H. Balakrishnan (2004). Fast portscan detection using sequential hypothesis testing. In *Proceedings of the 2004 IEEE Symposium on Security and Privacy,* pp. 211–225.

Kemmerer, R. and G. Vigna (2002). Intrusion detection: a brief history and overview. *Computer 35*(4), 27–30.

Kendall, K. (1999). A database of computer attacks for the evaluation of intrusion detection systems. Masters thesis, Massachusetts Institute of Technology.

Kharbat, F., L. Bull, and M. Odeh (2005). Revisiting genetic selection in the XCS learning classifier system. In *Proceedings of the 2005 IEEE Congress on Evolutionary Computation*, Volume 3, pp. 2061–2068.

Kim, J. and P. Bentley (2001). Towards an artificial immune system for network intrusion detection: an investigation of clonal selection with a negative selection operator. In *Proceedings of the 2001 IEEE Congress on Evolutionary Computation*, Volume 2, pp. 1244–1252.

Kim, J., J. Greensmith, J. Twycross, and U. Aickelin (2005). Malicious Code Execution Detection and Response Immune System inpired by the Danger Theory. In *Adaptive and Resilient Computing Security Workshop (ARCS-05)*.

Kovacs, T. (1997). XCS Classifier System Reliably Evolves Accurate, Complete, and Minimal Representations for Boolean Functions. In Roy, Chawdhry, and Pant (Eds.), *Soft Computing in Engineering Design and Manufacturing*, pp. 59–68. Springer-Verlag, London.

Kovacs, T. (2000). Strength or Accuracy? Fitness Calculation in Learning Classifier Systems. In *International Workshop on Learning Classifier Systems, (IWLCS'99)*, pp. 143–160. Springer.

Kovacs, T. (2002). What should a classifier system learn and how should we measure it? *Journal of Soft Computing 6*(3–4), 171–182.

Kovacs, T. and M. Kerber (2006). A Study of Structural and Parametric Learning in XCS. *Evolutionary Computation 14*(1), 1–19.

Koza, J. (1992). *Genetic Programming: On the Programming of Computers by Means of Natural Selection*. The MIT Press.

Lanzi, P. (1999). Extending the Representation of Classifier Conditions Part II:

From Messy Coding to S-Expressions. In *Proceedings of the Genetic and Evolutionary Computation Conference*, Volume 1, pp. 345–352.

Lee, W., S. Stolfo, P. Chan, E. Eskin, W. Fan, M. Miller, S. Hershkop, and J. Zhang (2001). Real Time Data Mining-based Intrusion Detection. In *Proceedings of DISCEX II*, pp. 89–100. Anaheim, USA.

Lee, W. and S. J. Stolfo (2001). A framework for constructing features and models for intrusion detection systems. *ACM Trans. Inf. Syst. Secur. 3*(4), 227–261.

Levin, I. (2000). KDD-99 classifier learning contest LLSoft's results overview. *ACM SIGKDD Explorations Newsletter 1*(2), 67–75.

Llorà, X. and K. Sastry (2006). Fast rule matching for learning classifier systems via vector instructions. In *Proceedings of the 8th annual conference on Genetic and evolutionary computation*, pp. 1513–1520. ACM Press New York, NY, USA.

Ludovic, M. (1998). Gassata, a genetic algorithm as an alternative tool for security audit trails analysis. In *Proceedings of the First International Workshop on the Recent Advances in Intrusion Detection, Louvain-la-Neuve, Belgium*.

Luo, S. and G. Marin (2004). Generating Realistic Network Traffic for Security Experiments. In *Proceedings of the IEEE SoutheastCon*, pp. 200–207.

Mahoney, M. (2003). *A Machine Learning Approach to Detecting Attacks by Identifying Anomalies in Network Traffic*. Ph. D. thesis, Florida Institute of Technology.

Mahoney, M. and P. Chan (2003a). An Analysis of the 1999 DARPA/Lincoln Laboratory Evaluation Data for Network Anomaly Detection. In *Proceedings of Recent Advances in Intrusion Detection (RAID) 2003*, pp. 220–237. Springer.

Mahoney, M. V. and P. K. Chan (2003b). Learning rules for anomaly detection of hostile network traffic. In *Proceedings of the Third IEEE International Conference on Data Mining (ICDM 2003)*, pp. 601–604.

Maloof, M. (2003). Incremental rule learning with partial instance memory for changing concepts. *Proceedings of the International Joint Conference on Neural Networks 4*, 2764–2769.

Martin, S. and A. Sewani (2004). Semi-supervised learning on email characteristics for novel worm detection. In *Conference on Email and Anti-Spam*.

Massicotte, F., F. Gagnon, Y. Labiche, L. Briand, and M. Couture (2006). Automatic Evaluation of Intrusion Detection Systems. In *22nd Annual Computer Security Applications Conference, 2006.*, pp. 361–370.

Maulik, U. and S. Bandyopadhyay (2000). Genetic algorithm-based clustering technique. *Pattern Recognition 33*(9), 1455–1465.

McHugh, J. (2000). Testing Intrusion detection systems: a critique of the 1998 and 1999 DARPA intrusion detection system evaluations as performed by Lincoln Laboratory. *ACM Transactions on Information System Security 3*(4), 262–294.

Michalewicz, Z. (1996). *Genetic Algorithms+ Data Structures= Evolution Programs.* Springer.

Michalski, R. (1969). On the Quasi-Minimal Solution of the General Covering Problem. In *Proceedings of the V International Symposium on Information Processing*, pp. 125–128.

Michalski, R., J. Carbonell, and T. Mitchell (1986). *Machine Learning: An Artificial Intelligence Approach.* Morgan Kaufmann.

Michalski, R., I. Mozetic, J. Hong, and N. Lavrac (1986). The multi-purpose incremental learning system AQ15 and its testing application to three medical domains. In *Proceedings of the Fifth National Conference on Artificial Intelligence*, pp. 1041–1045.

Miller, B. and D. E. Goldberg (1996). Genetic Algorithms, Selection Schemes, and the Varying Effects of Noise. *Evolutionary Computation 4*(2), 113–131.

Mitchell, T. (1997). *Machine Learning.* McGraw-Hill.

Mitchell, T., R. Keller, and S. Kedar-Cabelli (1986). Explanation-based generalization: A unifying view. *Machine Learning 1*(1), 47–80.

Mutz, D., G. Vigna, and R. Kemmerer (2003). An experience developing an IDS stimulator for the black-box testing of network intrusion detection systems. In *Proceedings of the 19th Annual Computer Security Applications Conference*, pp. 374–383.

Orriols-Puig, A. and E. Bernadó-Mansilla (2005). Class Imbalance Problem in UCS Classifier System: Fitness Adaptation. In *Proceedings of the 2005 IEEE Congress on Evolutionary Computation*, Volume 1, pp. 604–611.

Orriols-Puig, A. and E. Bernadó-Mansilla (2006a). A further look at UCS classifier system. In *Proceedings of the 8th annual Conference on Genetic and Evolutionary Computation Workshop Program*. ACM Press New York, NY, USA.

Orriols-Puig, A. and E. Bernadó-Mansilla (2006b). Bounding XCS's parameters for unbalanced datasets. In *Proceedings of the 8th annual conference on Genetic and evolutionary computation*, pp. 1561–1568. ACM Press New York, NY, USA.

Paxson, V. (1998). Bro: a system for detecting network intruders in real-time. In *Proceedings of the 7th conference on USENIX Security Symposium*, Volume 7, pp. 3–3. USENIX Association Berkeley, CA, USA. Available from, http://www.bro-ids.org/.

Pfahringer, B. (2000). Winning the KDD99 classification cup: bagged boosting. *ACM SIGKDD Explorations Newsletter 1*(2), 65–66.

Pillai, M. M., J. H. P. Eloff, and H. S. Venter (2004). An approach to implement a network intrusion detection system using genetic algorithms. In *Proceedings of SAICSIT '04:*, Republic of South Africa, pp. 221–221. South African Institute for Computer Scientists and Information Technologists.

Porras, P. A. and P. G. Neumann (1997). EMERALD: Event Monitoring Enabling Responses to Anomalous Live Disturbances. In *Proceedings of 20th NIST-*

NCSC National Information Systems Security Conference, pp. 353–365.

Quinlan, J. (1986). The effect of noise on concept learning. *Machine Learning: An Artificial Intelligence Approach 2*, 149–166.

Quinlan, J. (1987). Generating production rules from decision trees. In *Proceedings of the Tenth International Joint Conference on Artificial Intelligence*, pp. 304–307. Morgan Kaufmann.

Ramesh, A. and J. V. Mahesh (2001). PNrule: A new framework for learning classifier models in data mining (a case-study in network intrusion detection). In *Proceedings of the First SIAM International Conference on Data Mining, Chicago, IL USA, 5-7 April, 2001.*

Rechenberg, I. (1973). *Evolutionsstrategie: Optimierung technischer Systeme nach Prinzipien der biologischen evolution.* Frommann-Holzboog, Stuttgart.

Roesch, M. (1999). Snort-Lightweight Intrusion Detection for Networks. In *Proceedings of USENIX LISA*, pp. 229–238. Available from, url-http://www.snort.org/.

Sabhnani, M. and G. Serpen (2003). Application of Machine Learning Algorithms to KDD Intrusion Detection Dataset within Misuse Detection Context. In *Proceedings of International Conference on Machine Learning: Models, Technologies, and Applications*, pp. 23–26.

Sabhnani, M. and G. Serpen (2004). Why machine learning algorithms fail in misuse detection on KDD intrusion detection data set. *Intelligent Data Analysis 8*(4), 403–415.

Shafi, K., H. A. Abbass, and W. Zhu (2006). An Adaptive Rule-based Intrusion Detection Architecture. In *Proceedings of the RNSA Security Technology Conference, Canberra, Australia, 19-21 Sept., 2006*, pp. 345–355.

Sinclair, C., L. Pierce, and S. Matzner (1999). An Application of Machine Learning to Network Intrusion Detection. In *Proceedings of the 15th Annual Computer Security Applications Conference, 6-10 Dec., 1999*, pp. 371–377.

Sommers, J., V. Yegneswaran, and P. Barford (2005). Toward Comprehensive Traffic Generation for Online IDS Evaluation. Technical report, Dept. of Computer Science, University of Wisconsin.

Song, D., M. Heywood, and A. Zincir-Heywood (2005). Training genetic programming on half a million patterns: an example from anomaly detection. *IEEE Transactions on Evolutionary Computation 9*(3), 225–239.

Staniford, S. (2002). Practical automated detection of stealthy portscans. *Journal of Computer Security 10*(1), 105–136.

Stewart W. Wilson (2000). Get Real! XCS with Continuous-Valued Inputs. In P. Lanzi, W. Stolzmann, and S. Wilson (Eds.), *Learning Classifier Systems, From Foundations to Applications, LNAI-1813*, Berlin, pp. 209–219. Springer-Verlag.

Stolfo, S., W. Fan, W. Lee, A. Prodromidis, and P. Chan (2000). Cost-based modeling for fraud and intrusion detection: results from the JAM project. In *Proceedings of DARPA Information Survivability Conference and Exposition, DISCEX '00*, Volume 2, pp. 130–144.

Stolfo, S. J., W. Fan, W. Lee, A. Prodromidis, and P. K. Chan. (2000). Cost-based Modeling and Evaluation for Data Mining With Application to Fraud and Intrusion Detection: Results from the JAM Project. In *Proceedings of DARPA Information Survivability Conference*, pp. 130–144.

Stone, C. and L. Bull (2003). For real! XCS with continuous-valued inputs. *Evolutionary Computation 11*(3), 299–336.

Survey, E. (2006). CSO magazine, US Secret Service, CERT Coordination Center, Microsoft Corp, 2006.

Tandon, G. and P. Chan (2005). Learning Useful System Call Attributes for Anomaly Detection. In *Proceeding of the 18th International FLAIRS Conference*, pp. 405–411.

Team, M. (2006). The Metasploit Project. available from, http://www.metasploit.com/.

TeleGeography (2008). TeleGeography's Global Internet Geography. available from, `http://www.telegeography.com/products/gig/index.php`.

Tsang, C. and S. Kwong (2005). Multi-Agent Intrusion Detection System in Industrial Network using Ant Colony Clustering Approach and Unsupervised Feature Extraction. In *IEEE International Conference on Industrial Technology (ICIT)*, pp. 51–56.

Turner, A. and M. Bing (2005). TCPReplay: PCAP editing and replay tools for ∗nix. available from, `http://tcpreplay.sourceforge.net`.

UPI (2008). Study: New computer threat is emerging. United Press International, Science News,. `http://www.upi.com/Science_News/2008/05/05/Study_New_computer_threat_is_emerging/UPI-41851210008896/`, 5/05/2008.

Vigna, G. and R. A. Kemmerer (1999). NetSTAT: A network-based intrusion detection system. *Journal of Computer Security* 7(1), 37–71.

Wang, K. and S. Stolfo (2004). Anomalous payload-based network intrusion detection. *Proceedings of the Recent Advances in Intrusion Detection* 7, 201–222.

Wilson, S. W. (1987). Classifier systems and the animat problem. *Machine Learning* 2(3), 199–228.

Wilson, S. W. (1995). Classifier fitness based on accuracy. *Evolutionary Computation* 3(2), 149–175.

Wilson, S. W. (1998). Generalization in the XCS classifier system. In *Genetic Programming 1998: Proceedings of the Third Annual Conference*, University of Wisconsin, Madison, Wisconsin, USA, pp. 665–674. Morgan Kaufmann.

Wilson, S. W. (2001a). Compact Rulesets from XCSI. In *Proceedings of the 4th International Workshop on Advances in Learning Classifier Systems: Revised Papers*, pp. 197–210. Springer.

Wilson, S. W. (2001b). Mining oblique data with XCS. In P. L. Lanzi, W. Stolzmann, and S. W. Wilson (Eds.), *Proceedings of the Third International Workshop (IWLCS-2000), Lecture Notes in Artificial Intelligence*, pp. 158–174.

Wilson, S. W. (August-November 2005). Personal communications.

Wyatt, D., L. Bull, and I. Parmee (2004). Building compact rulesets for describing continuous-valued problem spaces using a learning classifier system. In I. Parmee (Ed.), *Adaptive Computing in Design and Manufacture VI*, pp. 235–248. Springer.

Yao, X. and Y. Liu (1997). A new evolutionary system for evolving artificial neural networks. *IEEE Transactions on Neural Networks 8*(3), 694–713.

Zhang, Y. and S. Bhattacharyya (2004). Genetic programming in classifying large-scale data: an ensemble method. *Information Sciences 163*(1-3), 85–101.

www.ingramcontent.com/pod-product-compliance
Lightning Source LLC
LaVergne TN
LVHW042331060326
832902LV00006B/113